THE LIMITS OF COMMUNITY POLICING

The Limits of Community Policing

Civilian Power and Police Accountability in Black and Brown Los Angeles

Luis Daniel Gascón *and* Aaron Roussell

NEW YORK UNIVERSITY PRESS
New York

NEW YORK UNIVERSITY PRESS
New York
www.nyupress.org

References to Internet websites (URLs) were accurate at the time of writing. Neither the author nor New York University Press is responsible for URLs that may have expired or changed since the manuscript was prepared.

Library of Congress Cataloging-in-Publication Data
Names: Gascon, Luis Daniel, author. | Roussell, Aaron, author.
Title: The limits of community policing : civilian power and police accountability in black and brown Los Angeles / Luis Daniel Gascon and Aaron Roussell.
Description: New York : New York University Press, [2019] |
Includes bibliographical references and index.
Identifiers: LCCN 2018030569| ISBN 9781479871209 (cl : alk. paper) |
ISBN 9781479842254 (pb : alk. paper)
Subjects: LCSH: Police—California—Los Angeles. | Police-community relations—California—Los Angeles. | Police—Complaints against—California—Los Angeles. | African Americans—California—Los Angeles. | Hispanic Americans—California—Los Angeles.
Classification: LCC HV8148.L55 G37 2019 | DDC 363.2/30979494—dc23
LC record available at https://lccn.loc.gov/2018030569

New York University Press books are printed on acid-free paper, and their binding materials are chosen for strength and durability. We strive to use environmentally responsible suppliers and materials to the greatest extent possible in publishing our books.

Manufactured in the United States of America

10 9 8 7 6 5 4 3 2 1

Also available as an ebook

To Teresa Mayfield and Niccolo Nazario. Rest in power.

CONTENTS

ABBREVIATIONS

BC	Business Car
BCA	Basic Car Area
BCP	Basic Car Plan
BLM	Black Lives Matter
CAPA	Coalition Against Police Abuse
CERT	Community Emergency Response Team
COPS	Community-Oriented Policing Services
CPAB	Community-Police Advisory Board
CRA	Community Redevelopment Agency
CRO	Community Relations Office/Officer
CRT	Crisis Response Team
DAP	Deputy Auxiliary Police
GRYD	Gang Reduction and Youth Development
HACLA	Housing Authority of the City of Los Angeles
HO	Hispanic Outreach
IAD	Internal Affairs Division
IG	Inspector General
LAPD	Los Angeles Police Department
OAD	Officer Appreciation Day
OIS	Officer-Involved Shooting
RLA	Rebuild Los Angeles
SLO	Senior Lead Officer
SNL	Summer Night Lights

LIST OF FIGURES AND TABLES

PREFACE

We wrote this book to deepen traditional understandings of community policing and police-civilian partnerships. Community policing became our focus specifically because it is a politically sound response to complicated questions surrounding protest, police brutality, racism, and problems that seem endemic to policing. After yet another public revolt against police practice, community policing remains the buzzword, but what does it really look like? Words like "community" and "partner" are thrown around in policy circles as well by well-intentioned reformists, but what do these ideas mean in practice?

Although we've presented some of these ideas in other places, ethnographies are best presented in book format, where the characters have room to express themselves and the setting can be presented in all its complexity. Our motivation was to get experience at the places where community and police come together (particularly in the place most associated with community policing—South Los Angeles), elevate perspectives from the communities most affected, and amplify the voices of the often-unspoken challenges of and to policing in this context. More than distributing surveys or counting bureaucratic output, this meant getting close and looking at social interactions on the ground. We spent a lot of time watching, talking, volunteering, and immersing ourselves in the spaces of community policing. We hope *The Limits of Community Policing* provides a rich and multifaceted look at the project, offering data that raises questions and produces conversations, even for those who may disagree with our conclusions.

This book begins with a history of the present of South LA, focusing on several specific themes: the evolution of LAPD, LA's key moments of mass violence, Black and Latin@ communities, and economic and demographic shifts. The remainder of the book outlines the social organization, key actors, routines, and challenges of community policing in LA. We start by looking at the police-community crime prevention meetings in one South LA neighborhood we call Lakeside. By the end of the book, readers will have met the diverse cast of characters who shape the community policing regime in Lakeside. Longtime residents of some of South LA's oldest Black neighborhoods, Gerry Torrance and Teresa Mayfield, offer these discussions much-needed historical context. Repeated heated exchanges between group leaders, the irrepressible Vera Fisher and commanding Hector Mendoza, illustrate South LA's contemporary racial and political landscape. Their contests, negotiations, and collaborations with a multiracial cast of police officers and administrators like the enigmatic White Senior Lead Officer Phil Hackett, the nepotistic Latino Sergeant David Guevara, and administrators like the relatable Asian American Captain Albert Himura, make up what LAPD calls the Community-Police Advisory Board (CPAB). Within the rich vein of legal and urban ethnographies, we explain the everyday work of the people in South LA who attempt to use community policing to improve their neighborhoods.

Our work is collaborative, which is not the norm in ethnography. Although we wrote the book together, we found it helpful to reproduce our fieldnotes directly (lightly edited for clarity) as a form of data to give the reader a flavor of the setting as well as our idiosyncratic ways of thinking, writing, and analyzing. There are stylistic differences between us—for example, Danny is descriptive, while Aaron hones in on dialogue—which we preserve. When transcribing residents' Spanish, we provide our own translations in brackets. Brackets also help us isolate our analysis of the setting from the action of the moment. Conversational exchanges occur frequently. Due to the nature of note taking, some considerable abbreviation is normal, but text that is quoted verbatim receives the requisite quotations marks—all else is summary.

Introduction

Questions about a police shooting interrupted our regularly scheduled community-police meeting, whose agenda was organized around preparing for the twentieth anniversary of the 1992 Rodney King Uprisings. A day earlier, Los Angeles Police Department (LAPD) officers had shot and killed an Arab American teenager they said was driving into oncoming traffic on the 101 freeway (Curwen and Blankstein 2012).[1] His killing came just two months after George Zimmerman, the self-appointed block club captain of a Sanford, Florida, neighborhood, stalked, shot, and killed a Black teenager named Trayvon Martin, sparking what would become the international Black Lives Matter (BLM) movement.

We began observing monthly community-police meetings at LAPD's Lakeside Station in South LA four years prior to these incidents. Community-Police Advisory Board (CPAB) meetings are the clearest example of community-police engagement that arose from the ashes of the 1992 LA uprising. Yet, given the intervening decades, neither of us expected that police brutality, particularly police killings, would again become front-page news when we began this research.

Thirty or more mostly elderly and middle-aged Black attendees, including as well a few Whites, Latin@s, and Asians, crowded around a square arrangement of tables in the Lakeside community room. The meeting chair, Captain Albert Himura, called the meeting to order, after which several residents shot up their hands to question the merits of police action. The group was animated, angry that Sanford police allowed a killer to walk free that night. Longtime attendee Nicole Williams claimed this questionable action reflected other problems, such as retaliation from police if people stand up for their rights: "They see the police as a gang," she said, referring to young people in the neighborhood. "If I turn [an abusive officer] in, his partner's gonna get me."

The Captain and several others pushed back. Captain Himura dismissed the problem out of hand: "Have them bring this to my attention," he said. "Or have them bring it to you and *you* bring it to my attention." Every police car was equipped with a mic and a camera. "Ninety-five percent of the time," he said, the tape vindicated his officers. But he was "absolutely" willing to "discipline his officers," particularly now that cameras had become ubiquitous. Several residents, including Vera Fisher, the civilian co-chair, were righteously indignant on behalf of police and dismissed the rallies and protests as underattended. Ms. Williams conceded that the young people she knows through her after-school police partnership program said they've noticed a difference in LAPD.

The sole Latin@ attendee was a first-timer named Enrique Alves. "Our justice system says Zimmerman's guilty until proven innocent," he said, stumbling over his words, "I mean, innocent until proven guilty." People nodded, ignoring the slipup but also his point. It seemed to regalvanize Himura however: "If people want to march, I'll facilitate it," he informed the group. They would have to let him know in advance though, or else a bunch of young people in hoodies might show up and his officers would think "It's a gang!"

A middle-aged Black woman raised her hand and cautiously noted that she sometimes wears a hoodie: "People *do* get profiled." She suggested that officers might be more successful if they were less intimidating. Right on cue, this prompted Williams to digress on "black-on-black violence." "There's no justice for *them*," she said heatedly, referring to victims, "and they're *right here* in our community." She argued that the homicide rate is rising in Lakeside and that only residents can keep their community safe. "The police don't live here."

Gerry Torrance's hand had been up forever, even while people jumped into the discussion right and left without waiting for Himura's recognition. He and several of the less excitable members were silently exchanging glances about this, while Gerry configured his raised hand entertainingly into a gun, a peace sign, and a radio antenna while waiting to speak. Once recognized, he began speaking slowly and deliberately: "I was here for the 1992 riots. And I was here for the 1965 riots as well. We need to go back . . . and find those people, find people that said good things about LAPD. Nothing came about from '65 or '92 . . . they [those involved in the violence] just went back into their houses." He continued, arguing that the fallout from the uprisings was a wasted opportunity—"All youth know now is to split!"—punctuating his remarks by slapping his hands past each other quickly and loudly.

Officers' responses to Gerry dovetailed. Captain Himura responded first: Lakeside needs to develop press contacts. He volunteered Mrs. Kwon, who had been very quiet, and her circle of Korean grocers as well as Nicole Williams and Gerry Torrance to attend a media event on April 29 at the epicenter of the 1992 violence. They were to talk about peace, improvements in safety in the intervening years, and how Lakeside didn't want to go back to "the way it was." "We're not *going* back," Williams affirmed sharply.

Officer Gus Fernandez, a community policing officer, asserted that the media were "poking around," trying to capture discontentment surrounding the anniversary. He asked those who wanted to relate a positive message about police to find him and he'd put them in touch with the media. The media was out there looking for confrontation, he said, and it isn't there. Almost as an afterthought he added: "It really had nothing to do with the acquittal of the officers anyway—mostly it was Damian Williams drunk out of his mind."

Interactions like these, between residents like Williams and Torrance, officers like Fernandez, and police administrators like Himura, help disclose the nature of community-police partnerships. In this example, the Captain positioned himself as the concerned patriarch, directing the conversation, channeling complaints, and finally organizing an event for the purposes of legitimizing LAPD's post-uprising efforts. Himura lauded Lakeside's complaint process, deflecting concerns and gesturing at technology as objective evidence of police trustworthiness. The disciplinary process was sound, he argued, because of his vigilance regarding discipline, while a breath later he admitted to finding the vast majority of civilian complaints baseless. Fernandez, a community policing officer known as a Senior Lead Officer (SLO; pronounced "slow"), was unusually trusted and empowered by the top brass. He extended the official messaging on police integrity by revising the historical record: one rebellious Black man, drunk and out of control, stirred up rioting for its own sake in 1992. The subtext for Fernandez was that there are few lessons to be learned from drunk and disorderly residents. The message of LAPD's trustworthiness and transparency advanced by

Fernandez and Himura was the same message disseminated at the anniversary media event ultimately orchestrated through Himura.

Community voices like those of Gerry Torrance and Nicole Williams reveal complex social dynamics. Torrance, a lifelong South LA resident, lived in the neighborhood where the uprisings broke out. He had grandchildren in rival gangs ("I don't give a shit, you are still relatives") and has made pointed comments about police use of racial profiling. While Torrance sometimes seemed to doubt LAPD's post-1992 changes, he also deferred to police and spread responsibility to community youth. Like Williams, who ran the Mission: Responsibility after-school program for disadvantaged youth, Torrance remained invested in groups like CPAB while accepting certain realities about the impact of police on his community. Likewise, Williams's plea for the community to address "black-on-black violence" seemed less a call for more aggressive policing than an expression of beleaguered feelings and a defiant hopefulness regarding the potential of partnerships like CPAB. This set of residents believed in their own power as well as the idea that they should not have to manage such problems on their own. As tax-paying residents, they felt reasonably entitled to safety, and that, in part, motivated their engagement. Still, as the comment about hoodies and other subtext suggest, attendees were caught in a catch-22, and the slice of residents involved in CPAB ran the gamut from police enthusiasts to mild skeptics.

Finally, the sidelining of Enrique Alves hints at questions of community belonging. Latin@ voices generally were marginalized within the official English CPAB meetings. The less official community-police meetings for Spanish speakers, held separately on different nights and with different goals, were called (sometimes) Hispanic Outreach (HO). There was little crossover between HO and CPAB meetings. CPAB was not welcoming to all Black residents either—although Himura had connections with gang leaders and interventionists, he did not encourage either group to attend. Less controversial groups than gangs fared poorly in CPAB, and one need not imagine the skepticism or even hostility that groups like BLM and LA's Coalition Against Police Abuse (CAPA) might engender.

* * *

LAPD holds hundreds of CPAB and other community-police meetings every year, and such efforts are ubiquitous in police stations, community centers, high schools, churches, and other public spaces around the country. The city of LA, the state of California, and the federal government have spent millions of dollars on community-based initiatives since the 1940s as the centerpiece of the police reform agenda. The federal government has invested millions more establishing community-based policing as a national model for police reform over the last forty years, now spearheaded by the Community-Oriented Policing Services (COPS) office chartered by the Clinton administration (Escobar 1999; Murakawa 2014; Sides 2003; J. Simon 2007). Departments across the country claim to be employing community-based strategies on a regular basis. US soldiers have also deployed community policing strategies abroad, referring to them as "counterinsurgency," while funneling surplus equipment and providing military training to domestic police departments (K. Williams 2011).[2] While lawmakers and reformists extol the virtues of community, the United States incarcerates more people and at a higher rate than any other nation in the world by a wide margin (Alexander 2010; J. Simon 2007). This book is an attempt to investigate what, precisely, community policing is and does, in the very place that made it a political buzzword in 1992—South Los Angeles.

We spent five years attending police-sponsored events to understand the inner workings of LAPD's community policing program in Lakeside Division. At these events we conducted participant observation, speaking with neighborhood residents, criminal justice practitioners, government officials, community activists, and LAPD officers and administrators. We also followed participants to citywide events and meetings in other divisions to better contextualize our findings. *The Limits of Community Policing* synthesizes hundreds of hours of observations and thousands of pages of fieldnotes, interview transcripts, and internal LAPD documents.

In this book, we address three main points. First, against the common narrative that community policing has democratized policing, we argue rather that the state has used community discourse to justify the expansion of policing initiatives and police power. Working with civilians to control communities is one way that police expand state power. Race "riots" throughout US history have moved communities of color to cry out for better relations with government institutions, even though police are often directly involved; brutality has been a weapon, a cause, and an outcome of these disturbances. In a race- and class-stratified society, police reinforce divisions and hierarchies. Complaints about police have provoked the contemporary "community policing era," but community discourse has worked mainly to strengthen criminal justice institutions. Police have deployed ideals about community to create and extend networks of individuals, organizations, and businesses across their territory, silencing antipolice discourse and becoming power brokers over neighborhoods' apparatuses of governance and social control.

Second, we argue that police governance over the community works to limit civilian power. Police attempt to turn civilians into appendages of the state—their "eyes and ears" on the street, as well as their "mouths" during crises. Such partnerships leave little room for the public's needs—or their authority. Co-governance becomes an exercise in repurposing community activists to share the responsibility of achieving police institutional goals. The meeting forum invites the public to share complaints, yet officers work hard to negotiate those complaints down to those most enforceable according to police standards. Information flows up to police from community partners, while messages about police integrity are pushed down to community partners. Small acts of resistance to these tactics by aggrieved individuals and groups are normal, but there is little internal avenue for them to coalesce into larger efforts.

Third, disputes about who does and does not count as "community" complicate mobilization. Under the umbrella of such a strangled partnership, internal community conflicts problematize intercommunity collaborations. People do not always consider themselves to be part of the same community just because they share space and can see the behavior of others as a nuisance or a danger that confirms their outsider status. In poor segregated urban neighborhoods already marked for social exclusion, these perceptions are often rooted in dominant racial interpretive frameworks and competition over scarce social and material resources. The promise of changing grim circumstances keeps residents engaged. Yet this engagement does not necessarily heal these divides but can encourage them instead.

Our observations suggest that interventions like CPAB have evolved within a long line of LAPD public relations tools—vehicles through which to showcase "goodwill and optimism," as SLO Fernandez put it—and widen enforcement capabilities while smothering independent community power. Contemporary community-based tactics are more similar to those that were implemented throughout the twentieth century than police and community policing scholars typically admit. While racial conflict appears to have improved on the surface, this is part of the community relations strategy. Outside of CPAB meetings, police continue to target neighborhoods of color while maintaining a rhetoric of accountability. Until police departments are forced to adapt directly to the needs of communities of color, grassroots organizations will lead initiatives that push for these changes. Below, we address these points in greater depth.

The Origins of Community Policing

Traditionally, criminological narratives position community policing as the third era in the evolution of US policing. In the "parochial" or "political" era, police were the direct tool of local politicians to acquire, maintain, and administer local political power. Police were not independent crime fighters, crime preventers, or public protectors, but rather tightly involved in the affairs of neighborhoods and accountable only to local political bosses (Kelling and Moore 1988; S. Walker and Katz 2002). Pelfry (2000) argues that the well-known New York Tammany Hall political machine perhaps best characterizes policing during this era. Officers corralled neighborhood groups to the polls and intimidated political opponents, as well as providing some limited social welfare services and suppressing or enabling vice depending on their own or their bosses' discretion. While LAPD's 1999–2000 Rampart scandal brings to mind very specific images of similar forms of police corruption, policing scholars regard the corruption of the police during the parochial era as epiphenomenal, insofar as officers were simply stewards of a larger politically corrupt system.

Kelling and Moore (1988) indicate that public dissatisfaction with this overall system led to a reform of police beginning in the 1920s. Political campaigns to reform police struggled to gain traction until several high-ranking and well-regarded police administrators took up the mantle. During this second era, which scholars refer to as the "reform" or "professional" era, police retreated from politics. To combat the parochial nature of the job, administrators professionalized policing, which involved not only insulating departments from the vulgarities of politics and providing job security for officers, but also outfitting departments with organizational technologies, such as patrol cars, radios, 911 systems, and standardized weaponry. Policing became less about order maintenance or political patronage and more strictly about reacting to crime; police training came to reflect this. Success became a matter of performance measurement instead of elections, orienting around criteria such as 911 response times and arrests. As one of our LAPD administrators, paraphrasing Kelling and Moore (1988), put it, the archetypical officer put forth the "just the facts, ma'am" detachment of *Dragnet*'s Joe Friday.

Collective acts of violence throughout the last century highlight how many problems in US policing persisted despite (or perhaps because of) attempts at professionalization. The twentieth century in the United States had more mass urban violence than any other period in history (Abu-Lughod 2007). The first half of the century can be characterized by massive outbreaks of White mob violence against Blacks and Mexicans, which mainly occurred in the quickly integrating northern and southwestern regions of the country (Bell 2013; Delgado 2009). In response to the larger problem of White supremacy, of which White mob violence was a key component, civil rights groups pressed the federal government to respond as they asserted their rights to full citizenship (Murakawa 2014). The relative intransigence of the White political establishment produced protest, and the rage of exploited Black and Brown communities exploded into a different wave of collective violence between the 1960s and 1970s. In contrast with White riots, where the actors were in many ways direct extensions of the White political establishment, the second wave produced political panic and eventually federal and state-level organized commissions calling for government institutions to build closer ties with minority communities (Abu-Lughod 2007).

Police were at the center of all these explosions of violence. Early in the last century, police sanctioned, aided, and facilitated White mob violence, some of which police officers themselves led. Largely White police forces tended not to be progressive bastions protecting the rights and bodies of communities of color, but rather stood in opposition to civil rights, maintaining a strict color line (Bell 2013; Sides 2003). Jim Crow, after all, was the law to be enforced, particularly for Blacks in the South and Latin@s in the Southwest, but segregationist policies underwrote urban development in the rest of the country as well. As civil rights legislation took hold in cities across the country and communities began integrating, White civilians regularly called police to interfere and disrupt these efforts with violent confrontations. Compared with the relative dearth of municipal services such as water, sanitation, education, and health, local police forces were built up and specifically began concentrating on enforcement in communities of color (Escobar 1999; Sides 2003). Incidents of police brutality and misconduct were high going into the 1960s, as was racially disparate treatment by the criminal justice system more broadly (Mirandé 1987; Sides 2003).

External oversight agencies throughout the twentieth century were largely responsible for forcing police to adopt reforms in what Walker and Bumphus (1992) call the "scandal and reform" process. Historically, a pattern emerged: Police engaged in some pattern or practice of misconduct or abuse that reached a boiling point, and the people responded with collective acts of violence. Soon after these events, the state organized a "blue ribbon" or "riot" commission to examine the causes of the outbreak. The formation of the Christopher Commission following the Rodney King beating incident, as we discuss in Chapter 1, remains perhaps the preeminent example of reforms brought on as a result of police misconduct in modern US policing. Walker and Bumphus (1992) explain that of all the various external oversight mechanisms, these commissions have the greatest degree of independence from the department. They typically (although not always) employ nonsworn, civilian staff to engage in fact-finding investigations, draft a report, and make disciplinary and policy recommendations.

Several reports found that a "siege mentality" had developed in some departments that produced violent and antagonistic relationships with the residents of the neighborhoods most subject to coercive policing practices (Greene 2000a; Pelfry 2000). As Kelling and Moore (1988, 8) put it:

> [D]espite attempts by police departments to create equitable police allocation systems and to provide impartial policing to all citizens, many minority citizens, especially blacks during the 1960's and 1970's, did not perceive their treatment as equitable or adequate. They protested not only police mistreatment, but lack of treatment—inadequate or insufficient

> services—as well. . . . [C]ivil rights and antiwar movements challenged police. This challenge took several forms. The legitimacy of police was questioned: students resisted police, minorities rioted against them, and the public, observing police via live television for the first time, questioned their tactics. More-over, despite police attempts to upgrade personnel through improved recruitment, training, and supervision, minorities and then women insisted that they had to be adequately represented in policing if police were to be legitimate.

From the perspective of these scholars, although professionalization was intended to morph policing into a respected occupation and legitimate the exercise of state power, the result was, frustratingly, a hardening of ungrateful attitudes—particularly residents in Black and Latin@ neighborhoods—toward police. This had some limited impact on White communities as well—"the public" in Kelling and Moore's formulation above was made distinct from "students" and "minorities"—and by the end of the 1970s, public dissatisfaction led to the advent of the "community policing" era (Greene and Pelfry 1997).

Criminal justice scholars argue that the community policing movement, although widely variegated in practice, had a core intent to engage the local community and bridge social distance between police and residents (C. C. Johnson and Roth 2003). Beginning in the mid-1980s, a flurry of articles emerged that defined programmatic, philosophical, and tactical elements, and were meant to institutionalize police-community engagement (Bayley 1986; Cordner 1995; Goldstein 1987; Morgan 1985; Skolnick and Bayley 1988). One element involved a visible, accessible, and caring police presence in the community. Block clubs, neighborhood watch groups, and community meetings organized by or with police were a centerpiece to this strategy. Scholars encouraged police patrols to enhance nonemergency service, intervening independently of emergency radio dispatch. Such patrols, particularly on foot and bike, were intended to improve communication and prevent crime, while mini-stations and mobile substations, liaisons with other public institutions, and "house calls" to area businesses and residences were also encouraged. Central to these deployments was enhanced flexibility and ability for officers to solve community problems directly and holistically rather than just responding to atomized 911 calls "on the queue."

Scholars recommended decentralizing the police command structure to empower individual officers to engage neighborhood problems and follow through over the long term, rather than using performance measures such as arrest or citation quotas.

Finally, scholars stressed the idea of increased police accountability to the public. Rather than self-assessments or periodic political purges, community policing required a dialogue with the policed. As a carrot to untrusting residents, policing began to incorporate ideas about "procedural justice" (Sunshine and Tyler 2003; Tyler 1990)—that is, opportunities for residents to participate in the policing project directly and democratically. Tyler (1990) and his colleagues argue that public perceptions of legitimacy increase when people feel they have been treated with respect and can voice their opinions about an event or interaction. When civilians trust the police, they are more likely to obey the law, be respectful and cooperative, accept proceedings, such as an arrest, and call the police in the future (Walker and Archbold 2014). Research suggests that civilians, in other words, are more concerned with having their day in court than with the outcomes they receive.

Police evolution from a parochial to a professional to a (now) community-engaged institution has become close to disciplinary gospel. Yet the institution of US policing is embedded within its own set of political and historical contexts and operates according to certain logics that are lost in such a narrative. While we take these up specifically relating to LA in Chapter 1, we rehearse the argument here. Policing has become the hard edge of executive power, gradually absorbing its methods and subjects from the military, militias, and slave patrols as the United States established itself as a nation that encouraged enslavement, expanded its borders at the expense of native populations, and became a powerhouse of capitalist production (Hadden 2003; Mirandé 1987; Rousey 1996; K. Williams 2007). To imagine a reverse scenario, policing's priorities have never been to protect the enslaved from their enslavers, native and Mexican land from Anglo prospectors, or the working class from exploitation.

In a basic sense, police are chartered to maintain order. Because social progress—pushing back against oppression—is usually somewhat disorderly, "order" tends to maintain the existing social and political investments in capitalism and White supremacy. As Reiman (1979) expresses it, police focus closely on the conduct of the "dangerous classes," while mainly ignoring the crimes of the powerful. While officers' daily tasks are more mundane than this suggests and they can individually effect genuine protection, this is not the cornerstone upon which their authority rests.

To maintain order, police must have the latitude to identify threat. When charged with guarding against unspecified threat, proscribing the conduct of state agents is counterproductive. Quoting Supreme Court Justice Samuel Miller, Wagner (2009) argues that the power of police as protector is essentially infinite: "The [police] power is, and must be from its very nature, incapable of any very exact definition or limitation" (6). The lurking danger identified by Wagner is the threat of race, but the legal architecture established as a result has its echo in class, anti-Muslim, and other antiprogressive suppression (Mirandé 1987; Sexton 2010; S. Smith 2006; K. Williams 2007). The result of this is police immunity from public accountability at the systemic level as well as the level of the line officer.[3]

Executive agencies have always crafted internal policies within their broad mandates. Known as administrative law, such policies can be curtailed by judicial review, yet the deference to the police continues here as well. Alexander (2010) has documented the series of court cases that demonstrate how police departments craft their own policies divorced from any dialogue with the law or the citizenry. Due to the publicization of various abuses, the US Justice Department and federal courts have required a number of local departments to submit to consent decrees. Although this oversight imposes a variety of rules, enforcement evaporates as soon as federal oversight ends. Civilian oversight boards, when established, tend to rubberstamp police procedures and are often resisted by officers (Human Rights Watch 1998; Skolnick and Fyfe 1993). Police chiefs and federal oversight come and go, but by and large police agencies retain their autonomy.

Co-opting the Community

In the community policing era, ideals regarding community, democracy, and accountability quickly become the talking points for police reform. What Vitale (2017) calls the "liberal approach" to police reform tends to emphasize individual "bad apples" acting within an otherwise sound organizational structure. The current crisis in policing has, however, expanded the focus from the individual to the organization, while deploying the same tools to address the problem. In Vitale's words:

> If entire police departments are discriminatory, abusive, or unprofessional, then [the liberal approach] advocates efforts to stamp out bias and bad practices through training, changes in leadership, and a variety of oversight mechanisms until legitimacy is reestablished. They argue that racist and brutal cops can be purged from the profession and an unbiased system of law enforcement reestablished in the interest of the whole of society. They want police to be better trained, more accountable, and less brutal and racist—laudable goals, but they leave intact the basic function of the police which has never been about public safety or crime control. (2017, 33)

Beyond individualistic approaches of training and purging bad apples, the liberal approach also focuses on institutional measures, such as community policing. Such reforms embrace police organizations, again, as fundamentally sound, requiring only internal tweaks to correct occasional injustices and restore police legitimacy. Criminologists have traditionally encouraged this perspective, treating police as an organ of the state that is consistently sensitive and responsive to changing community needs. Policing, in this view, is constantly reshaping and adjusting itself to align with what the public wants with respect to police service.

A key example of these assumptions of the liberal paradigm is the final report of former President Barack Obama's Task Force on 21st Century Policing (2015). Convened in response to the flood of national coverage on police killings of young Black people and the resulting urban rebellions, the Task Force produced a document calling for increased education, training, and technology for officers, but also the institutional rebuilding of trust, legitimacy, and oversight between police and community. It is far from clear that such a relationship has cooperative roots to which it should return, however. Yet the answer to questions involving racism and police brutality, the Task Force hints, is community policing—largely the same sets of reforms that were ubiquitous by the 1990s.

During the civil rights era, federal lawmakers similarly moved to reinforce police legitimacy in ways they argued would benefit marginalized communities. The Safe Streets Act of 1968 defined local crime as a problem for federal intervention. Unlike civil rights legislation, Safe Streets targeted Black and Brown subversion rather than White aggression, committing four hundred million dollars to remake local police, courts, and correctional systems. Safe Streets, built on the fear of Black protest, dictated the adoption of community-oriented approaches, such as "team policing"; lowered requirements for eavesdropping and wiretapping warrants; and facilitated the creation of federal and local crime control partnerships. Through Safe Streets, the federal government began auctioning off military equipment and integrating military tactics and personnel into local agencies (Balko 2013; Domanick 2016; Kraska 2007). Community integration on the one hand, militarization on the other.

Community governance scholars point out that state-civilian collaborations, intended to improve the state's legitimacy, often result in the expansion of its enforcement and regulatory capacities (Foucault 2010; Rose 1996; Vitale 2017; Wacquant 2009). The genesis of this approach can be found in the twin discussions of crime and protest during the civil rights era. When Black and Brown protesters took to the streets to demand their rights as Americans—at the same time as antiwar, socialist, and feminist protesters who were often White rose up—government at all levels struggled with how to react, ultimately (and grudgingly) granting new federal civil protections against discrimination. The seeds of a new era of social control were planted. Black protesters were first framed as schizophrenic (Metzl 2011); after it became clear that pathologizing individuals was insufficient, protest was rearticulated as criminal activity. Community demands could be engaged in a process of endless dialogue, while militants became enemies of the state. Out of this crucible came new strategies: the creation of a police state in the poor communities of color and the turn to community partnerships to help manage it.

At the same time as criminal justice scholars were defining the community policing canon, proponents of the War on Drugs and tough-on-crime politics were justifying the need for saturation policing and surveillance. The Violent Crime Control and Law Enforcement Act of 1994 was one response, extending the Safe Streets legacy of federal support for strengthening local law enforcement capacities. The act provided funding to put one hundred thousand more cops on the street, toughened sentencing laws, enshrined a host of new criminal offenses, and allocated nine billion dollars for prison construction (J. Simon 2007; US Department of Justice 1994; US Government Accountability Office 2005). The 1994 Crime Bill also established the federal COPS office, which has provided thirty billion dollars to local jurisdictions to support community policing, an undisclosed amount of which almost certainly went to militarization efforts (Balko 2013). In addition to providing a militarized response to drugs within poor communities of color, these laws also helped to concretize the new face of community under which law enforcement was to operate. This has become a standard—police departments now risk losing legitimacy if they do not claim to practice at least some sort of community-oriented approach (Walker and Katz 2002). Yet under this mandate police have also incorporated a drastic turn to saturation patrols, intrusive surveillance, and criminalization in Black and Brown communities (Stuart 2016; Wacquant 2009). Both community policing and mass incarceration have attracted an impressive number of commentators, but are seldom in the same conversation (but see Vitale 2017); the extent to which these trends move together and support one another has been largely neglected.

What we do know about mass incarceration, however, is that it plays a significant role in maintaining contemporary racial hierarchies. Richie (2012, 3), for instance, argues for a broader concept, the "prison nation," that expands prison logics of exclusion society-wide: "A prison nation refers to the dimensions of civil society that use the power of law, public policy, and institutional practices in strategic ways to advance hegemonic values and to overpower efforts by individuals and groups that challenge the status quo. . . . A prison nation depends on the ability of leaders to create fear (of terrorists or health reform); to identify scapegoats (like immigrants or feminists); and to reclassify people as enemies of a stable society (such as prisoners, activists, hip-hop artists)." It is not just the expansion of prisons that is the concern, but rather the expansion of all of the enabling processes that leverage community resources—surveillance, spatial regulation, broken windows policing, and the capitalization of urban space. At a fundamental level, the prison nation relies upon governmental and civilian collaborations to identify ever-growing numbers of enemy outsiders who must be contained, controlled, and removed from the community.

The Eyes, Ears, and Mouths

Governmentality scholars refer to the processes by which civilians adopt state-centered sensibilities and collaborate within state-sponsored institutions as the "responsibilization" of the citizenry (Garland 2001; Herbert 2006; Rose 1996). Such institutions reeducate the public to govern themselves according to state-oriented logics. Under public pressure, police agencies began admitting their failings, alluding to the many constraints upon the policing institution that limit its capacity to fight crime. From there, policy makers began asserting that "crime control is beyond the state" (Garland 2001, 123). The final turn institutionalized community-based programs that connected nonstate actors to formal governmental processes. Community policing is a prime example.

Community-based policing initiatives are intended to integrate residents of police-controlled territory into various police projects. Community-police meetings are an ubiquitous tactic, operated either by the department or precinct directly or by a civilian review board. In the federal COPS survey of community policing practices, Johnson and Roth (2003) report that by 2000 more than 93 percent of large agencies and over 55 percent of small municipal/county agencies reported holding regular community meetings; over 56 percent and nearly 21 percent of the same agencies reported the presence of "citizen action/advisory boards." They also note that the field teams sent by COPS to observe "community-policing practices," including meetings and community boards, found that these terms "turned out to have wide ranges of meanings in actual practice" (C. C. Johnson and Roth 2003, 5–3). Federal money may have enabled the spread of community policing, but it did not ensure its standardization—a concern or a feature, depending on one's perspective.

Although the promise of community partnership envisions democratic and cogovernance styles of community partnership, police afford themselves considerable latitude in constructing such partnerships, while civilian power is much more contingent (Goldstein 1987; Morgan 1985; Skolnick and Bayley 1988). One style is to create for civilians the role of police "eyes and ears." Skogan and Hartnett (1997, 134) evaluated community meetings in Chicago, where police informed residents of the best collaborative practices: "A sergeant described the [Chicago community policing program] to residents by telling them, 'You're the eyes and ears. . . . But we do the need the whole body. We are the hand and feet. We are the ones who chase and arrest them.' . . . As another sergeant put it, 'We need your input and information about felons, drug corners. We need you here every month.'" Such a role envisions community members as an extension of the police corpus, filling needs for intelligence around which police can form strategy and tactics.

Yet research suggests that resident complaints, one key outcome of the eyes and ears function, do not always result in the enforcement that residents might prefer. At meetings, residents complain about a wide range of community problems from graffiti to drug dealing to violence. Herbert's (2006) ethnography of police-community meetings in Seattle found that police were more likely to resort to traditional patrolling strategies than community-based strategies when identifying and responding to crime. Officers attending meetings frustrated the public with their slow and inefficient responses to complaints, while some officers avoided meetings altogether. Skogan's (2006) evaluation of community policing in Chicago found police similarly resistant to mobilizing in response to public request.

In addition to the eyes and ears, police also position civilians as "mouths": those who will volunteer to partner with police and take back messages of police support to their communities. It is no secret that community policing is often adopted or revamped by departments facing periods of crisis. The effort is seen as crucial to building police legitimacy. In analyzing the parallels between overseas military counterinsurgency and domestic efforts at policing, Williams (2011, 98) identifies the federal Weed and Seed program as comparable to the military strategy of Clear-Hold-Build, outlined in army field manuals: "Create a secure physical and psychological environment. Establish firm government control of the populace and area. Gain the populace's support." Weed and Seed similarly involves the "weeding" of gangs and other oppositional groups and "seeding" the area with groups friendly to and cooperative with the state. Community policing uses civilian nonprofits to recruit its own membership groups and uses them to push its messaging back to such nonprofits and then back out onto the streets. Together, the eyes, ears, and mouth functions produce responsibilized citizens that serve to protect police legitimacy, provide intelligence, and represent police viewpoints to skeptical neighbors.

Responsibilization of residents is always a work in progress, often interrupted by political events or crises precipitated by police themselves such as police killings of residents known as "officer-involved shootings" (OISs). The management of these interruptions can hinge on the success of volunteers' internalization of their roles. People's feelings about the police vary within any community, so responsibilization can be complicated. Many people in impoverished communities believe that police cause more harm than good, while those who live in constant fear of deportation or criminal profiling often avoid contact with law enforcement altogether (Coutin 2003; Rios 2011). These orientations toward law enforcement not only condition who composes the face of community policing by volunteering to attend meetings and staff initiatives, but also how they will engage once they attend.

Intercommunity Conflict

Communities undergoing rapid social change often experience conflict between the settled and settling populations. Research suggests that investigating the relations between groups—such as rules implicit to a particular neighborhood—can tells us much about the way communities change and engage with both formal and informal social control (Ewick and Silbey 1998; Greenhouse, Yngvesson, and Engel 1994; C. G. Martinez 2016). For instance, Ewick and Silbey (1998) discuss how parking practices in a neighborhood could provoke an informal community response. Neighbors claimed the parking spaces they dug out of the snow by placing chairs in them. A neighbor who moved a chair would violate community rules and would be subject to informal sanction. Similarly, Martinez's (2016) ethnography shows that rules of racial avoidance are deployed in a transitioning neighborhood in South LA to prevent violence. The violation of such carefully crafted rules can trigger violence between Black and Latin@ residents. Although the characteristics of neighborhoods differ, the nature of localized disputes can reveal the boundaries of social order.

Disputes between Black and Latin@ neighbors over social and material resources are becoming increasingly common (Kun and Pulido

2014; Telles, Sawyer, and Rivera-Salgado 2011). Segregation meant that large urban centers around the country were recognized as Black spaces in previous eras, but these are beginning to Latinize at an accelerating rate (Bonilla-Silva 2004). Negative racial attitudes between these groups emerged within a larger context of White supremacy, such that each group can reproduce pervasive stereotypes emphasizing Black danger or Latin@ illegality (Feagin and Cobas 2014). Conflicts over limited economic opportunities often erupt in the most strained sections of large cities, although there is little reason to believe that Blacks and Latin@s are in direct competition for employment opportunities (Telles, Sawyer, and Rivera-Salgado 2011).

Internal conflicts problematize community governance. Herbert (2005) argues that in a community policing context, the community is a political "trapdoor" that buckles under the weight of the responsibilities police place upon it. From their perspective, police confront a community that is politically ill equipped, disunited, or resistant to police expectations. This reduces the community's capacity to perform crime control. Studies show that historically bad police-community relations, racial/ethnic diversity, and intragroup conflicts can impede sustained public involvement in community partnerships (Grinc 1994). Language differences can also reinforce existing social cleavages, further entrenching residential disunity (Herbert 2005).

Conflicts occur not only between groups of residents, but also between residents and businesses in yet another dimension of localized conflict. Herbert (2005) shows that White business owners have significant influence over partnership operations in communities of color, which can work against the residential population. He explains that scholars have reason to be skeptical regarding community governance due to concerns that "localized associations will run roughshod over the desires and rights of those less well organized" (2005, 856). The potential threats that new businesses pose to the community become clearest when their interests are at odds, as we discuss in Chapter 4. While many of our study participants welcomed the arrival of new businesses for the promises of improving the local economy, businesses that sold alcohol were thought to potentially amplify existing crime and disorder and were less welcome. Despite this, and given that some businesses directly support LAPD, police advocated for new business franchises.

Studying Police-Community Collaborations in South Los Angeles

Communities of color such as South LA have been the subject of sociological study since W. E. B. Du Bois's Atlanta School and later the Chicago School produced their first ethnographies around the turn of last century (Morris 2015). Common sense of the time showed neighborhoods with large concentrations of migrants and ethnic and racial minorities, removed from communities of assimilated Whites, to be the natural order, but the closer sociologists have looked, the more they have found invisible hands designing urban life. Much of the public as well as many researchers continue to see poor urban communities as strange, dangerous places where undesirable people live in undesirable conditions and engage in undesirable conduct. When scholars identify neighborhoods like Lakeside as the product of social and economic forces, urban policing is often the point of application by which such forces exert influence. Given its history and LAPD's prominence, Lakeside is an ideal setting in which to deepen our understanding of the social processes through which police govern communities.

The South Bureau is the largest of the four LAPD bureaus that divide the city of Los Angeles—the others are Central, West, and the Valley. Within these bureaus are twenty-two police divisions or areas (i.e., precincts), each with its own centralized station and distinctive community policing style. The Lakeside Division station, where our fieldwork began, sits on the corner of a heavily trafficked street a full floor higher than the surrounding buildings. Squad cars line the streets around the station and helicopters sometimes land on the roof. Fast-talking young men roam the building's front steps, handing out bail bond information from their vans plastered with advertising decals, a cutthroat service made necessary by the legal system's principle of wealth (or credit) for freedom (L. D. Johnson 2015). Through the glass doors of the front entrance is the lobby where two officers peer down from behind a tall desk and direct the two lines of civilians queued in front of them. Pictures of notable police administrators stare down from the wall across from the main desk.

Lakeside, cut out of LA's geography along census tract borders for easy statistical tracking, is a distressed community. Census numbers during our research placed unemployment at about 40 percent, while about 30

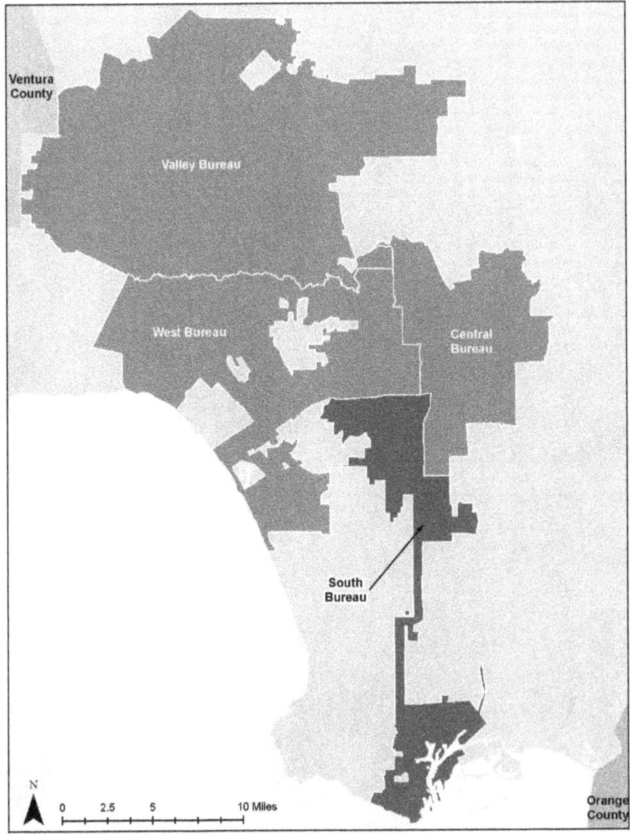

Figure I.1. Map of the four LAPD bureaus.

percent of residents lived under the poverty line. Public services were strained as a result and private investment was limited. In 2011, organizers felt that no other facilities were capable of hosting a job fair, so Captain Himura agreed at the last minute to host five hundred job-seeking residents at the station. Schools with some of the nation's lowest graduation rates sat only a few blocks away. Many structures were in physical disarray—burned out, boarded up, or needing repairs. Secondary streets were lined with single-family, ranch-style homes and two- and three-story apartment complexes. Some homes were freshly painted with manicured lawns down picturesque palm-tree-lined streets, and many were also wrapped in wrought iron and had barred windows. Used tires,

Figures I.2 and I.3. A tree-lined street and a helicopter over a house in South LA.

mattresses, clothing, and trash lined many alleyways. Lakeside sometimes served as an informal way station into and out of LA's Skid Row, and a growing population of homeless people began to shelter there and set up tent cities along the nearby freeway.

South LA's racial makeup was changing quickly. Popularized in song and film, South LA historically had been a Black community, but the Black population had dropped dramatically since the mid-1980s, accompanied by a simultaneous rise in the Latin@ population. Blacks fled poverty, police harassment, and gang warfare while also being subject to forcible removal through incarceration. Many moved outside the city, to places like Antelope Valley to the north and San Bernardino to the east (Sides 2003). Fleeing poverty, military repression, and civil war in their homelands around the same time, Central American migrants moved to central city areas like Boyle Heights and Pico Union, as well as Lakeside, sharing space with both long-term and newly arrived Mexican immigrants (Vigil 2002). The few hole-in-the-wall southern-style restaurants that remained competed with new fast-food restaurants and *taquerías*. Schools began hiring more Spanish-language personnel and organizing events to connect with Latin@ parents. On weeknights, Black kids rode their skateboards in local parks and Latin@ kids played soccer on the tennis courts nearby.

Crime and punishment were interwoven throughout the social fabric. Residents complained of trash dumping and graffiti, car and home burglaries, and physical violence and homicide. They linked much of this to gangs or the homeless. Following a national trend, fear of crime remained high despite historic lows in the actual crime rate (Baumer and Wolff 2014). Despite the relative lows, South Bureau divisions routinely ranked among LA's highest in terms of property, violent, and particularly gang crime.[4] Although such statistics should be examined skeptically, South LA has the largest concentration of gang members registered in the statewide gang-tracking database.[5] Despite crime levels that rivaled the lows of the early 1960s or those of wealthier, Whiter communities in more crime-prone times, Lakeside's police presence remained undiminished. Wailing sirens, buzzing helicopters, and the occasional crack of gunfire contributed to the neighborhood soundtrack. Various groups, such as neighborhood associations, civil rights groups, community organizations, and government-run groups, organized public safety initiatives with various goals, but all recognized Los Angeles as hosting one of the most active criminal justice systems in the United States. LA sends more people to state prisons than any other county in California. Most of the people in the system are Black and Brown. Blacks are vastly overrepresented, while Latin@s are by far the most numerous group under formal correctional supervision (Muñiz and McGill 2012). Crime and overincarceration do not have a simple cause-and-effect relationship. Structural

Figures 1.4 and 1.5. Kids playing soccer and the "no soccer" sign.

disruption of this magnitude cannot help but increase crime and poverty, producing physical and mental health challenges, reducing employment and earnings, disrupting families, increasing debt, destabilizing housing, reducing informal social control, and elevating legal cynicism within such neighborhoods (for a review, see D. S. Kirk and Wakefield 2018).

South LA is like segregated areas in other large cities in many respects. Like LA, cities in the Northeast and Midwest were among the largest recipients of Black migrants during the Great Migration from southern states. All developed distinctive segregationist policies restricting Black and Brown life and erupted into "race riots" in the twentieth century. Other US cities too became large industrial centers that began shedding manufacturing jobs in the 1970s, while replacing some with service positions, which accompanied large influxes of Latin@ migrants. Other cities also have hyperactive criminal justice systems and cases of police brutality that have become national symbols (Taylor 2016). While none of these things mean that our findings necessarily are generalizable to all urban US cities, the problems that confront civilians and police on South LA streets are often similar, in kind if not degree. Our observations may deepen future understandings of these common social processes.

This collaborative investigation draws on field data collected between summer 2008 and spring 2013 in one South Los Angeles Division. Armed with notebooks and pens, we began by attending public safety meetings and events at the Lakeside police station. We soon expanded to other specialized public safety forums and neighborhood associations within the division. We observed and participated in community carnivals, emergency preparedness fairs, day-in-the-park events, Officer Appreciation Day (OAD) celebrations, and other community events. Quests for ride-alongs and interviews took us all over the division, as we sat down with gang interventionists, resource providers, community leaders, and school teachers, observing social dynamics in schools, parks, and churches.

With time, we began walking into the station past the guarded front desk and through "Personnel Only" doors without question. We submitted to fingerprint and background screenings to obtain the name tags and nameplates that identified us at the station. Group leaders and police officials knew us as doctoral student researchers from the University of California, Irvine. But new participants or officials did not know this until we introduced ourselves.[6] Upon meeting us, several were surprised that we were not undercover detectives, "or at least a probation officer," as one SLO told Danny.[7]

We were both in our mid- to late twenties when we began fieldwork. Looking back through the eyes of a meeting participant, it is perfectly logical that two people matching our description would be cops. Most LAPD officers are Latin@ or White (in that order) and in their late twenties or early thirties (LAPD 2017). The two of us probably looked like buddy cops right out of a Hollywood movie. Danny is the Latino guy, Aaron the White guy. Our dress depended on the formality of the event, but we often wore jeans. Danny usually wore an untucked collared shirt, Aaron usually a blank T-shirt under an unbuttoned collared shirt with the sleeves rolled up. Aaron has the build of a long-distance runner, lean and tall. Danny has the build of a weekend *futbolista*, solid and imposing.

Collaborations are rare in ethnographic research. Most scholars recognize ethnography as a solo venture of situated scientific discovery (Gupta and Ferguson 1997). Traditionally, cooperative ethnographies have been produced by husband and wife teams (for a critical review, see Ariëns and Strijp 1989). But multiresearcher ethnographies examining marginalized populations (Bourgois and Schonberg 2009) and criminal justice settings (Conley and O'Barr 1990) are becoming more common. Bourgois and Schonberg (2009, 12) explain that ethnographers perform at least two functions in the field: "Ethnography is an artisanal practice that involves interpretive and political choices. On the one hand, the researcher merges into the environment, relaxing into conversations, friendships, and interactions and participating in everyday activities. On the other hand, the observer is mentally racing to register the significance of what is occurring and to conceptualize strategies to deepen that understanding." The ability to have two ethnographers doing this simultaneously is invaluable.

We almost always collected field data together. After conducting observations, we would each expand our notebook jottings into typed fieldnotes. Our typed accounts described each meeting, summarizing the exchanges and sometimes transcribing the dialogue. As a practical matter, we often wrote separately to preserve the first-person nature of ethnographic accounts and let the fieldnotes express how our personalities and positionalities shaped the social dynamics we observed. Sometimes we cowrote fieldnotes to construct thicker descriptions of especially lengthy or complex gatherings. We each developed closer relationships with different police and community participants. This allowed us to gain broader access and coverage and generated distinct perspectives on the same events. Collectively, our observations amounted to hundreds of hours of fieldwork and thousands of pages of fieldnotes.

We always exchanged fieldnotes. Collaborative research lends to the validity of data collection methods, offering thicker description through coinciding accounts (Emerson, Fretz, and Shaw 1995; May and Pattillo-McCoy 2000). We systematically compared our observations to identify significant departures in action and language, skipping purposefully over minor deviations in personal or spatial descriptors. When comparing notes, we paid closer attention to interactions and language use. We did not always agree on the specifics of what we heard, saw, or felt, so when inconsistencies emerged, we discussed how they deepened our understanding of the setting. We think that these disagreements add robustness to our fieldwork (see Bourgois and Schonberg 2009, 11). In practice, for most major issues there were few significant departures. In either case, both sets of fieldnotes stand as finalized data, and we both stand behind the data and interpretations, no matter the author. Rather than a challenge to validity, diverging accounts highlight the complexities of different social worlds. The "truths" that ethnographers observe depend on the personal and academic background of each ethnographer, and different interpretations may be equally true (Emerson, Fretz, and Shaw 1995; May and Pattillo-McCoy 2000).

We organized and analyzed our fieldnotes using qualitative data analysis software, systematically coding fieldnotes for significant and recurrent themes. When identifying a key theme, we adopted a two-stage process for fleshing out its meaning. We began by first elaborating on the theoretical significance of an individual fieldnote excerpt in a short, preliminary memo. Then we wrote lengthier, more substantial memos relating two or more excerpts or memos to explain their theoretical significance.

To situate our observational findings within a larger context, we analyzed LA City and LAPD documents. In 2009, we obtained an informal archive of community policing documents from the files of Dr. Cheryl

Maxson at UCI.[8] Some are easily accessible in the public domain, while others are internal memoranda and administrative directives. Our goal was to understand LAPD's plans to implement community policing in the early 1990s. These documents are, in some cases, more than twenty-five years old. Because they are physical copies, we sorted and hand-typed all passages that dealt directly with the organizing concept of "community policing" through our open coding procedure. The themes gleaned from these documents informed interviews with former and current LAPD administrators who shepherded the community policing project in its early years and were integral to crafting parts of Chapters 1 and 3.

We also collected in-depth interviews. We employed a sampling method for those attending various community policing functions that was part purposive and part convenience. The former reflected our desire to speak with key stakeholders, while the latter acknowledges the inaccessibility of some desired interviewees. Interviewees included community residents and activists, police officers, and prosecutors.[9] Our conversations with them lasted between thirty minutes and three hours and took place in coffee shops, restaurants, business and government offices, personal residences, and borrowed interrogation rooms. Study participants consented to be tape-recorded, with a few exceptions. When participants (nearly always police officers) gave consent for interviews but not recordings, we handwrote notes during the interview and typed out detailed reports immediately afterward. We steered research participants to talk about what community meant, what problems they confronted, and who should take charge of the response and how. Many conversations continued long beyond the formal interviews. We use pseudonyms for all participants as well as places and landmarks in all fieldnotes and transcripts to protect the privacy of the people who were so generous with their time.[10]

Organization of the Book

The world of community policing is removed from more spectacular police violences in kind but not in logic. The task of community policing is not only to rebuild bridges that may never have existed but also to repair social systems that have never fully materialized and heal rifts between marginalized populations caused by the state in the first place. Our job in the succeeding pages is to understand the relatively mundane world of community policing in light of shifting political, economic, and demographic contexts.

We begin by looking back at LA's history of change, conflict, and police intervention. Chapter 1 traces the dynamics of policing in Black and Brown LA and its shaky foundation going back to the 1940s. This intersecting history demonstrates not only how similar and cyclical mass violence has been but how the department's responses have been patterned as well and what that means for contemporary community policing. Chapter 2 continues by looking through the eyes of Ms. Mayfield, a CPAB member, to examine change and conflict in Lakeside. We look back at how the neighborhood has changed at the social, economic, and demographic levels. Then we explore how racial attitudes and intergroup conflicts have emerged as a result. We end by discussing the past and present of Black-Latin@ solidarity.

Then we explore the social arrangements of community governance internal to and outside of the station. Chapter 3 focuses on the power dynamics involved in organizing community meetings, focusing on Lakeside Captains Himura and Patton. We discuss the split between English and Spanish meetings, their goals, and the techniques that Captains employ to responsibilize the community. Chapter 5 examines the role of Senior Leads and the Community Relations Office in governing the business community. Officers define businesses as members of the community and claim to serve them as they would any other civilian. In the process, officers criminalize their customers to maintain a stable market environment, while leveraging their authority as gatekeepers to shape both the security and composition of Lakeside.

We open the doors of the meeting room and focus on the contests and challenges of police-community collaboration. Chapter 4 reveals how community status shapes complaints. We juxtapose three complainants—Mr. Palmer, Ms. Carter, and Sra. Santos. Their encounters in meetings demonstrate how much police restrict residents in their capacity as the faces of community policing. Through three meeting leaders—Mrs. Fisher, Sr. Mendoza, and Ms. Coleman—Chapter 6 explores how power struggles with police and racial antagonisms between Blacks and Latin@s problematize the goals of community policing. These can diminish the influence community leaders have in shaping police action and their relationships to community groups more broadly. The chapter ends by examining the experience of Ms. Coleman, who attempts to hold LAPD accountable for their treatment of community volunteers.

This book concludes by taking the reader through another discussion of race, crime, and policing in the community. This time we explore the 2013 Christopher Dorner case and demonstrate that the CPAB is not an adequate forum for police oversight and accountability. Policing as an institution remains largely unaccountable, and the past fifty years of legal decision making at the federal level have solidified, not dissolved, this impunity. Despite a wealth of community rhetoric, collaborative meetings, like other community-based initiatives, reflect mainly the needs of the state. Community policing remains the state's response to mass protest surrounding issues of police brutality and maintenance of the racial order, but if it remains undemocratized, democracy itself will again take to the streets. We turn now to LA as the site of our research.

1

Roots, Rebellion, and Reform

> Building trust and nurturing legitimacy on both sides of the police/citizen divide is the foundational principle underlying the nature of relations between law enforcement agencies and the communities they serve. . . . Law enforcement cannot build community trust if it is seen as an occupying force coming in from outside to impose control on the community.
>
> —President's Task Force on 21st Century Policing (2015)

After the 2014 uprisings died down in Ferguson, Missouri, President Barack Obama's Task Force on 21st Century Policing identified what it considered to be the source of the problem: mutual distrust between police and civilians.[1] Investigators from the US Department of Justice (2015) concluded the same. DOJ presented evidence that both police and city agencies had for years been systemically targeting Blacks in the poorest neighborhoods of Ferguson with increased police contact and court-imposed financial penalties for minor offenses. Such treatment, found throughout the suburbs and East St. Louis, effectively locked much of the Black community into a cycle of poverty and imprisonment. Young Black men like Michael Brown saw police as an "outside force" that both feared them and used them to extract scant resources, while police saw young men like Brown simply as criminals (Balko 2014). While DOJ investigated Ferguson, there were similar cases in large cities across the United States; Clevelanders shouted the name of Tamir Rice, New Yorkers rose for Eric Garner, and the people of Waller County stood up for Sandra Bland. Reactions coalesced into the Black Lives Matter movement, which identified the staggering numbers of Blacks killed by police; simultaneously, police and conservative commentators produced increasingly negative reactions to such public pressure. All of this attested to a widespread and deeply rooted mutual distrust (Taylor 2016).

Closely examining three of LA's biggest violent disturbances—the 1943 Government Riot (popularly known as the Zoot Suit Riots), the 1965 Watts Rebellion, and the 1992 Rodney King Uprisings—reveals that government appeals to mutual trust and collaboration are among the most common post-disturbance police reforms. Each civil disturbance in LA motivated the creation of a state-organized commission to spearhead reforms that sought to rebuild the public's confidence in the police. Building on Vitale's (2017) examination of liberal police reforms in the United States, we look back at each commission report to understand the nature of their recommendations with respect to enhanced training, workforce diversity, and improved public accountability and community relations. From one commission to the next, report authors recommended that LAPD integrate additional training measures, such as cultural sensitivity or Spanish-language skills; they recommended the Department hire more officers of color; they recommended greater oversight by local government, greater sensitivity to the needs of communities of color, and the introduction of collaborative, non-enforcement-based strategies to reduce crime in strained areas of the city. Although the United States is well into the "community policing era," it would seem that each of these landmark events in LA's history produced a similar series of police and legal reforms that quieted public resentment. Subsequent uprisings, however, call their effectiveness into question.

To contextualize these reports, we look back at the preconditions of each disturbance and how these shaped LAPD's post-disturbance reform agenda. Collective violence in LA repeatedly involved young men of color whom police and the press perceived as violent and dangerous criminals. From the 1960s onward, Black and Latin@ rage at structural conditions took the place of White hatred in motivating civil disturbances in LA (Abu-Lughod 2007; Valle and Torres 2000). Successive waves of new migration further destabilized LA's social and racial order. Periods of economic growth lured new migrants to the city with the promise of greater opportunities, but these promises were seldom realized. LA made few accommodations for the rapidly expanding population, and subsequent economic downturns plunged many newcomers back into poverty. LAPD was intimately involved in such urban governance efforts, repeatedly organizing specialized units to criminalize priority enforcement targets as the public image of the criminal evolved from subversive labor union organizer to dangerous and drug-selling gang member—usually a young man of color (Abu-Lughod 2007).

LA's history of violent disturbances reveals that community governance discourse is a public confidence-building project. The rhetoric each time of rebuilding strained relationships between police and communities of color was a misstatement of the problem—there is no period of tranquility and harmony to which relations can return. Prior to 1992, post-disturbance reforms could not reorient police priorities or make police more responsible to the most heavily policed communities because the relationship between communities of color and the state remained (and remains) one of oppression and exploitation. To maintain and reinforce this dynamic without invoking violent resistance, LAPD officials in the wake of each of these disturbances found just cause to strengthen and expand their policing capacity. As the twentieth century wore on, LAPD became a leader in militarized domestic police operations, even after officially adopting community governance strategies. Police created inroads into poor Black and Brown communities and became more thoroughly integrated into community life, facilitating the criminalization of those groups in the process (Murakawa 2014; J. Simon 2007).

Government Riot

Early in June 1943, ten drunken Navy servicemen stumbled, beaten, back to Chavez Ravine where they were stationed. A naval commander at the time claimed that several "pachucos," an umbrella term for those perceived to be Mexican American gang members, blindsided his men in an alley. Later, naval commanders discovered that another group of White servicemen and civilians were the real culprits (Escobar 1999). Angered by the incident, other Navy servicemen took matters into their own hands and set off what would later be called the Zoot Suit Riots. Mirandé (1987), however, recognizing that this blames the victims of the violence, refers to it as a "government riot." Between June 3 and 10, more than two hundred Navy servicemen and off-duty police officers conspired to commit acts of vigilante violence. They descended into Mexican barrios in a fleet of rented taxis and pulled young Chican@s from bars, restaurants, theaters, and dance halls, exacting their revenge. After harassing and beating young Chican@s, they ritually stripped them of their zoot suits and left them bloodied in the street. Police sanctioned these attacks. While some participated in the violence directly, most on-duty police purposely arrived late to the scenes, ultimately arresting six hundred Chican@ (and some Black) victims on suspicion of robbery and assault. Taking their cue from police, newspapers also blamed the victims for the violence and claimed this incident was proof of a Mexican "crime wave" (Escobar 1999).[2]

Henry "Hank" Leyvas, a Mexican American teenager from East LA, was at the center of the city's growing anti-Mexican hysteria during World War II. A year prior to the outbreak of the Government Riot, "pachuco madness" caught fire. Police arrested Hank and seventeen other Mexican American teenagers for involvement in the homicide of Jose Diaz, a Chican@ teenager from another barrio. They dubbed the group the 38th Street Gang and fingered Hank as the leader. LA County Judge Charles C. Fricke charged the gang with murder and conspiracy (Mirandé 1987). Anti-Mexican attitudes among LA's law enforcement community were laid bare throughout the trial. Police-Chican@ conflict was particularly intense given the rookie status of most line officers, who had been forced onto the streets when LAPD's most experienced officers went off to war. Police, the larger White community, and LA's media all believed the youngsters were guilty prior to the trial, with the latter circulating "zoot-suit gangster" and "pachuco killer" headlines (Escobar 1999).

The emergence of zoot-suit culture was a direct response to police brutality but also to the larger racism of White society embodied in the war effort. The zoot-suit style was seen as un-American. In 1942 the War Production Bureau imposed fabric rations and specifically forbade their manufacture and sale, so when White serviceman saw young men of color wearing zoot suits, they took grave exception. Whites and servicemen perceived young men of color as draft dodgers, purposely avoiding a "White man's war," which further justified their resentment (Kelley 1996). Zoot suits, car clubs, and street gangs became primary cultural expressions for marginalized, alienated, and oppressed youth of color.

Donning zoot suits was a cultural awakening for Chican@ Angelenos who increasingly saw themselves as "Mexican Americans."[3] Many were war veterans who rejected the labels of "foreigner" and "illegal alien," and refused to accept the second-class citizenship and the conditions of Jim Crow LA (Escobar 1999). Emboldened by the antisegregation movement, which eventually led to such legal cases as *Brown v. Board* in 1954, zoot-suiters rejected a subservient role in society and embraced a subversive culture (Kelley 1996). The suit embodied their nonconformity and resistance (Kun and Pulido 2014). Their desire to integrate into public spaces made them vulnerable to White hatred and precipitated violent police encounters. Zoot-suiters soon began countering police aggression by mouthing off, resisting arrest, and fighting with officers (Escobar 1999).

The Brown Scare

White hatred toward Chican@s increased as the population grew between the two world wars. Just over fifty thousand in 1890, the Mexican population in LA jumped to over five hundred thousand within thirty years and grew by two million more when Mexican rural peasants migrated to the city, fleeing the violence and economic dislocation of the Mexican Revolution (Escobar 1999; Vigil 2002). Since the 1930s, the second largest Mexican population outside of Mexico City has resided in LA, and this remains true today. Whites at the time viewed all "foreigners" with intense suspicion, but particularly Mexicans, who were seen as German allies. White fears encompassed proximity to the border, the growing population, and the belief that socialist revolutionary rhetoric was spreading among Mexican Angelenos. Later, due to the heavy participation of Chican@s in the labor movement, the nationwide Red Scare merged with anti-Mexican sentiment to become the Brown Scare in LA (Escobar 1999).

LA's White power structure had taken shape decades before when White industrialists, local police, and the local news media forged an alliance. Most White immigrants were foreign-born Europeans. The disappearance of adobe structures and replacement with Protestant churches in the aftermath of the Mexican-US War signaled a shift in LA's racial order. In the 1920s the city's economy became heavily dependent on manufacturing, which was concentrated along Central Avenue in South LA. City governors, trying to tempt new industrialists, labeled the city the "citadel of the open shop" and promised to maintain this antiunion reputation. Business associations formed to combat the growing labor union activity and sought help from the LAPD to ensure city officials fulfilled their promises. News accounts condemned Mexicans as drunk, volatile, and irresponsible and condemned labor unions as communist recruiters. They also called for organized vigilantism and the formation of a "safety committee" composed of business owners who would advise the chief of police on the handling of Mexican unionists (Escobar 1999).

Jim Crow laws restricted almost every aspect of Mexican social life and were resisted by the Mexican American community. Segregationist policies and White intimidation confined Mexicans to either "Sonoratown"—the city's original town plaza—or the neighborhoods east of the LA River. But they also crowded around "company towns" in smaller pockets along Central Avenue, in Watts, and in the Harbor area. Living conditions in these barrios were among the worst in California. Neighborhoods were overcrowded. Houses were dirty, cramped, and dilapidated. Children suffered malnutrition and respiratory problems. White teachers prohibited Chican@ students from speaking Spanish in schools and "tracked" them into remedial classes purportedly due to their lesser abilities (Vigil 2002). Discriminatory hiring practices restricted Mexican employment. Mexicans were significantly underemployed and unemployed when compared to other racial groups. Openings tended to be for work that Whites refused: seasonal, menial, and low wage. Homelessness and hunger meant that many Mexicans depended upon government food trucks for sustenance during the Great Depression (Escobar 1999).

Mexican labor leaders fought back against their economic and racial oppression and developed a sophisticated radical movement that integrated churches, mutual aid organizations, businesses, and neighborhood associations (Vigil 2002). Civil rights groups joined in the struggle against discriminatory and exploitative labor practices. When these groups organized strikes, there were few victories due to the relationship between police and local industrialists. Civil rights groups charged the LAPD with being anti-Mexican and practicing acts of misconduct and abuse, ranging from the use of racial slurs to sexually harassing and groping women and arbitrary field searches and brutality. Mexicans distrusted police and saw them, accurately, as the violent enforcers of Jim Crow segregation (Escobar 1999).

Judge Fricke and the Red Squad

The prosecution of Hank Leyvas and the other youth of the so-called 38th Street Gang in 1942 was known as the Sleepy Lagoon Trial. Steeped in controversy, the trial exposed systemic anti-Mexican racism. Judge Fricke was widely known as both anti-Mexican and a proponent of law and order. He refused to allow defendants to change out of their clothes or to confer with their defense attorney throughout the trail. Defendants wore their zoot suits—by the time they got to court, their clothes were dirty, scuffed, and bloody, after the violence meted out on the streets and the LAPD beatings administered during their interrogations (Escobar 1999). Prosecutors argued that the defendants' distinctive clothing was important evidence in this case, while critics pointed to this as an attempt to bias the jury. Police testimony revealed the extent of their anti-Mexican beliefs as well: police viewed Mexicans as poor, lazy, and immoral troublemakers, whose violence was rooted in their "Aztec heritage" (Mirandé 1987). The courts accepted these views and convicted the group. In 1944, while Leyvas and others were serving prison sentences in San Quentin, California's Second District Appeals Court overturned all seventeen convictions due to a lack of evidence and charged Judge Fricke with "severe misconduct" (Escobar 1999).

In the years leading up to the Sleepy Lagoon Trial, LA's Chiefs of Police cycled in and out, forced to resign mainly as a result of corruption and brutality scandals that reflected the pervasive violence of White racism in law enforcement. In 1923, for example, city officials discovered that LAPD's Chief was an active Ku Klux Klan (KKK) member, which came to light only because several other officers and Klansmen had been killed while conducting an unsanctioned vice raid (Sides 2003). Police also worked directly with business owners to maintain union-free "open shops" for unrestricted labor exploitation, practices resisted by unions (K. Williams 2007). Another Chief accepted increased departmental funds from beet growers in exchange for breaking farmworker strikes—an institutional rather than personal quid pro quo (Escobar 1999). The creation of LAPD, meant to curb the violent vigilantism of the LA Rangers police-militia in the post–Mexican-US War era, in some ways institutionalized and amplified the danger posed to non-Whites and the working class.[4]

Reflecting national trends in police expansion, LAPD began developing specialized police units specifically to counter Mexican radicalism (Escobar 1999; Sides 2003; K. Williams 2007). Buoyed by federal anticommunist laws, LAPD's Red Squad worked to quell radicalism after union organizers, frustrated by the LA business community's ruthless antiunionism, bombed the *LA Times* building in 1910. The Red Squad disrupted union activity through surveillance, investigation, and arrest, as well as espionage, sabotage, strike breaking, intimidation, harassment, physical violence, and their own bombings. LAPD imposed a gun and liquor embargo on Mexicans and, in its first efforts at diversity, set up a "special police force" mainly composed of Mexican officers to infiltrate, surveil, and suppress criminal and radical activity in Sonoratown. City officials also enacted "sumptuary laws" to reduce vice, targeting Mexicans disproportionately for alcohol consumption, prostitution, and gambling, producing further racial exclusion (Escobar 1999). Police also performed dragnet operations, wherein hundreds of officers would walk block by block arresting "suspicious characters" for minor offenses (Domanick 2016). Several "riots" erupted after the Red Squad responded to labor disputes with force (Escobar 1999).[5]

Other government agencies enhanced their exclusion of the Mexican population in the early 1930s. The Great Depression prompted the federal government to create general relief programs, but racial preferences in many programs resulted in what Katznelson (2006) refers to as "welfare for Whites." In rhetoric recognizable today, Anglos saw Mexican migrants as scapegoats, perceiving them as economic competitors and an overall drain on the US economy (Balderrama and Rodriguez 2006). California state law expanded its efforts to prohibit companies from hiring "foreign" and "alien" workers in an effort to stem White unemployment while at the same time denying Mexicans public relief and compounding their economic vulnerability. With the support of many Whites, immigration agents began a massive deportation campaign in East LA, seeking to remove Mexican "undesirables" and "illegal aliens." Agents conducted neighborhood roundups and stormed into family homes; LA City Council, meanwhile, refused to officially allow LAPD to enforce federal law and prohibited direct police involvement in these deportations. Meanwhile, private business quietly prepared for the country's economy to stabilize once more, since they would again need cheap Mexican labor (Escobar 1999).

The McGucken Committee

In some ways, LA was not surprised by the Government Riot. Prior to the violence, the city government was already trying to rein in police corruption, vice, and abuse. August Vollmer, widely considered the father of police professionalism, left the Berkeley Police Department briefly to assume the role of Chief in 1923 after LAPD's KKK scandal (Sides 2003). Before leaving after one year, disillusioned, Vollmer established professional standards, requiring screenings, education, and guidelines for criminal investigations, in order to prevent corruption and abuse. He also enhanced police infrastructure, opening new jails and stations and outfitting them with phones and other communication systems (Escobar 1999).

Days after the Government Riot, Earl Warren, the newly elected Governor of California, appointed Auxiliary Bishop Joseph T. McGucken of the LA Archdiocese to head a Citizen's Committee that would investigate the causes and advise the government on next steps. The McGucken Committee found that the riot had largely been the result of pervasive anti-Mexican racism and boiling resentment among Mexican American youth toward the deplorable conditions into which LA's White power structure had forced the community. While the committee concluded that "[n]one of the warring elements has clean hands" (McGucken 1943b, 1), the report went out of its way to note that although juvenile crime had increased, there was nothing to suggest that this was a uniquely, or even primarily, Mexican American (or African American) problem. Indeed, to its credit, the committee took strong stands against racial discrimination both generally and by law enforcement specifically. LAPD came in for special scrutiny. The report uncovered many cases in which police officers willfully disregarded the complaints of innocent Chican@ youth mistaken for gang members and attacked solely due to their Mexican (or Black) appearance. LAPD was also reprimanded for its enforcement methods: "Mass arrests, drag-net raids and other wholesale classifications of groups of people are based on false premises and tend merely to aggravate the situation. Any American citizen suspected of crime is entitled to be treated as an individual . . . regardless of race, color, creed or the kind of clothes he wears" (McGucken 1943b, 3–4).

The McGucken Committee recommended that LA law enforcement agencies improve their training methods, hire more Chican@ officers, and adopt community-based approaches to build better relations with young Chican@s.[6] The committee recommended that juvenile courts, underlined as one major contributor to the riot, draft and implement policy to deal with enhanced numbers of minority youth and that police train officers such that arrest decisions reflect misconduct rather than racial makeup. Further, the McGucken Committee recommended that officers undergo specialized training on Spanish-language skills, "Mexican psychology," and appropriate law enforcement techniques for juveniles (McGucken 1943b, 5). Within four months of the McGucken Report, the University of Southern California created and taught specialized courses for LAPD officers on these subjects as well Chican@ history and Caló, or Pachuc@ slang (Escobar 1999). LAPD officials also introduced racial sensitivity training and wrote a manual on how to respond during civil disturbances (McGucken 1943a). Complying with the committee's recommendation to diversify the police force was not difficult. It was already standard Red Squad practice to recruit a small contingency of police officers of color to infiltrate the community as part of their strikebreaking operations (Escobar 1999; Sides 2003). But LAPD responded further to the committee by hiring additional Chican@s, particularly war veterans, to serve (Escobar 1999; McGucken 1943a).

Although public accountability measures were not directly discussed in the McGucken Report, the final and lengthiest recommendation edged in that direction. The Citizen's Committee recommended that their group morph into a formal governmental entity called the "Interracial Council" that would assist in addressing "such serious problems as the acute housing shortage, the present housing quota imposed upon minority groups, race discrimination in the use of public facilities, unfair publicity [of defendants, preadjudication], and all other concerns which merely aggravate and inflame the groups concerned" (McGucken 1943b, 1). However, the committee was unable to recruit enough financing and leadership representing the interests of groups of color to collaborate (McGucken 1943a).

Inspired by Vollmer's earlier work, LAPD also established a youth-oriented program aimed at building social and civic capacities. Vollmer's Police Crime Prevention Division sought to address delinquency and was guided by his belief in the "perfectibility" of young Anglos through rehabilitative programming (Escobar 1999). The new Deputy Auxiliary Police (DAP) program, on the other hand, targeted gang-involved Chican@s, which impressed the McGucken Committee (McGucken 1943a). Participants underwent Americanization programming and learned the tenets of good citizenship, the virtues of cooperating with law enforcement, and leadership skills. DAP engaged participants in "wholesome leisure activities," such as handicrafts, sports, camping, and group picnics. DAP youth also received counseling, visited crime labs, and received lectures from FBI agents and gun maintenance instructions from representatives of the National Rifle Association. As participants in a proto-police program, DAP youth also engaged in crowd and event control (Escobar 1999).

As historians argued, however, Vollmer's progressive values continued to reinforce White supremacy. His delinquency prevention programs were largely reserved for White youth and helped normalize the presence of law enforcement in LA's public life (Escobar 1999). Such juvenile programs, criticized by Platt (1977) for their deference to market discipline, were not available to Black and Mexican youth, who were seen as deficient and suited only for domestic surveillance, cultural degradation, and exploitative labor (Chávez-García 2012; Ward 2012). Late to the Progressive Era, LAPD would eventually become known for its professionalism, which co-occurred with a violent enforcement of a strict class and color line. Even on those infrequent occasions when courts would issue injunctions or rule in favor of complainants of color, they could not control the rampant abuses that inherently characterize racialized enforcement (Escobar 1999).

Neighborhood Rebellion

On the night of August 10, 1965, a California Highway Patrolman pulled over Marquette Frye, a twenty-two-year-old Black man, and his brother on suspicion of driving under the influence. Though they were only a few blocks from their home, police insisted on impounding the car, which belonged to Marquette's mother, Rena Price. Reaching the scene, Price implored police to give her the vehicle and release her son, but police refused and attempted to take Marquette and the car into custody. A scuffle ensued and police struck Marquette and his brother with batons. Neighbors gathered while police called in reinforcements. Police arrested all three as well as a bystander.[7] Within a few hours, the crowd swelled to over a thousand residents, stoned passing cars, pulled out White motorists and beat them, and damaged an LAPD field office. Twenty-nine were arrested. By the next morning, 261 buildings, stretching from Watts to the neighboring city of Compton, had burned. Home and business owners in some neighborhoods resisted the violence and began taking up arms to defend their property (Abu-Lughod 2007; McCone and Christopher 1965; Sides 2003).

The night after Frye's arrest, community leaders organized a meeting to calm widespread discontentment, but eventually Watts would be considered the most destructive urban uprising in US history up to that point. Away on business, neither LA Mayor Sam Yorty nor LAPD Chief William H. Parker attended the meeting. Blacks interpreted their absences as callousness, and the meeting broke down. For the next six days violence, destruction, and confrontations with police worsened. LAPD set up a perimeter around the epicenter of the disorder, instituted a "curfew zone" to restrict movement, and labeled the violence a full-fledged rebellion. Parker eventually called in the National Guard. Black residents, including World War II and Korean War veterans, took up sniper positions on rooftops and drove away police and firefighters. Police responded by shooting to kill in the crowded streets. On the final day police allowed churches, community groups, and government agencies to distribute aid to residents. The rebellion resulted in thirty-four deaths, some by police gunfire, thousands of injuries, and more than forty million dollars in damages. Almost four thousand men and women were arrested during the violence for burglary and theft, five hundred of whom were under eighteen. The vast majority of those charged either were acquitted or had their cases dismissed (Abu-Lughod 2007; Sides 2003).

Young Black men in street clubs played a key role in the outbreak of violence; they, like zoot-suiters, had materialized as a defensive response to White racism and police aggression.[8] Street club members, angry at police aggression, derived a sense of pride, dignity, and racial empowerment from confronting police in the rebellion, calling it the "last great rumble" (Hunt and Ramón 2010). Barred from the Boy Scouts of America in the 1940s and 1950s because White troops resisted Black participation, young Blacks in South LA formed clubs like the Slausons, the Businessmen, and others (Peralta 2008). Soon they had to defend themselves as they faced violence from groups of young White hot rodders known as "Spook Hunters." Veritable extensions of the KKK, they opposed racial integration and intimidated and attacked Blacks in schools and out on the street (Alonso 2004).

The Undesirables

Blacks and Afro-Mestizos were among the city's founders, but the largest numbers of Blacks arrived throughout the Great Migration, which actually comprised two waves. Sides (2003) explains that the first wave, occurring around the time of World War I, comprised a group of well-educated middle-class Blacks hoping to achieve their class potential. The second, occurring around the time of World War II, included a much larger population of poor, rural, less educated Blacks, drawn by industrial jobs, which could lead to home ownership and other middle-class markers. Migrants boarded trains along the "sunset route" linking New Orleans, Houston, and Los Angeles, and the population grew from just about two thousand in 1900 to almost forty thousand by 1930. Most arrivals were rural southerners, who settled along Central Avenue and in Watts due to restrictive housing practices. Train operators forced Blacks to disembark at Central Avenue, the last train stop before downtown LA's segregated Union Station. The Black population of LA grew tenfold between 1940 and 1970, eventually totaling over 763,000 (Sides 2003; Vigil 2002).

Although World War II brought the city unprecedented economic growth, LA's antiunion, "open shop" environment exacerbated its uneven distribution. Forty-three million dollars in steel production and government ship and plane building contracts grew LA's manufacturing base during the war, and two billion dollars in construction and manufacturing investments expanded development afterward. Between the 1940s and the 1970s, LA gained tens of thousands of both low- and high-wage jobs. Quickly expanding opportunity created labor shortages; coupled with federal legislation that forced industry to loosen hiring requirements and the increasing power of organized labor, industrial employment could become a stepping stone to the middle class.

Although these gains were realized solidly by Whites, workers of color began to benefit from them as well.[9] By the 1950s, the stretch of factories from Central Avenue to the Port of Los Angeles became known as the "industrial corridor." Freeway construction into the 1960s fueled the auto industry and the region's driving culture, which facilitated access to growing suburban employment for those who could afford cars. LA became second only to Detroit in automotive production and related industries. Suburbanization simultaneously "killed" public transportation in South LA, leaving large portions of the population there isolated and stranded (Sides 2003).

Compared to the rural South, LA was seen by Black workers as the "promised land," a much more hospitable place, but that image faded over time (Sides 2003). Prior to the war, anti-Black violence was limited and Black home ownership was as high as that in any northern urban city—that is, better, but still outpaced by Whites. Black men worked largely as servers, train porters, and menial laborers; a few were musicians and entertainers. Black women worked almost exclusively as housekeepers. Still, southern transplants were employed at relatively higher rates, bought homes, and carved out a public life. Some achieved middle-class economic status into the 1950s. Together with the comparatively hospitable environment of Southern California, these opportunities made this postwar era the "Golden Age" of Black Los Angeles (Sides 2003).

Central Avenue was the heart of Black Los Angeles, but Watts would also become an important enclave. Though Central Avenue was known for its collection of Black-owned jazz clubs, restaurants, hotels, and other businesses, more than twenty-two thousand Mexicans lived in the neighborhood as well. By the 1950s, conditions were increasingly overcrowded and recent migrants lived behind storefronts, in shacks, garages, and old crates, and along back alleys, while small children played on neighborhood streets near industrial debris and runoff (Kun and Pulido 2014). Many Blacks had settled into Watts, or what was then called Mudtown, as early as the turn of the century; Pacific Electric built a company town there, attracting Anglo and Mexican laborers and Black homesteaders (Abu-Lughod 2007; Sides 2003). The Watts community grew as the interurban railway system grew, connecting downtown to outlying regions, including the San Pedro harbor farther south. Watts, by the 1940s, was about a third Black and half White or Chican@, with much smaller numbers of Mexican migrants and Asians. These groups lived in mixed, multicultural neighborhoods and shared a public life. Living this way shielded Blacks in part from the social and psychological detriments of segregation. Further, compulsory interracial contact helped Blacks forge communal bonds with other non-Whites (Sides 2003).

Anti-Black racism throughout South LA rose sharply as the Black population grew and Whites employed move-in violence and segregationist policies to maintain the racial hierarchy. Racial barriers of this period may not have been a coherent set of rigid policies, but they were no less pernicious. Black, Mexican, and other "undesirable" children had to wait for International Day to use public pools, which were subsequently drained and cleaned for White children the following week. In fact, many public spaces—theaters, dance halls, and amusement parks, not to mention neighborhoods—were segregated. White neighborhood associations formed, and the KKK reemerged to intimidate, attack, and terrorize Black integrationists. White mobs vandalized or bombed Black homes. In one case, a uniformed LAPD officer led a group of Whites in issuing death threats to a newly arrived Black family before burning a twelve-foot cross on their lawn (Sides 2003). The promise of a Golden Age never became a reality for large numbers of Blacks who settled in LA.

Chief Parker and the Color Line

William H. Parker, arguably the most influential figure in LAPD's history, served as Chief from 1950 to 1966—LAPD headquarters bore his name for decades until 2009. A decorated Army veteran, Parker first rose to prominence in the department when he was appointed to head the newly formed Internal Affairs Division (IAD). To keep pace with the post-Prohibition increase in organized crime, the Red Squad was renamed the Gangster Squad. Before long, a federal grand jury investigation revealed that the Gangster Squad was protecting a brothel run by a local vice lord (Escobar 1999). LAPD leadership created the IAD to maintain police independence and persuade the city not to establish a civilian oversight review board. Although IAD was not usually a popular division among officers, Parker's stern, uncompromising, rule-oriented approach to investigating corruption allowed him to springboard from head of IAD into the Chief position by discouraging bribery, blocking promotion for officers with misconduct records, and promoting uniformity in training standards. Recruits attended a military-style boot camp and adhered to strict standards in cleanliness, uniformity, and physical conditioning. He also expanded Vollmer's screenings for education, age, height, weight, and psychological fitness, while increasing salaries to help prevent corruption (Domanick 2016).

Parker officially institutionalized crime fighting as LAPD's official mission. His IAD experiences made him suspicious of close relationships between police and the larger community, reasoning that such coziness bred corruption. He rejected the notion of police as "social workers" involved in preventive and rehabilitative programming and discontinued many pre-1943 youth programs (Cannon 1999). He preferred officers to be socially distant, action-oriented, business-like professionals who spent their time patrolling, responding to the highest priority calls and making plentiful arrests of "enemies" on the street (Balko 2013; Cannon 1999). Parker regularly asserted that LAPD was the "thin blue line" between civilization and chaos, ingraining his officers with an "us-versus-them" attitude. Parker's belief that "everyone is a stranger" complemented his officers' "siege mentality"—the perception of LAPD as understaffed and overwhelmed by the city's population and sprawling geography—a mind-set that persisted well into the future (Greene 2000b; Herbert 1997). Anyone who looked "out of place" or "suspicious" suffered beatings and arrests at the hands of his officers. Young people of color tended to fit this description (Cannon 1999).

While taking strong stands against certain forms of corruption, Parker was proudly racist and fiercely opposed the racial integration of LAPD.[10] From its beginning as the White supremacist LA Rangers militia, policing in LA was founded on segregationist principles. While Parker was still an officer, LAPD established a "Black Watch" composed solely of Black officers, responsible for patrolling Black neighborhoods, joining the "special police unit" that patrolled Mexican neighborhoods (Cannon 1999; Escobar 1999). Officers in these units were not coequal and were used by the top brass mainly for jobs that other officers disdained, gathering intelligence and suppressing non-White communities. Rather than expand "specialized units," Parker went to great lengths to recruit southern White military veterans, many of whom refused to work with officers of color anyway (Cannon 1999; M. Davis 2006). Among other things, Parker believed that Mexicans were too short for the rough-and-tumble brand of law enforcement he envisioned (Morales 1972).

Parker's desire to maintain a strict color line extended into the streets. Shortly after he took office, for instance, Parker ordered a blockade in front of Dolphin's of Hollywood, a Black-owned record shop and recording studio on Central Avenue. Police warned Whites to stay away because it was "too dangerous." Parker was well known for making racist public statements, saying that young Mexican Angelenos were "not far from the wild tribes of Mexico" and likening Blacks to "monkeys in the zoo" (Balko 2013; Escobar 1999). Later he would launch an "all-out war on narcotics" in East and South LA to prevent marijuana and heroin from reaching White communities, an ethos and set of tactics that his successors would emulate (Sides 2003). Much like Vollmer in the Progressive Era, Parker was convinced that Black and Chican@ boys became hardcore criminals by their teenage years. The only way to deal with their misbehavior, in contrast to that of salvageable White youth who needed stricter discipline, was through physical intervention and incapacitation (M. Davis 2006). In the 1950s, police patrolled Alameda Boulevard, which separated Watts from the White communities of South Gate and Lynwood, and would stop, question, and harass young Black men who crossed (Sides 2003). But even when officers were found guilty of brutality in a court of law, there was often little recourse from Parker's LAPD.[11]

Police had several confrontations with the Black community, who, by the 1960s, were growing increasingly angry at their continued oppression by the police, especially after legal advances in their civil rights. As public space slowly integrated, Blacks were exposed directly to more White hostility, and police acted quickly to enforce racist norms. Yet as part of the growing national ethos toward self-determination and rejection of racist abuse, Blacks confronted police terror and began to retaliate. In 1961, four officers were injured in Griffith Park after police refused to release a Black teenager arrested for riding an amusement park ride without a ticket. A small crowd gathered and pelted police with rocks and flipped the patrol car. A year later a gun battle broke out between police and Black Muslims in front of a South LA mosque, leaving one Muslim dead and three Muslims and an officer wounded. Two years later another small riot touched off when police tried to arrest a Black teenager at Jefferson High School (Sides 2003).

The McCone Commission

Unlike the McGucken Committee, the McCone Commission, chartered by California Governor Edmund Brown to address the Watts Rebellion, exonerated LAPD from any wrongdoing in the buildup to the rebellion (McCone and Christopher 1965).[12] The report demonstrates a calculated confusion regarding the "distrust" and "hate" of Chief Parker by his Black critics who "carefully analyze for anti-Negro meaning almost every action he takes and every statement he makes" (28).[13] The McCone Commission concluded that Watts residents "resent" and "hate" police not due to their discriminatory treatment or officers' KKK affiliations, but rather because police represented a "symbol of authority" (2). In addition to willfully misrepresenting Parker and his critics, the report's authors also reacted defensively to more than seventy police brutality complaints that civilians registered to them directly. They lauded the internal LAPD oversight process for setting the "highest standards" and "conscientiously" enforcing them. Community demands for an independent civilian review board were dismissed summarily, as the commission reasoned that an outside board would have "likely deleterious effects on law enforcement" (31).

Instead, the commission recommended that LAPD increase officer diversity and improve existing accountability measures. Report authors believed that LAPD should hire more Black and Brown officers to avoid being perceived as an occupying force and improve the department's responsiveness to the community's needs. Beyond this, the commission recommended increased funding and staffing for the sluggish Board of Police Commissioners and replacement of the IAD with a military-style Inspector General, which would only expand existing internal processes. Though the report's authors praised LAPD for implementing community-based policies since the disturbance, recommendations included further expanding such measures. Parker was commended for appointing a Coordinator of Community Relations Activity and Community-Police Relations Advisory Committee as well as increasing the staff of the Community-Police Relations unit. Report authors also lamented Parker's elimination of the DAP and recommended that it be reestablished. Another suggestion was to expand existing school visitation programs from elementary to junior and senior high schools. Although the Commission loudly deplored racial discrimination, including an entire section titled "An End to Discrimination," there was no discussion of such within or by LAPD. Perhaps gesturing toward this, the report also recommended expanding human relations training for officers and that police hold open forums and workshops to discuss law enforcement with the community.

Parker's sudden death due to a heart attack in 1966 provided a brief opportunity to diversify policing strategies. New chief Thomas Reddin oversaw the rise of team policing, which he thought could improve community relations by involving civilians in the development of police enforcement practices (Escobar 1999; Sides 2003). In theory, team policing a dedicated unit of officers revolved around who would respond to one particular neighborhood without interference from other units. This unit was supposed to hold monthly meetings with residents, share information to identify crime without relying on traditional policing techniques, craft community-led solutions, and assess their progress. Reddin grew the department's community relations unit from four to over a hundred officers, implemented racial sensitivity training, reinstated foot patrols and some youth programs, and recruited more Blacks and Latin@s. To enhance police intelligence and communication, he held meetings with local moderates, radicals, and militants and employed ex-convicts as police-community liaisons (Bloch and Specht 1973). Trained under Parker, however, many officers worried they would become "social workers with guns," and Reddin's approaches were unpopular. After two short years in office, Reddin left LAPD to become a TV commentator (Cannon 1999; Domanick 2016).

Citywide Uprising

Just after midnight on Sunday, March 3, 1991, Rodney King, a twenty-five-year-old Black man, drank a tall can of beer, hopped into his Hyundai, and sped onto the freeway. Highway Patrol clocked him traveling above 110 miles per hour and tried to pull him over. A parolee at the time, King was anxious to avoid a return to prison and attempted to lose officers through a high-speed pursuit. LAPD joined the chase and took control as King exited into the Foothill neighborhood in LA, where he was finally stopped by cars yielding to the sirens. As police approached his vehicle, King's behavior was hard to read—perhaps still attempting to avoid a ticket, he sweated but smiled. Officers later claimed he was on PCP, but urinalysis revealed only alcohol in his system. Frustrated by his semicompliant behavior and hot from the chase, the officers tasered him twice and "swarmed" him to complete the takedown. At this point George Holliday stood on his second-floor balcony nearby and began recording the scene with a video camera. Footage shows one officer batting King in the head, knocking him to the ground. Several officers surround King, striking him about the head, body, and extremities (Cannon 1999), despite his pleas for officers to stop. King sustained numerous broken bones, skull fractures, and permanent facial nerve damage. Nearly thirty officers milled about watching the scene unfold. Finally, officers cuffed King, hog-tied him, and dragged him facedown across the pavement toward a squad car.

Public pressure created the atmosphere necessary for a trial against the four most culpable officers, but the case lingered in court. Without video footage and the massive public audience, it is doubtful that any prosecution would have taken place. If the beating itself revealed the casual violence that undergirded LAPD's policing of Black Angelenos, the court's treatment of the defendants' actions revealed the degree to which racism pervaded LA's entire criminal justice system. The case was initially assigned to downtown LA, where there would have been a substantial chance of Black and Latin@ representation, but court officials reassigned it to Simi Valley in Ventura County, a majority-White, pro–law enforcement community twenty-five miles away, on the grounds that media exposure would taint the jury pool. The trial dragged on due to "falsified" police reports, "frustrated" attempts by King's brother to file a police report, and continual questions over King's mental state at the time of the beating (Independent Commission on the Los Angeles Police Department 1991).

More than a year later, on April 29, 1992, South LA was on a razor's edge when the jury pronounced the defendants not guilty of misconduct. Within minutes, protesters began marching, chanting "Rodney King!" and "Fuck the police!" even while police cheered the verdict in their station houses (Domanick 2016). The corner of Florence and Normandie in South LA became the epicenter of the disturbances when a group of young Black men looted Tom's Liquor. The streets of the surrounding neighborhood brimmed with angry residents. Bands of young Black men gathered, shouting and throwing objects at passing cars with non-Black motorists. They bashed in car windows and pulled out motorists and beat them (Abu-Lughod 2007).[14] The first officers who arrived to the chaotic scene attempted to calm the angry crowd but were quickly overwhelmed by a hail of insults, rocks, and bottles. Later, Metro Unit officers engaged in an hour-long gun battle with residents of a Watts housing project, before evacuating (Domanick 2016). Korean-owned businesses in South LA—liquor stores, supermarkets, retail stores, and banks—also became the targets of Black rage, and Korean shopkeepers took up arms to defend their property (Domanick 2016). By the next morning, the uprising spread to the entire city and several other cities across the country (Abu-Lughod 2007). Tom Bradley, former LAPD officer and LA's first Black Mayor, imposed a citywide curfew and called in the National Guard, the Marines, and more than twenty thousand law enforcement personnel from agencies throughout the Southwest. The uprising lasted five days before Bradley lifted the curfew. Forty-five people were killed, mostly by civilian gunfire. More than twenty-three hundred were injured and the city sustained more than one billion dollars in damages. Just like the Watts Rebellion three decades prior had been, the 1992 uprising was at the time and remains the deadliest and costliest civil disturbance in US history (Cannon 1999; Domanick 2016).[15]

Young men of color involved in the violent uprising were already LAPD's priority enforcement targets. Gang violence and drug consumption had come to replace the brief economic respite of the preceding decades, as the vestiges of Johnson's War on Poverty finally eroded in South LA under the politics of the New Right. Inter-neighborhood conflicts increasingly ended in serious injury and death (Alonso 2004; Hunt and Ramón 2010). Forty Black street gangs were at war with one another by 1978 (M. Davis 2006; Hagedorn 1988), but within four years there would be 151 in South LA alone. Shootings spread beyond the poorest sections of the city and into traditionally White spaces, such as Magic Mountain, Disneyland, and the Santa Monica Pier. When Karen Toshima was killed by a stray bullet near UCLA, the media frenzy and public outrage elevated LA's gang violence to the national consciousness

(Hunt and Ramón 2010). Black community leaders wondered why police, media, and policy makers seemed to care less about the young Black men being shot and killed en masse (M. Davis 2006).[16]

The "Great Melodrama of Race Relations"

Despite the brief relief of antipoverty remedies in the late 1960s that brought thousands of permanent and part-time jobs to South LA, the 1970s saw many industrial plants shut down.[17] Jobs up and down the industrial corridor disappeared as racialized working-class exploitation turned to ghettoization. Rubber, steel, and automotive factories that had been some of the largest employers of low-wage labor in South LA began disinvesting in domestic production and moved operations abroad (Sides 2003). As manufacturing employment left, job availability grew mainly in the high-tech and textile industries, sectors that largely excluded Blacks (Costa Vargas 2006). Aircraft and aerospace employers began to grow operations in the suburbs, establishing new company towns that barred Blacks and restricted Mexicans from accessing housing and employment. Antipoverty job training programs not only were radically reduced in the conservative backlash, but were underfunded and ill equipped to prepare those in poverty for high-skilled aerospace and electronics jobs (Sides 2003). The lack of adequate training programs plus persistent employment discrimination meant the Black working class fared poorly. On the other hand, textile employers preferred hiring Latin@ and Asian migrants over Blacks because employers knew migrants were willing to accept low pay and unsafe or exploitative working conditions, whereas Blacks would not (Costa Vargas 2006). By the 1980s, 80 percent of the employees in this sector were undocumented, while an equal percentage of factory operations violated state and federal health standards (Sides 2003).

LA's population growth since the 1960s mostly comprised influxes of Mexican, Central American, and Asian migrants. Blacks in South LA in the 1970s made up 93 percent of the total population, but by 2000 Latin@s made up 60 percent. By 1980 Black enclaves crystallized in South LA and to a lesser extent in Altadena and Pacoima to the north, while East LA, Compton, Inglewood, and Lynwood in South LA and the Harbor region were becoming Latin@ enclaves (Kun and Pulido 2014).

As the city's racial landscape changed, interracial tensions grew. Black-Latin@-Korean conflict composed the "great melodrama of race relations" in Los Angeles, a discourse that Valle and Torres (1992) argue ignores entirely the great economic inequalities that produce such conflict. Although media tended to frame these conflicts simplistically without referencing the White power structure that shaped them, these tensions emerged between marginalized groups forced to compete in a system that circumscribed their success. The perception among Black South LA residents that they were competing with Latin@ migrants for low-wage work led to feelings of resentment, and they began to reject the Latin Americanization of their communities (Costa Vargas 2006). The LA County Commission on Human Rights observed that beginning in the 1980s Black-Latin@ hate crime intensified, especially among gang-involved youth, and that social and economic factors undergirded this trend (Kun and Pulido 2014), although other sources suggest that the competition argument is much overblown (Telles, Sawyer, and Rivera-Salgado 2011). We examine Black-Latin@ conflict more closely in the next chapter.

By the early 1990s, conflict between Blacks and Koreans was perhaps even more intense. Possessing some limited capital and integrated product distribution networks, Koreans began to take the place of the Jewish shopkeepers of the previous era in South LA's small business community (Abu-Lughod 2007). Although proprietors of integral businesses, including grocery and liquor stores, Koreans preferred family labor and neglected to hire local Blacks. Shop owners often came across as prejudiced, abrasive, and distrustful toward Black youth, who resented such treatment (Domanick 2016). Only ten days after King's beating by LAPD, Korean liquor owner Soon Ja Du shot fifteen-year-old Latasha Harlins in the back of the head after inexplicably mistaking her attempted purchase of orange juice for theft, inflaming tensions.[18]

Chief Gates at War

Daryl Gates, perhaps the most influential LAPD figure after Parker, served as Chief from 1978 until his ouster from office in 1992 under the cloud of numerous scandals culminating in the King disturbances. Gates joined the force the year before Parker's appointment to Chief and quickly became his chauffeur and protégé (Domanick 2016). After Parker's heart attack, Chief Reddin came under heavy criticism from the public and city officials for the police clubbing of protesters at a rally before a visit from President Lyndon Johnson. Reddin responded by creating Metro Division, responsible for riots, protests, and visits by foreign dignitaries, and put Gates in charge. Gates quickly grew Metro from 50 to 220 specially trained officers, using his new invention, the Special Weapons and Tactics (SWAT) Unit, as the centerpiece. Naked militarism would come to define Gates's leadership (Balko 2013).

Emergency situations during Gates's early career served to justify militarization—the late 1960s were a key turning point for both the LAPD and police agencies nationwide. The Watts uprising and subsequent events convinced Gates that LAPD needed more aggressive options to handle similar situations without relying on the military or National Guard. Gates began informally consulting with Marines stationed at Chavez Ravine on the principles of guerrilla warfare. Initially the top brass rejected increased militarization as a threat to public relations, but Gates persisted. He sifted out the best marksmen in the department and secretly trained his new unit in the San Fernando Valley alongside military units from Camp Pendleton (Balko 2013). Young Blacks, meanwhile, politicized by the rebellion, established an LA chapter of the Black Panther Party—a revolutionary civil rights organization that emphasized militancy, education, and self-defense—and opened its Central Avenue headquarters in 1968 in the middle of South LA. Gates, not coincidentally, put SWAT's no-knock raid technique to the test the following year against the Panthers after conflicts between police and the Party became widely publicized in the media (Alonso 2004; Bloom and Martin 2013; M. Davis 2006).[19] The raid set the foundation for future SWAT missions. By 1968, LAPD was "stockpiling" armored vehicles, helicopters, and high-powered rifles as Gate's SWAT unit became a national model that eventually would conduct no-knock servings of warrants, raids, and mass arrests as a matter of course. Within two decades, the Department of Defense was giving police departments grenade launchers for everyday use (Balko 2013).

Gates's militaristic innovations gained traction and began to integrate with LAPD's post-Watts strategies. Chief Ed Davis (1969–78), whom officers described as hard-nosed and Parker-like, was particularly impressed by these aggressive tactics and merged them with Reddin's team policing, which he called the Basic Car Plan (BCP) (Cannon 1999). On the one (community) hand, Davis favored attaching officers to particular beats, rather than having them roam the entire city. He divided the city into Basic Car Areas (BCAs) consisting of reporting districts of a few square blocks (see Greene 2000b).[20] As Figure 3.1 depicts, a Senior Lead Officer (SLO) took charge of each BCA and about a dozen BCAs made up a division, overseen by an Area Captain. SLOs, accountable for crime and disorder within their BCA, directed the operations of patrol officers out of their Basic Car (Los Angeles Police Department 1997). Such a setup, reasoned Davis, would help cultivate not only trust, identification, and familiarity between police and residents but also a sense of officer responsibility.

On the other (militarized) hand, the BCP was more a tool for patrol allocation than any grassroots effort at community self-determination or democratization of policing. Although officers met regularly with block clubs and other public safety groups, the BCP deemphasized dedicated community-police meetings as a central practice to the point that one evaluation specifically declared that the BCP was "Not a Neighborhood Police Team Program" (Bloch and Specht 1973). Instead, vehicle patrols limited community interaction and SLOs regularly went outside their territory to improve call response time. Meetings, held at officers' convenience, were simply one option within the larger paradigm that Davis erected. The few community meetings organized by SLOs were more formality than genuine partnership. Ignoring community input and the advice of their line officers, commanders made decisions about patrol allocation based on crime data and call-for-service analyses (Cannon 1999).

Davis organized SLOs around the "territorial imperative," where officers were directly responsible for all that occurred on their turf. The "territorial imperative" was not Davis's original creation—rather, he adapted it from Robert Ardrey (1966), an amateur anthropologist, and his then-popular text, *The Territorial Imperative: A Personal Inquiry into the Animal Origins of Property and Nations*. Ardrey argued that a theory of animal territoriality could apply to human affairs, using animal comparisons to demonstrate that humans are inevitably destined for violent conflict over geographic control. If territorial aggression is just human nature, then colonialism, segregation, and ethnic cleansing are justifiable self-protection rather than immoral preemptive genocide. Davis absorbed this ethos of coercive peace into a sense of territorial responsibility that, he felt, would yield information from residents and knowledge on the part of officers (Cannon 1999).[21] Combined with LAPD's ingrained "siege mentality," this created an atmosphere of aggressive police dominance over specific geographic areas. Officers became responsible for reducing crime in their areas, and institutional pressures forced them to handle these problems alone, which only heightened aggression.

When Gates took control of LAPD, he phased out community-oriented programs that had been established by previous administrations. Parker's protégé had little use for community or team approaches, regardless of their aggressive potential. Gates used statewide Proposition 13 budget cuts as an excuse to cut team policing and return to the model he found more comfortable—a roving and action-oriented police force like Parker's (Cannon 1999). Fiercely antidrug, he once commented to the *LA Times* that "casual drug users ought to be taken out and shot" (Ostrow 1990). Despite his dislike of community initiatives, Gates was sufficiently disturbed by the issue of drugs to found Drug Abuse Resistance Education (DARE), a deterrence-based educational program geared toward K–12 youth, in 1983. Its curricula focused around awareness and prevention of drug use, gang membership, and violence. DARE officers walked into school classrooms in full uniform, equipped with speeches and horror stories about the dangers of drugs. Gates even encouraged young people to turn in their parents for drug use, though there are few indications this occurred in large numbers (Domanick 2016).[22]

Gates's main project, however, was fighting LA's gangs by any means he found necessary. As fear of drugs soared, restraining forces in both the government and the citizenry were increasingly willing to accept aggressive policing. SWAT's paramilitary tactics came to epitomize LAPD's "proactive" gang and drug enforcement by the mid-1980s (Cannon 1999).[23] The war on gangs was not figurative and included significant collateral damage, as officer aggression and high arrest statistics became vital for career advancement. Gates purchased an armored personnel carrier in 1984, affixed to it a battering ram, and on its maiden deployment rode shotgun while it broke through the wall of a Black family's home in a failed drug raid (Balko 2013; Domanick 2016). LAPD deployed the first

CRASH Unit (standing, unbelievably, for Community Resources Against Street Hoodlums) in 1980 to conduct no-knock raids and Red Squad–style dragnet operations to apprehend potential drug-selling gang members (M. Davis 2006; Hunt and Ramón 2010).

Indeed, it seemed as though LAPD was determined to escalate violence through the tactics of occupation. Pioneered in 1988, Operation Hammer was a "gang sweep" wherein a thousand officers in tactical squads would barricade a neighborhood, preventing entry or exit, and storm in, rousting anyone they suspected of criminal activity. Hammer resulted in more than twenty-five thousand arrests of mostly Black men for mainly trivial offenses, such as parking and other traffic violations (M. Davis 2006; Domanick 2016). The city attorney's office supported these occupational tactics by establishing its own antigang policies and defending police in brutality cases involving suspected gang members. LAPD's intervention did little to reduce crime rates, and succeeded mainly in stirring the pot by encouraging gang warfare and incapacitating and stigmatizing large numbers of Black and Brown Angelenos by mass arrest (Cannon 1999; M. Davis 2006; Domanick 2016).[24]

As an inevitable function of the institutional occupation, complaints of police brutality, principally against South LA's Black community, doubled between 1983 and 1988 (Domanick 2016). Between 1980 and 1986 police perpetrated 372 shootings, but no officers were indicted and only one was fired. Dog-biting incidents also rose steadily.[25] Between 1977 and 1982, fifteen people, mostly Black, were killed by police choke holds.[26] Gates waved away these choking deaths, arguing alternately that police had not been properly trained on the arm-bar hold, that victims had overdosed on drugs, or that the victims' racial makeup was at fault: "We may be finding that in some blacks when [the choke hold] is applied the veins or arteries do not open up as fast as they do in normal people. There may be something arresting the ability of the blood to flow again" (Domanick 2016, 101). No LAPD policy changes followed the declaration of these supposed vulnerabilities; rather, after a series of choke hold deaths, City Council and a state court banned LAPD from using the choke hold except in life-or-death situations, elevating them to the same level as firearms use.[27] Baton usage replaced choke holds, and baton injuries soon began to increase considerably (Domanick 2016).

There were few checks on Gates's authority from either the Police Commission or city government and even less so from the public, despite outcry from the South LA community. Settlement payments for police abuse rose from just about nine hundred thousand in 1980 to over fourteen million dollars by 1991 (Domanick 2016). Continuing Parker's tradition of ignoring the Police Commission, Gates was allowed to write his own performance reviews, which were meekly accepted to maintain a positive working relationship. Meanwhile, Gates recruited the most street-hardened cops into Metro Division and publicly defended their most aggressive actions, making him wildly popular among rank and file officers and conservative White voters (Domanick 2016).[28]

The Christopher Commission

Months before the 1992 uprising, the King beating provoked a nonpartisan commission investigation similar to the McCone Commission. It even reprised some of the same personnel, empaneling Warren Christopher, co-chair of the McCone Commission, as its chair. The Christopher Commission, however, reviewed more than a million pages of documents and months of electronic communications from patrol cars and interviewed hundreds of stakeholders in its investigation of LAPD's operations, organization, complaint system, and reputation for brutality. The report concluded that "a significant number of officers in the LAPD . . . repetitively use excessive force against the public and persistently ignore the written guidelines of the Department regarding force" and that these problems were "aggravated by racism and bias" (Independent Commission on the Los Angeles Police Department 1991, iii).[29]

These charges led the commission to conclude that LAPD should improve their training methods and hiring practices. Report authors praised Gates and LAPD for maintaining a high-quality training facility and recommended that the curriculum include additional courses on human relations, cultural awareness, and Spanish verbal skills. Formal standards, additional training for those in the academy, and field training for officers also featured among the recommendations. The department's hiring practices had come into question long before the Christopher report. Several employment discrimination lawsuits and a federal consent decree in 1981 forced Gates to hire more women and people of color, trends that the commission urged the department to continue. Commission authors were most shocked, however, by the sheer number of officers who had long records of sustained public complaints and noted LAPD's lackadaisical approach to psychological evaluation of recruits. The commission urged that LAPD screen their applicants more thoroughly for emotional and psychological characteristics associated with violent behavior and that commanders terminate any officers with problematic disciplinary records (Independent Commission on the Los Angeles Police Department 1991).

Apart from management and personnel tweaks, the Christopher Commission believed that LAPD leadership lacked public accountability and suggested making the department more responsive and responsible to citizens. First, it recommended genuine civilian oversight of LAPD. In practice, LAPD created an Inspector General position to be the inquisitor of the department. The Inspector General would serve under the control of the Police Commission, outside the LAPD hierarchy. The Internal Affairs Division would no longer be solely responsible for reviewing public complaints against officers; instead the Inspector General would perform annual audits of the disciplinary system to determine whether commanders were taking appropriate action. The Inspector General's report would then go directly to the Police Commission without prior intervention from the Chief. Authors of the Christopher Report also recommended increased funding and staffing for the Board of Police Commissioners and an expanded capacity to remove the Chief for failing to respond to the public's and the Police Commission's demands.

Gates (and many officers) believed that the commission's recommendations were specifically intended to remove him. At the time, the Chief position was a civil service job—Gates could be removed only by a "full, fair, and impartial hearing . . . for good and sufficient cause" by the Police Commission, which essentially ensured life tenure for the position, barring egregious interpersonal conduct (Independent Commission on the Los Angeles Police Department 1991). Gates intended to remain as Chief in spite of the commission's findings, but the subsequent uprisings painted him as incompetent and the commission as prescient. The city moved to shift the Chief position to a contract, allowing the commission to fire Gates, but he resigned first. One former LAPD administrator we interviewed explained that officers and brass saw this as scapegoating a community problem onto police, and Gates became something of a martyr.

Resentment over Gates's ouster made the commission's next major recommendation—the official adoption of community policing—difficult to implement with an intransigent workforce, although it certainly would have been difficult under Gates anyway. However, administrators had little choice but to accept the idea, regardless of its unpopularity among line officers. LAPD brass composed a new set of mandates and cleared them through City Council (Los Angeles Police Department 1992; W. L. Williams 1995a). Implementation began in September 1992 under Chief Willie L. Williams,[30] Gates's replacement and LA's first Black Police Chief—his job was not an easy one. Perhaps to make change more palatable, Williams and the top brass planned to largely recycle the post-Watts reforms and "rejuvenate" the territorial imperative. Rebranding the old territorial imperative as "community policing," LAPD overlaid a concern for "community" on top of existing departmental structures (for additional details, see Roussell 2015b). While LAPD publicly touted community policing as the innovation that would solve LA's race and policing problems, much of the community policing "paradigm shift" was a return to the 1970s (Pelfry 2000). We discuss the on-the-ground implementation of the commission's recommendations in more detail in Chapter 3.

Loud and public commitment to community policing since 1992 has overshadowed the fact that LAPD continued to rely on (and even escalate) traditional aggressive street tactics to control crime. Williams's successor, Bernard Parks, LAPD's second Black Chief and heir to the community policing charge, exited under a cloud of scandal in LAPD's Rampart Division. More than seventy CRASH unit members and other Rampart officers engaged in drug dealing, blackmail, torture, suspect framing, aggravated assault, and the deliberate wounding and murder of LA residents. The Rampart CRASH unit's criminal abuses seemed to be a continuation of the Gates era and a direct repudiation of the department's commitment to community policing. Indeed, the report of the Rampart Independent Review Panel (2000, 7) succinctly stated that "[c]ommunity policing—which must be at the heart of Department's efforts to reestablish its credibility with the public—remains more a slogan than a reality. The LAPD still fails to treat the communities it serves as full partners in its mission." While federal intervention after 1992 had been avoided by adopting community policing in accordance with the Christopher Commission Report, in 2000 the US Department of Justice entered into a consent decree with LAPD at the behest of City Council (M. Kirk 2001; Stone, Foglesong, and Cole 2009). LA's City Council appointed William "Bill" Bratton, a White man fresh from his oversight of the New York Police Department, in 2000 to finish the implementation of community policing reforms and the federal consent decree. Bratton immediately reinforced the territorial imperative with Compstat, a geographic crime tracking and management system, and managed LAPD through the implementation of the federal consent decree. He announced his departure only after DOJ lifted the decree in 2009.

Legacies of Reform

In a superficial sense, LAPD's changes and reforms over the past century resemble the traditional academic narrative—the parochial era gives way to professionalization, which in turn gives way to a final regime of community policing. Although the eras of policing correspond neatly to the various reform commission reports and responses, one major element is missing from the story: mass violence and public protest. Each mass riot or uprising was caused by societal oppression of marginalized Angelenos encapsulated in police brutality. Each outbreak resulted in a governmentally empaneled commission that evinced varying degrees of sympathy for those protesting their social exclusion. Each commission's proposed changes to policing resemble Vitale's (2017) characterization of "liberal" reforms: additional training measures (e.g., cultural sensitivity, antidiscrimination, Spanish language skills), increased officer diversity, greater oversight by local government, greater sensitivity to marginalized communities of color, and rhetoric and gestures at community collaboration and accountability. The technology and the character of each era differ, but the general pattern is the same. Indeed, as the recommendations of Obama's Task Force on 21st Century Policing, issued in the wake of Ferguson, suggest, this may not be a cycle unique to LA.

One conclusion to be drawn from these observations is that while community policing may be a relatively new label, its basic tenets comprise the commonsense reforms used to placate any group of people aggrieved by government oppression. Two related observations emerge as well. First, the police institution seems to embrace such changes halfheartedly and incompletely and retreats from many of them after sufficient time has passed. It seems clear that the McGucken Report was far from Chief Parker's mind when he aggressively enforced the color line, just as Gates's response to Watts was not to enhance diversity measures but rather to create SWAT and Operation Hammer. Second, these reforms, to the extent that they are implemented, seem fairly ineffective—LA has the dubious distinction of being home to some of the largest and most expensive uprisings in US history. Casting an anxious eye to the future, each set of reforms seemed only to push the matter into greater violence down the road.

This is not to suggest that LAPD has remained static. Policing in general, and with LAPD in particular, has changed considerably from the 1930s. LAPD has been a national model of police professionalism, principally as a result of its world-class training facilities. After 1943 and 1965, the department expanded its training materials and practices as well as its departmental diversity. In the struggle to contain its sprawling municipal geography, LAPD also developed a "command and control" strategy—the territorial imperative—only to roll it back, relabel it, and return to it under the label of community policing.

The likelihood of future mass violence notwithstanding, LAPD has mastered the strategy of codeveloping community discourse and military infrastructure side by side. Since the beginning of the Civil Rights Movement, community discourse has been a key governmental tool for the control of dissenting populations, and this remains the case for the contemporary LAPD. Meanwhile, LAPD developed and refined its capacity for community occupation in the form of SWAT and Metro. Indeed, according to a 2015 *LA Times* report, two hundred additional officers were assigned to Metro, while forty more formed a new specialized community policing division (Jamison and Reyes 2015).

Law enforcement has not built community trust because police have historically proved to be an occupying force that comes into communities of color to impose social control. Community policing is a policy within a larger repository of post-disturbance reforms that leverage community rhetoric to reassure the public that police take the concerns of marginalized populations seriously and that only by working together can they bring about a racially harmonious future. But LAPD Chiefs have instead mainly created internal accountability measures that insulate the department from community oversight. Threats to the contemporary order are seen to reside in Black, Latin@, and laboring populations, and the repression of these groups has not much lessened over the past century, although the faces of officers themselves have changed considerably. The lesson that LAPD and many other municipal departments appear to have learned is that community-friendly programs can be deployed alongside militarized ones. Before we discuss the social organization of community policing in Chapter 3, our next chapter focuses on the impact of social, economic, and demographic changes from the community's perspective.

2

The Making of Lakeside

My community is a good community. My community is a cooperative community. And my community wants a good quality of life in it. People want to return to the old ways, which is totally gone. You're not going to be able to sit on your porch or whatever because you never know what is going to happen. . . . We want quality treatment. We want equal treatment. We want the respect that we give.
—Teresa Mayfield

Teresa Mayfield is an elderly Black woman and a concerned citizen. She is exactly the sort of person who seems a natural fit in organizations like LAPD's Community-Police Advisory Board (CPAB). She liaises between police and her neighbors. When other residents see problems in the neighborhood, they call Ms. Mayfield because they know she has police connections. As she puts it, this community "wants a good quality of life," and maintaining an open line of communication with police is important for concerned citizens. With information from such community residents, police, theoretically, tailor their patrol and enforcement strategies to fit each neighborhood's idiosyncratic sense of morality. But in neighborhoods that have undergone significant and rapid demographic changes, the ability to define a unified local moral order becomes complicated.

This chapter looks through Ms. Mayfield's eyes at a generation of conflict and change in Lakeside. First, we discuss the impacts that social, economic, and demographic changes have had on the former heart of LA's "Black Belt" and the conflicts that have emerged as a result. Lakeside's Black community is divided in a number of ways. In the post–World War II era, the slowly increasing diversity of job prospects offered to Blacks led to increasing economic stratification within the Black community. Further internal conflicts developed when large numbers of southern Black migrants poured into the city. Many were absorbed into the lowest skilled, lowest paying, and least secure job sectors, growing the number of Blacks toiling in poverty. Economic restructuring worked to erode the Black middle class that had arisen, and soon after the Black population began to polarize even further. As the 1960s and 1970s wore on, Black labor and economic prospects dwindled as the growing Latin@ migrant population further divided Lakeside. The lack of familiarity and communication between these groups reinforced social and cultural differences.

When Ms. Mayfield laments the loss of the "old ways," she is referring to the end of an era in the Lakeside neighborhood. Lakeside has endured many socioeconomic and demographic transformations, not all of which have been peaceful. Rather, each successive wave of new migrants, whether Black or Brown, endured varying degrees of contest and conflict. Suttles (1968) warns of the need to develop an inclusive moral order in diverse communities, but the settled and settling populations of Lakeside found uneven middle ground. Instead, they disliked, resented, and occasionally attacked one another. The growing Latin@ population is the most recent wave of demographic change, and their presence has elicited increasingly negative attitudes toward newcomers (G. T. Johnson 2013; Kun and Pulido 2014). Ms. Mayfield's desire for "respect" reflects a frustration shared by many Blacks in the CPAB and throughout South LA, wherein she and others feel Latin@s do not recognize the history of struggle that went into defining the social, economic, and geographic boundaries of the neighborhood. Their lack of recognition is seen as disrespectful to those who identify community with such history.

Yet LA was born of ethnoracial intermingling (G. T. Johnson 2013). Black and Brown people have lived together, struggled together, and shared experiences of marginality. While the nature of these struggles changed midcentury as newer Latin@ migrants brought new experiences, new struggles, and new civil rights agendas that changed community interactions, there is also clear evidence of solidarity movements. Many in Lakeside see that the fates of Blacks and Latin@s are linked and seek to forge alliances across racial and cultural barriers to construct an inclusive moral order. Let us begin by learning more about Ms. Mayfield to get a sense of the changes the Black community has undergone and how Blacks in Lakeside have reacted to these changes. We then move to discuss economic and cultural conflict and end by tackling the reality and possibility of solidarity.

Change

Ms. Mayfield was over eighty when we first met her, and she has lived in South LA for more than half a century. She was much quieter than other CPAB members, particularly compared to high-profile figures such as Vera Fisher and Ms. Ruby Carter. Before meetings were called to order we often saw Ms. Mayfield slowly moving about the room silently setting out nameplates. When meetings were in full swing she was similarly quiet but came alive when called upon to discuss her volunteer work. A stickler for procedure, hierarchy, and definition, Ms. Mayfield would let other attendees know if there was a problem. Early in our fieldwork, we both declined Ms. Mayfield's invitation to sit at the boardroom table with the rest of the CPAB members after she had set out our yellow nameplates. "No thanks! Don't want to take away seats from residents," we said. "I believe in infrastructure," she shot back, staring at us as if we had just said something stupid. Abashed, we sat behind our nameplates. Similarly, when CPAB held a potluck, she took a hard line on planning, folding her arms obstinately: "It's a potluck. We'll see what we get. That's why we call it a 'pot-luck.' If we get all desserts, then that's what we get!" She would joke occasionally, taking shots at other board members and the Senior Lead Officers (SLOs). She once called Ms. Carter "Miss Deep Pockets" after Ms. Carter seemed flippant about the Officer Appreciation Day budget. And she exchanged playful banter with a SLO over the previous night's college football game between a Midwestern college and Lakeside University, where she spent several decades on staff. Lakeside U lost, but she wrote it off as a fluke due to the rain.

Originally from Mississippi and educated in Louisiana, Ms. Mayfield moved to LA to escape conditions under Jim Crow. As a young woman, Ms. Mayfield became politically active in the fight to secure equal voting rights for Blacks in her home state. Town officials had imposed a poll tax on Blacks, which officials claimed was legally justified. Angered that barely literate Whites could vote without restriction, she and a group of activists poured over legal documents in search of the relevant passages.

After a long and drawn out battle with local officials, the group was successful in lifting the tax. In spite of this victory, Ms. Mayfield elected to flee the South after a Klansman murdered her friend and noted civil rights activist Medgar Evers. Stopping briefly in the Midwest and Sacramento, she arrived in South LA in 1969, lured by rumors that LA was a more hospitable place for Blacks than the South. She found instead that LA had a more "hidden" form of racism rather than Mississippi's naked oppression. She confronted this while working at Lakeside University, where she was time and again passed over for promotion while less qualified Whites moved up the ranks instead. When we asked why, she explained simply, "Because I am Afro-American."

Ms. Mayfield is one of several board members police recruited to join the CPAB after the formal embrace of community policing in 1992. Many of the longest serving and most committed board members joined in this way, she says. Police took notice of Ms. Mayfield while she worked on a local block club, which she joined in the mid-1970s upon witnessing escalating gang violence, but they did not reach out to her to join the CPAB until the mid-1990s. Ms. Mayfield believes she was "recommended" to join because she was "involved in the community," was in "good standing," and knew "how to deal with people."

During our research, Ms. Mayfield was a CPAB leader who previously served as the CPAB secretary—though she maintains she was "suckered into it" after once suggesting how the agenda could be modified—and headed the History and Outreach subcommittees as we left the field. For the latter, she and other board members made numerous phone calls to publicize police and CPAB events; this also included sending letters soliciting donations. For the former, she acted as a researcher alongside compatriot Bruce Palmer, contacting former CPAB participants to secure photos and documents. Outside of meetings, Ms. Mayfield saw herself as a community liaison between her local SLO and the neighborhood. When people heard gunshots, saw abandoned cars, or passed new graffiti, they would notify Ms. Mayfield. Her role was to contact her SLO to coordinate a plan of action to resolve the problem and prevent future incidents.[1]

Ms. Mayfield explained that "community" refers to a group of people who over time forge a strong bond—a kind of kinship. Kinship of this sort was built upon a shared sense of struggle as Black Los Angeles evolved due to a convergence of social and economic pressures. Community is legible through its past, while geographic boundaries are important to residents mainly for their historical significance. Up through the 1970s, geography officially determined where Blacks could live, and those de jure boundaries have come to shape the ongoing de facto segregation in South LA (M. Davis 2006; Sides 2003). Neighborhood resistance against White racism helped shape Lakeside into a resilient Black community, and that history continued to bind, creating a strong sense of solidarity. Residents like Ms. Mayfield, whose struggle was not just physical and emotional but also geographical and historical, remained emotionally attached to South Los Angeles.

Greenhouse, Yngvesson, and Engel (1994) suggest that community and history are tightly interwoven but can also be at odds. History in a rigid sense is a matter of the temporal arrangement of events; within the valence of community, however, it is remembered more as a categorization of ingroups (community) and outgroups (others):

> To the extent that "community" is predefined as harmonious, conflict must be located outside of the community. . . . To the extent that history is the history of the present moment, and, even more so, to the extent that history is the story of the transformation of controversy and dispute over time, history and community become mutually exclusive. Any recognition of the salience of the temporal dimensions of community would, in effect, blur the very distinction that is so important to local people, the one that divides them from the newcomers and the others who make the present so unlike the past they prefer to remember. (Greenhouse, Yngvesson, and Engel 1994, 168)

As Ms. Mayfield's experiences with employment discrimination may have suggested, anti-Black racism in LA rose sharply while the Black population grew throughout the Great Migration. Whites employed move-in violence and segregation policies to maintain separate White and non-White communities. Racial barriers of this period may not have been stamped into the state legal code, but they were no less effective for that. Housing covenants labeled White neighborhoods "restricted," separating White and non-White neighborhoods (Sides 2003). Though they had been used in LA beginning in the 1890s—even the California Real Estate

Association endorsed housing restrictions for non-White "alien races"—the use of restrictive covenants peaked as the Black population grew. Housing covenants involved both informal and institutionalized practices. Blacks would be required to make higher payments than Whites to buy in White neighborhoods, and lenders set unrealistic loan repayment plans for Black families. Real estate agents would refuse to show Black families homes in White neighborhoods at all; when this failed, White home owner associations would pool funds and pay off home owners to dissuade them from selling to Black buyers. When these measures failed, White supremacist groups would employ more direct terrorist intimidation tactics, issuing death threats, organizing cross burnings on front lawns of Black home owners, and bombing Black homes (Sides 2003).

Together, these practices created an "invisible wall" that Black home buyers crossed at their own risk (Sides 2003). The US Supreme Court cases aimed at ending such housing discrimination in 1948 and again in 1955, although decided favorably, could not completely curtail housing covenant practices. Whites and elites continued using racial housing covenants to restrict Black and other non-White home buyers, even though they were declared unconstitutional in *Shelley v. Kraemer* (1948). The Court made a fine distinction: although the state was not allowed to enforce housing covenants under the Equal Protection Clause, this did not mean that private parties were completely barred from entering into housing covenants—such agreements simply involved extralegal enforcement, and Blacks were unable to seek judicial relief. Lakeside's Black population understood these factors well. Dr. Cynthia Stacy—a CPAB member, longtime South LA resident, and professor at a local college—explained how housing covenants affected her and Ms. Mayfield's generation: "The older [Black residents] really have this nasty grind because of the covenant of the restriction, particularly on the west side of the freeway, on the property. You could not sell property to people of color—and that did include Brown and Black people—on the west side of the freeway."

Determined Blacks, with some governmental support, finally began to break down these barriers, but such victories provoked yet more racist White resistance. Some resistance took a more passive form. Increased Black residential mobility prompted Whites to retreat from newly integrated neighborhoods, and soon "White flight" in LA precipitated the formation of the Black Belt (Sides 2003). White flight began in the 1950s in direct response to the small but increasing number of Blacks who began moving into LA's "restricted" neighborhoods. Between the 1950s and the 1970s, more than 125,000 Whites (and to a lesser extent and for different reasons, the Black middle class) left the central city area, particularly after courts began supporting racial integration (e.g., Boustan 2010). In a sad irony, "transitional" or racially integrated neighborhoods of Latin@s, Asian, and other nonprivileged groups barred from the White racial order began to disappear, and South LA slowly coalesced into the city's Black Belt. Black Angelenos in Lakeside and surrounding neighborhoods became increasingly isolated, similar to East LA Mexicans decades before.

The city government set up a major housing initiative to accommodate the rapidly growing population and built more than a dozen projects, confining the poorest Blacks, those most desperate for reasonable employment, to Watts. Prior to World War II, the Housing Authority of the City of Los Angeles (HACLA) had a policy of building geographically dispersed projects from East LA to San Pedro precisely to prevent concentrated poverty. In 1954, HACLA reversed that policy and set up a major housing project experiment, building Imperial Courts, Jordan Downs, and Nickerson Gardens in Watts. As a result, more than ten thousand people moved into Watts, a neighborhood of just over twenty-six thousand residents. By the end of the decade, one-third of Watts residents—most of them poor, Black, and desperate for employment—lived in housing projects. Housing policy efforts had not untangled housing from larger issues of resource allocation, however—Whites, in control of LA's corporate and industrial finance and occupying the upper echelons of employment since before the turn of the century, took these things with them to the tax base of the LA suburbs. When Whites fled, work opportunities, unemployment, foreclosures, and the municipal infrastructure worsened dramatically. These erosions also contributed to sharp increases in crime and gang violence (Sides 2003).[2]

Once manufacturers began to deindustrialize and disinvest in domestic production in the late 1960s, Black Angelenos fared the worst, particularly those employed in low-wage manufacturing. Attached to a thriving private university, Ms. Mayfield personally avoided the unemployment that topped 40 percent in Lakeside, but watched as her friends and neighbors suffered. Southern Blacks continued to migrate to LA,

TABLE 2.1. LA Socioeconomics 1970–2007 (average percentage over census tract).

	% in Poverty			% Unemployed			% with Bachelor's Degree		
	LA	South Bureau	Lake-side	LA	South Bureau	Lake-side	LA	South Bureau	Lake-side
1940	—	—	—	—	—	—	4.6	3.1	2.9
1950	—	—	—	—	—	—	5.5	4.4	3.7
1960	—	—	—	6.5	8.4	8.1	6.1	4.2	3.2
1970	9.1	17.0	16.6	6.6	8.9	8.9	7.5	3.5	2.4
1980	14.1	23.7	25.1	6.5	10.2	11.4	11.5	5.2	3.4
1990	15.0	26.0	27.3	7.7	12.6	13.6	15.2	6.6	4.1
2000	18.0	29.7	31.0	8.9	13.2	14.8	24.9	11.5	7.4
2007	19.2	25.2	24.8	8.4	10.8	12.5	28.7	13.8	9.4

but, together with poor Mexicans, could hope to find only low-wage and seasonal work into the 1970s. In the wake of economic restructuring, LA's increasingly shuttered industrial corridor became a hub of unemployment and crime (Sides 2003). Ms. Mayfield's memories of the days when the availability of manufacturing jobs meant the potential for an improved quality of life, the end of entrenched employment discrimination seemed possible, and the elderly could feel comfortable sitting on their porches in peace—the "old ways"—became a vital piece of what Ms. Mayfield saw as her community.

The census data in Table 2.1 compare the extreme marginality of Lakeside to both the larger South Bureau area and the city of LA over the course of several decades. Unemployment in Lakeside, nearly twice the figure for LA, reached a peak of about 15 percent in 2000, the same year that poverty rates reached nearly one-third. In 2007, nearly a quarter of Lakeside residents still lived under the already-anemic federal poverty line, not far from the 27 percent rate just before the 1992 uprisings. College education, though rising in Lakeside, remained under 10 percent in 2007, low compared with South Bureau as a whole (nearly 14 percent) and LA (29 percent).

Meanwhile, LA's population growth after the 1970s was due primarily to Mexican, Central American, and Asian migrants. The Black Belt began to dissolve, with the largest Black concentration still in South LA and smaller enclaves in Altadena and Pacoima to the north (Sides 2003). Conditions for new Latin@ migrants were remarkably similar to the experiences of in-migrating southern Blacks decades prior. The Pico-Union district, a hub of Latin@ migration in LA, became the city's most densely populated area and is now the most densely populated area west of the Mississippi River (Domanick 2016; Vigil 2002). Living conditions there were deplorable for the largely Mexican, Guatemalan, and Salvadoran residents, who endured overcrowding and high rates of illiteracy, crime, and gang violence (Vigil 2002). Many Latin@ migrants were deported by federal immigration enforcement agencies, which sometimes worked with LAPD to facilitate removals (Zilberg 2011). Latin@ migrants in Pico-Union suffered from their clandestine existence; they lived in perpetual fear of arrest and deportation, avoided calling police in cases of victimization, and had little to no access to government and social services; domestic abuse and child neglect became rampant (Kun and Pulido 2014). Due to the complications that developed regarding the cooperation of undocumented immigrants, Chief Gates issued so-called Special Order 40 (Gates 1979). Phrased specifically to speak to these complaints, Special Order 40 directed that officers (1) should not "initiate police action with the objective of discovering the alien status of a person" and (2) should not report "undocumented aliens" to federal officials unless they committed a felony, a "high grade" misdemeanor, or multiple previous offenses.[3]

Conflict

> People who routinely occupy the same place must either develop a moral order that includes all those present or fall into conflict.
>
> —Gerald Suttles, *Social Order of the Slum* (1968)

Another way to interpret Ms. Mayfield lamenting the loss of the "old ways" is the threat that some in the Black community perceive from Latin@ in-migration. To several CPAB members, including Ms. Mayfield, the growing presence of Latin@s is worrisome and sometimes a thing to be policed. Several participants shared the frustration that Latin@s compete with Blacks for work, sap resources from Black businesses, and displace Blacks from their family homes. Research shows at least some of these frustrations to be misplaced, yet such feelings are shared by many Black Angelenos (Kun and Pulido 2014; Telles, Sawyer, and Rivera-Salgado 2011). While the economic and employment picture is more complex than simple displacement, the reality is that the Black community's economic and spatial decline coincided with an influx of new South LA neighbors from Mexico and Central America.

Accompanying these rapid demographic shifts came an increasingly sour view of these outsiders among residents like Ms. Mayfield. "Community" refers to a whole history and struggle that went into creating what Ms. Mayfield sees as the Black community, a time before new Latin@ migrants arrived. If history is a collection of stories and experiences, having a past makes locals part of the community because they have a collective memory of the struggles the group has endured.

Dr. Stacy explained to us Blacks' reactionary feelings about the relatively recent influx of Latin@s into South LA in light of these attachments: "We have got some of the bigotry from the African Americans toward them [Latin@s], particularly in our seniors, our older African Americans, who are ticked off that their whole community has been 'taken over' or 'invaded.' They feel invaded, the older citizens, because historically, these were all African American communities. Given the history of the struggles here and what they deal with—the lack of respect for their history—they're pissed!" For Black residents like Dr. Stacy, South LA represents a site of contest and struggle—a history that was hard fought, hard won, and is now inundated with people who seem unaware of that history. Historically, tensions between Blacks and Latin@s are rooted in labor concerns between two groups marked for exclusion and low-status work as well as anti-Black racism and anti-Latin@ nativism (Kun and Pulido 2014; Sides 2003). These residents long not for Jim Crow, but for South LA as the center of the city's Black Belt. Since the 1970s Blacks have increasingly come to fear the influence Latin@s have had and will continue to have over the fate of the Black community. First, they fear being displaced from South LA, a real anxiety given the trends of "forced migration" through incarceration and gentrification (Costa Vargas 2006; N. Smith 1996). Further, they fear that Blacks are declining in political importance, particularly given the shift toward Latin@ representation in city government and in the city's political agenda (Kun and Pulido 2014; Telles, Sawyer, and Rivera-Salgado 2011).

Though Black geographic isolation grew throughout the 1960s and 1970s, new Latin@ immigration led to increased contact with Blacks in the 1980s (Vigil 2002). The precarious Black middle class that emerged after World War II dwindled just as quickly as manufacturing jobs left South LA. Those who were last hired were first fired, and those who had previously been in the middle class reentered the working class and *lumpenproletariat* due to relegation to and then exclusion from the low-wage labor market (Sides 2003). Although the initial pattern had been concentrated poverty in South LA's Black communities, at the same time Latin@ isolation was sharply increasing due to the scale of in-migration and patterns of enclave settlements. Between 1984 and 1989, however, LA County built more than two hundred thousand new public housing units due to growing demand (Kun and Pulido 2014). These were scattered throughout LA, but especially in poor, Mexican neighborhoods with organized gangs. Soon many Blacks moved into federally subsidized (e.g., Section 8) housing in Latin@ neighborhoods, and as families vacated homes and apartments in formerly Black sections of South LA, they were replaced by Central American migrants (Kun and Pulido 2014).

The slow dissolution of South LA's Black Belt left some Black residents wondering about the impact on community solvency. The sense of history and shared struggle that infused notions of community for Ms. Mayfield and other Black residents extended to a collective sense of neighborhood wealth. Business disinvestment harms the community, regardless of an individual's relationship with that business. New business investments are often expressly discussed as "investments in the community," and this produces tension with Latin@s who may contribute to business and community in a different way. Many, though certainly not all, street vendors in Lakeside are Latin@. They sell tacos, produce, T-shirts, and trinkets on the sidewalks of the crowded retail districts. As street vending was illegal in Los Angeles during and prior to our research, they were unregistered with the city, although they sometimes possessed LA County Health Department approval of their product.[4] CPAB co-chair Vera Fisher is one of the most vocal CPAB members about this issue. After a CPAB meeting in which illegal street vending was a prominent topic, she explained how unregistered vendors cheat the Black community:

Aaron's fieldnotes

Vera Fisher is still furious about the vending issue. Her main concern, she says, is that they don't pay taxes. Of course they pay sales taxes, which is a conversation she has apparently had with Abril Solis and Hector Mendoza at the Spanish CPAB meeting, but there are taxes that legitimate businesses have to pay too.

Vera also has a huge problem with remittances to Central America and Mexico. She describes the local economy as a circle, with money circulating through consumers to local businesses to employees who become, or somehow pass on that money back to, consumers. Danny suggests that major corporations like Walgreens and El Pollo Loco centrally process their earnings and don't really put much money back into the community either, but Vera somehow manages to agree with that statement and make it support her argument as well. Remittances, in her eyes, are sucking money right out of the community and putting it into the places they [the vendors] came from.

For residents like Ms. Fisher, vending stood in for their frustrations with declining economic opportunity. Legitimate local businesses, many Black owned, suffered as a result of the transitioning market and the decline of Black labor opportunities, while the proceeds of unregistered businesses were funneled, untaxed, back to Mexico and Central America. Feagin and Cobas (2014) argue that Blacks sometimes adopt dominant White frameworks through which to perceive and respond to other groups of color. In this respect, anti-Latin@ sentiment among Lakeside Blacks reflected some of the same negative stereotypes normally (and originally) produced by Whites. That is, they viewed Latin@s as lesser than and as invaders of US society. Given the ubiquity and popularity of food vendors (even some police Captains admitted to patronizing street *taquerías*), Fisher saw illegal vending as siphoning money away from her community to foreign countries, even as the labor market for Black US citizens deteriorates. Resident Latin@s were thus seen as standing outside the South LA community, firmly planted in their countries of origin. Fisher interpreted the social networks along which remittances flow as external and alien, rather than broadening and strengthening community linkages, disqualifying Latin@s as a part of the community. This is consistent with what she saw as a refusal on the part of Latin@s to join the community into which they had migrated—a Black community. Vera, sensitive to depredations against her embattled community, also raised questions about whether undocumented Latin@s, connected more to their countries of origins through remittance channels, were worthy of belonging to the Lakeside community.

By the 1980s, more than a million low-wage jobs had disappeared from South LA. As manufacturing left, job availability grew mainly in the high-tech and textile industries that largely excluded Blacks (Costa Vargas 2006; Sides 2003). While the Watts Rebellion had secured anti-poverty programs, including job training for a brief time, the political conservatism that gripped both California and the nation saw these reduced considerably and poorly adapted for the changing market (Sides 2003). Sweatshop laborers, overworked and underpaid, took over the low-wage employment sector, but these employers increasingly preferred undocumented workers as the 1980s wore on. Citizens, able to lay claim to employment protections, were disfavored as employers preferred tractable employees who would not report factory operations for violating state and federal health standards (Costa Vargas 2006; Sides 2003). Like Whites, many Blacks felt as though US citizens should not have to work under unsafe and exploitative conditions, even had they been eligible.

Such job market racialization further diminished Blacks' job prospects. Dr. Stacy explained that one reason for the Black community's antipathy toward Latin@s is the perception of the "crisis of Black employment" that saw Black jobs go to migrants working for subpoverty wages: [W]hat would happen is that immigrants would come in—and this is why I have some issues from an economic perspective—they started to undermine the native, the American-born, whether they be Black or whatever, for wages. You know, you're in business and you're trying to be competitive, now if all your competitors are hiring these people for lower wages, . . . who are you going to hire?" Of course, a narrative of community that emphasizes history and social location, as Ms. Mayfield posits, is complicated by the perception that an influx of new people has heralded the very economic shifts that have contributed to the decline of the Black community. Dr. Stacy continues, describing the difficulty of watching opportunities for Black youth dwindle.

STACY: The janitors have this whole thing with the unions, the Blacks dominated that . . . [they] became unionized and then have been undermined by the Latin@ workers and there is tension there—it's economic. Now our kids—there are no Black kids working at McDonald's or even many younger kids, high school age kids working in the service industry, in the food industry, around our area because the adults [Latin@s] who are more available, are more employable. And they are working in fast food, so our kids have fewer opportunities for employment. . . . I could go down the street [when I was younger] and there were my classmates working at the store, the drug store, the grocery store, whatever, it doesn't happen anymore.

Blacks' perceptions of displacement by Latin@s were not entirely inaccurate—there are several reasons Latin@s were more likely to be employed over Blacks. Employers preferred to hire exploitable labor compared to young Blacks. Zamudio and Lichter (2008), among others, have documented the LA service economy's methods of discrimination against Blacks in favor of undocumented Latin@s. They suggest that employers used the trope of "soft skills"—ostensibly the ability to better work with and relate to customers—to screen out Black applicants in favor of Latin@ migrants. Such reasoning is not particularly persuasive, given that recently arrived migrants usually spoke little English; rather, the workforce was seen as more acquiescent to poor working conditions due to the constant threat of immigration enforcement. Additionally, employers often relied upon informal networks for job referrals. Latin@ migrants formed tight social networks, which facilitated securing not only employment but also housing and social services. Sides (2003) suggests that poor Blacks, in contrast, did not forge such networks due to distrust and competition as they watched the job market crumble. Young Black males, particularly high school dropouts, became the most economically dislocated.

Recent studies, however, show that contemporary employment patterns are less a matter of failed competition with the undocumented and more about disqualification from labor market participation entirely. While there has been a decrease in Black employment and an increase in Latin@ employment in low-wage jobs, there have been simultaneous increases in Black labor participation in specialized service work (see Telles, Sawyer, and Rivera-Salgado 2011). More importantly, the contracting labor market has rendered those with various levels of criminal justice contacts ineligible for many types of employment altogether (Manza and Uggen 2006; Western 2006). As the low-wage labor market shifted and contracted over the past four decades, the possession of a criminal record increasingly began to dictate hiring patterns. Although this phenomenon affects those of all races and ethnicities, it affects Black men at an elevated rate—Pager's (2007) data, for example, put the employment opportunities of Black men without a criminal record near those of White men who have a criminal record for entry-level positions, while the opportunities offered to Black men with a record were only slightly above zero. Even so, frustrations over the lack of job opportunities for Blacks have complicated community solidarity.

Black antipathy is not unique. As neighborhood prosecutor Dakari Hendricks said during an interview, "It's invidious racism and its goes both ways." Latin@s regularly expressed anti-Black attitudes. Sometimes this was reactionary. In a similar way that Blacks reproduce the White racial frame and express anti-Latin@ attitudes normally attributed to Whites, Latin@s too absorb White frameworks from mainstream society and reassert that Blacks are criminals, calling them "*ladrones* [thieves]," "*drogadictos* [drug addicts]," and "*pandilleros* [gang members]." Just as Blacks' negative reaction to what they perceive as Latin@s' role in the employment "crisis" complicates neighborhood solidarity, so too does Latin@s' perception of being the potential victims of Black criminality. Crime, of course, as always, remains a largely intraracial phenomenon, and South LA is no exception (Hipp et al. 2010; Hipp, Tita, and Boggess 2009).

Coalition

The development of Los Angeles is an Afro-Mexican story.
—Gaye Theresa Johnson, *Spaces of Conflict, Sounds of Solidarity* (2013)

There is no doubt that some elderly Black residents are aware of and resent the shifts that have shaped South LA's population and job opportunities. But shared experiences of poverty and marginalization based on race and class have created the possibility—and sometimes the reality—of community solidarity. In addition to the formation of zoot-suit culture and car clubs among Blacks and Chican@s in resource poor South LA, as we discussed in the previous chapter, their shared struggles are rooted in resistance to their marginalization (Escobar 1999; Kun and Pulido 2014; Sides 2003; Vigil 2002). In contrast to Ms. Fisher's view above, another CPAB member, Bruce Palmer, in a thoughtful defense of illegal vending, demonstrated discursive solidarity: "I know about poverty. I've been poor my whole life, I shined shoes . . . I would do it too [illegal vending], I would get out there and sell bacon sandwiches." Adriana Sanchez, who came to South LA from El Salvador with her family when she was six years old and now works as a childcare coordinator at a local nonprofit, agrees with Mr. Palmer, albeit from a more structural perspective:

> BRUCE: Well, I think that usually when we talk about race relations I always tend to think more along the lines of the economy more than anything else. Because there is so little resources in the area, I think that people tend to confuse race problems or problems between the races as having it be racial, when it's actually more economic. A lot of the issues around the area, I think the whole idea of race is sometimes put out there in the media especially . . . "Oh such and such happened, there was a big problem, there was a fight because of race." It's not necessarily always the case that it's race, it's actually more of resources I think than anything else. So when people say that there was a racial tension in the area, I don't tend to take it at face value when they say stuff like that.

Prior to World War II, South LA was one of the most racially integrated areas of the city. Many Blacks lived in multicultural, non-White neighborhoods, or in "transitional" neighborhoods buffering or surrounding smaller, concentrated pockets of Blacks. At the time of the first Great Migration as many as twenty-two thousand Mexicans lived along Central Avenue. South LA high schools, such as Fremont and Jefferson near Central Avenue and Jordan in Watts, were among the most integrated in the city prior to the Second World War. And despite increasing White discontentment, these schools were also among the first in the country to impose antisegregation policies, even prior to the *Brown v. Board* decision, which ruled de jure school segregation unconstitutional (G. T. Johnson 2013; Sides 2003).

Since World War II Black and Brown integration has continued in South LA. There have been shared civil rights struggles and shared resistances expressed in music (Pulido 2006). Johnson (2013) found that Blacks and Chican@s have interfaced in South LA for nearly a generation, sharing, mixing, and exchanging social and cultural life. LA's Black and Chican@ musical groups have had a significant influence on one another, protesting common experiences of marginalization. These musical and cultural formations have mirrored and drawn inspiration from the development of Black and Brown civil rights agendas, from the response to the Sleepy Lagoon Trial to solidarity with international counter-colonial struggles through the Black Panthers and Brown Berets. Both groups endured shared struggles throughout the twentieth century. The very same processes of systemic racism forced displacement and the destruction of Mexican barrios by public housing and freeway construction as well as provoking Black ghettoization. Both groups endured discrimination in employment and housing as well and endured the LAPD's brutal treatment throughout the century (G. T. Johnson 2013).

Antoine Johnson, a program director at a local job coordination organization, explains how Black investment in protesting against Latin@ marginality is necessary due to the similar persecution of Blacks but nevertheless remains unacknowledged by many Latin@s and Blacks. Here Johnson discusses his own experiences at the city's annual May Day demonstrations: "What [the media depicted] was Latin@s: all Mexicans, no Blacks. . . . But my friend is Black and when they were down there protesting she was laying on the train track as a part of the protest when I was there. . . . So what I would say to you is if they're allowed to do it to the Mexicans, we're next. So when they had the protest downtown about immigration reform or what not, I was there. They didn't show my picture, they didn't show my face, and I know other Black people down there too. And some of the Mexicans were confused." In Johnson's estimation, both establishment journalists and Latin@ protestors were confused by the sense of solidarity advanced by Black activists. While support for immigrants' rights remains ambivalent among Lakeside's

Black residents, Johnson and Palmer demonstrate that some believe that the fates of the Black and Brown communities are inextricably linked.

In recognition of their shared marginality, some Black residents are willing to speak on behalf of Latin@s. Bruce and Lydia Palmer, both officers in their neighborhood council and influential CPAB members, explain their ability to represent Latin@s in governmental affairs:

> AARON: What groups do you represent in this community? Which ones are there, which one do you see prevalent here? Latinos?
>
> BRUCE: Latinos.
>
> LYDIA: Latinos.
>
> BRUCE: Population-wise—
>
> LYDIA: Seventy percent.
>
> AARON: Seventy percent? Is that right?
>
> BRUCE: Right.
>
> LYDIA: African Americans is thirty percent. . . .
>
> AARON: But in terms in how it actually plays out in day-to-day life with all your constituents, does that happen or not? Do they get along, not get along?
>
> BRUCE: . . . I worked for twenty-one years at the local elementary school, and so of that twenty years and still living in the same community for forty years, you get to know everybody, generations of Africans and Latinos. And so the way that we make up the profile of the neighborhood council, you might use the word like "*Mi casa, su casa, mi niños, su niños*," My house, your house. . . . My house cannot stand without support from your house. . . . So I feel about your child like I feel about my child. I feel about your house like I feel about my house.

Embedded in the Palmers' explanation of their ability to represent Latin@s are themes that again reveal community as history and struggle: mutuality ("My house cannot stand without support from your house") and longevity ("twenty-one years at the local elementary school"). Bruce's long history of service to the local school system and his four-decade presence in the neighborhood provide him with a sense of history and changing local context that he sees as important for representation. On the other hand, prerequisites like tenure and official civic involvement can make it difficult for immigrant Latin@s to be seen as anything other than constituents by Black representatives as opposed to full partners.

Similar to the Palmers, Adriana Sanchez discusses the need for interracial political representation, while also acknowledging shared struggles over time:

> SANCHEZ: It's historical. [African Americans] were here for a lot of years and a lot of people that are coming here are immigrants, so I think that that kind of makes sense because some of the people are just kind of feeling out the area. They are just kind of getting adjusted. And part of coming in as an immigrant is getting adjusted. African Americans have been here for many years so they have more of an understanding of the community. So that's why they would be in more leadership roles.
>
> DANNY: Do you think that they are able to represent the interest of some of the other groups?
>
> SANCHEZ: Yeah, I think so. I think there is always representation from Hispanics as well, so I think that it's workable. They are living in the same type of situations. They understand the community because they have lived in it for many years so I would say yeah. They know the needs because they've lived here for so many years.
>
> DANNY: There is no friction between them, they really just represent the needs of everybody in the community?
>
> SANCHEZ: I guess the biggest thing right now is understanding an immigrant's needs. You don't get as many services as an immigrant because they are not legally here. So that is a problem because a lot of the services that are being offered are not offered to illegal immigrants. As we all know there is a lot of immigration happening and often times it's not legal. They aren't getting the services and it's difficult in some situations to express the need and not being able to fill it. You can express the fact that these people still need services and they still need jobs but what's to show for it? But how to you do that? There's no real solution to the problem at least not as far as illegal immigration is concerned.

Sanchez explicitly recognizes the relevance of the qualifications referenced by the Palmers and even agrees on their importance. However, she also recognizes the unique issues faced by an immigrant population as the first obstacle to such an arrangement. In seeking to enhance services and opportunity for the disenfranchised, Black residents' organizational efforts, she suggests, have tended to focus around solutions uncomplicated by the intersectional issue of immigration status. We take these issues up again in Chapter 6 by focusing on the sorts of problems that emerge when police and group leaders in Lakeside coordinate Black-Latin@ collaborations.

The Contested Meaning of Community

Lakeside is a divided community. It has undergone several cycles of rapid growth and change. Both Blacks and Latin@s have been newcomers to the city and in turn settled populations reacting to new migrants. Large numbers of Black migrants, fleeing the conditions of Jim Crow violence and poverty between the 1940s and 1960s, and Latin@ migrants, fleeing the conditions of war and crushing poverty in Mexico and Central America between the 1970s and 1990s, have forever changed Los Angeles. Neighborhoods that were once White became Black and then became Brown. This has resulted in a dynamic tension between each of these groups, complicating the very questions of community and history that Ms. Mayfield stressed were primary indicators of her feelings of kinship among a group of people and a place.

After the Mexican-US War set the stage for White accumulation of capital, each successive wave of non-White migrants entering Los Angeles endured hostilities from the settled population. Incoming Blacks suffered the violent reactions of Whites throughout the 1940s and 1950s. Having endured these hostilities before Whites fled South LA and then suffering the job market's collapse, Blacks became defensive of the area as their home, their rightful community—one forged by a shared struggle. Lakeside has long been recognized as a Black place—the heart of the city's Black Belt. As Ms. Mayfield and others assert, Blacks become protective over the community's geographic boundaries and resentful of the incoming Latin@ migrants "invading" the community. While there is evidence to suggest that negative feelings "go both ways," this chapter has highlighted the reactions of Blacks to the decline of the Black community and their perceptions of the role Latin@s played in this. They reacted to the perception that Latin@s are displacing Blacks from neighborhood homes, in the local labor market, and in city politics, notwithstanding the empirical basis for these assessments (Telles, Sawyer, and Rivera-Salgado 2011).

In spite of these hostilities, there is a segment of the Lakeside community that is seeking to forge multicultural coalitions that yield mutual benefits. Some Blacks and Latin@s see the fates of the two communities, whether regarding historical experiences with poverty and marginalization or contemporary struggles over governmental persecution in the form of immigration and police control, as intertwined. Yet while there are participants involved in attempting to construct an inclusive moral order, there are many in both the Black and Latin@ communities who do not acknowledge or actively retard these efforts.

Given this tempestuous history, we must acknowledge the reality that rapid demographic change and intergroup conflict will inevitably complicate any efforts at urban cogovernance. Multicultural coalitions have the potential to strengthen the capacity for both communities to respond to deleterious social conditions and bring about change (G. T. Johnson 2013). But how likely are the two communities to agree on what constitutes disorder? Are police even willing or able to address these concerns? We will discuss in later chapters how and why Blacks identify Latin@s as both illegal and problematic and why they feel Latin@s should be a prime target for police enforcement. Similarly, we will also explore how and why Latin@s identify Blacks as both criminal and problematic and why they feel Blacks should be targeted for similar reasons. In the next chapter, however, we first discuss how police have shaped and organized police-community meetings in Lakeside.

3

Organizing the Division

Danny and Aaron's fieldnotes

Captain Albert Himura proceeds to run through the CPAB by-laws, explaining the rules that allow expulsion of members for "good cause," but mentions that everyone should try to attend meetings as often as possible. He gets to the section on elections and spontaneously throws open the position of resident co-chair (he's the permanent chair). Members have the option of electing a new chair or retaining Vera Fisher, who says nothing on her own behalf, but only Bruce Palmer evinces any interest. "Okay, but only for one year," he says, and Himura admits that Fisher has agreed to stay on if nobody else wants to do it. Himura warns Palmer that if he takes the position, he's going to throw a lot of responsibility his way. Palmer nods, accepting the challenge, but his offer is passed over somehow without any further discussion and Fisher remains co-chair.

The position of secretary comes up next, and the younger woman sitting across the room shouts "Bernadette for secretary!" There seems to be general support for this proposition and it passes with Bernadette Ayers's caveat that there be a backup secretary as well.

The sergeant-at-arms position is the next opening requiring a volunteer. Palmer mentions that J. D. Evans used to hold the position officially and still speaks up and raps the table when residents are talking over one another ("*Hssst!* One at a time!"). Ignoring this, Himura inexplicably nominates John Peters, the quiet, heavyset man in his forties—the youngster of the group—for the position. When asked if he's comfortable assuming the responsibility, Peters says, "Well, you elected me, so I guess I have to," a joking reference to the "legal" nature of the Captain's bylaws. There is no vote, only Himura's nomination.

Captain Himura resumes reading the three-page by-laws document aloud line by line. A few things stand out, particularly various measures that reserve control of the meetings for the Captain, including veto power should the board make any recommendations that contradict the Captain's opinion of appropriate community policing activity.

In the above excerpt, Lakeside Captain Albert Himura oversees the CPAB's organizational power structure. Both Fisher and Himura occupy social roles created in the departmental reorganization after 1992. LAPD's "Strategic Plan on Community Policing" (Parks 1999) identifies the Division Captain as the key power broker of community policing, directly responsible for overseeing an area's problem-solving apparatus. In charge of all policing operations in Lakeside, Himura is the meeting's focal point. The excerpt demonstrates the co-chair position, ostensibly a coequal position held by a resident, to be subordinate and contingent upon the Captain's approval, which Mr. Palmer failed to garner. Himura leans heavily on volunteers to coordinate a wide range of community outreach activities. He determines whether someone is fit to take part in community meetings and whether members can continue to take part.

This chapter focuses on the structure of community meetings and some of the power dynamics involved by examining the leadership of Albert Himura and his predecessor Rick Patton. The Captains frame the two major sections of this chapter. We explore the structure of community meetings under Captain Himura, who is jolly yet demanding. The Captain represents broader trends in the evolving social role of police in the neoliberal/post–civil rights era. The transition between the Captains also demonstrates the degree to which LAPD maintains a nearly dynastic control over the CPAB despite differences in personality and leadership styles. Wacquant (2009) argues that, similar to transformations in police operations inspired by zero tolerance, community-oriented approaches involve three organizational changes. The first change involves decentralized services, flattened hierarchies, and devolution of responsibility, in this case to Area Captains whose promotions are based in large part on crime reduction statistics. Second is significant expansion of local and national law enforcement capabilities. Wacquant argues that it involves significant financial expenditures; others would add that enlisting the public to share the responsibility for crime control is another way of expanding police powers (Garland 2001; Gascón and Roussell 2016; Lyons 2002). And the third change is increased use of new technology, such as Compstat, and corporate reorganization of daily police operations to improve efficiency and resource management through directed, problem-solving, or proactive patrols.[1]

One of the Captain's main goals is to cultivate the capacity for the community to control crime, which begins with identifying pro-law-enforcement collaborators. Community-based policing initiatives work principally to redistribute the responsibility for local crime control (Garland 2001). The 1960s were a key turning point in the shift toward community governance. One of the first tasks of policy makers (including police administrators) was to identify responsible parties; these individuals would undergo public education and be trained on various modes of self-government. Governmentality scholars refer to the process by which residents come to share the responsibility for state-centered crime control as "responsibilization" (Garland 2001; Rose 1996). Volunteers, business owners, and residents began to share the burden of responsibility for locally based crime-prevention efforts. While police can capably deal with serious and chronic offenders, they admit defeat in enforcing random, opportunistic, or "everyday" crime.

We also discuss the symbolic boundaries of meetings—who is allowed to participate, the agenda, and what messages should be circulated within and outside of meetings—to further explore how police shape and restrict the role of the civilian in crime prevention. Captain Patton reveals how police exclude felons and undocumented migrants from the crime prevention community; he keeps to a strict agenda and restricts the flow of conversation; and he normalizes the presence of crime and the need for law enforcement in the community. This approach shifts the responsibility for the outcomes of police service onto the "customers"—that is, the public (Garland 2001). These partnerships and their activities are intended to coproduce public security so as to diffuse responsibility from the government. In a sense, the Captain asks residents to take "ownership" over some crime-prevention responsibilities in the ways he asks his SLOs to control crime on patrol.

Himura admits that established community divisions create a management problem for police and hinder the community's capacity to respond to crime. Herbert (2006), in his study of police-community partnerships in Seattle, explains that devolution of political power to the community can reinforce existing social and economic conditions in that community. Community political conflicts inevitably surface in the process of developing this self-governing potential. Not all citizens accept their posts as easily as Mr. Peters. Instead, they believe that police should extend themselves further to serve the public. Even assembling a single group into the community room to have a discussion sometimes poses a challenge to police; in Lakeside, the solution is to separate community groups by language.

Regular meetings demonstrate that LAPD wishes to collaborate, but at the same time the Captain and SLOs favor LAPD's traditional crime-fighting project. The Captains favor maintaining community order through problem-focused and data-driven enforcement strategies. Policing in the post–civil rights era has increasingly involved a shift from more traditional reactive to more proactive policing tactics (Balko 2013; Domanick 2016). This includes engaging in problem-oriented or order-maintenance-based strategies through targeted vehicle or foot patrols to more thoroughly criminalize disorder, criminal incivilities, and misdemeanors. In theory, community-based practices enable officers to interact with civilians on a regular basis and to consult with them on the problems affecting the neighborhood and facilitate a more direct form of public accountability (Garland 2001). Compstat helps define community problems without involving community members, identifying crime hot spots. This enables police agencies to adopt a "smarter" approach to crime, or at least one that improves the efficiency of police service delivery.

But an important yet less examined feature of the police-community partnership is personal relationships. Beyond the conflicts that we will discuss between community leaders, we refer here to the interpersonal relationships between the Captain and the participants. On many occasions Captains acknowledge the elevated degree of mistrust in Lakeside and surrounding communities, which historically have some of the greatest mistrust of police. And Captains whom civilians like and who are open to trying new things tend to be promoted or rotated out before they can institutionalize their programming. Their project ends abruptly and seems unfinished. Further, the revolving cast of leaders prohibits civilians from building lasting and productive relationships with LAPD decision makers. This, in particular, reveals how police can, actively or passively, isolate the community from police action. To better understand these dynamics, let us begin by discussing how community meetings are organized under Captain Himura's command.

Captain Himura—Mobilizing the Partners

Albert Himura is a stocky Asian American man with a florid complexion and a friendly face. A veteran South LA cop, Himura started his career patrolling Lakeside and working his way up through the ranks in two adjacent divisions. Most of our observation days Himura dressed in formal blues, with or without a bulletproof vest underneath. Once he wore a suit and tie to a community meeting when some of the top brass attended, and it stood out. The Captain was usually very polite and conciliatory. He was very accommodating toward us, probably because when he took command of Lakeside, co-chair Vera Fisher repeatedly referred to us affectionately as "our graduate students," making us a permanent fixture in the CPAB, which helped smooth the transition. At first there was some confusion over how to pronounce his name—HIMura or HimURA—so some just call him "the Captain." Often a deep thinker who shared his musings with us, Himura sincerely tried to balance his departmental and community responsibilities, although he favored the former despite his friendly demeanor toward residents. In proper community policing fashion, he tried to normalize the presence of law enforcement in the community, smoothing over LAPD's hard edges when they surfaced. Himura had a deft community touch and was skilled at running a room, able to get civilians behind him in an affable, I'm-a-good-guy-here-for-you kind of way. For example, Himura was on a first-name basis with one of the local gang leaders, Larry, who was busted for drugs in a federal drug raid coordinated by Himura's second in command, Carlos Macias. Due to their relationship, Larry asked Himura for a letter of support during a phone call at four o'clock in the morning:

Aaron's fieldnotes

Himura agrees, although he says that he cannot do it in his official capacity as an LAPD Captain—he has to do it as a private citizen, who just happens to work at LAPD in the position of Captain. This is exactly what he does, on his own letterhead (not LAPD's). He offers to show it to me, and summarizes it. It mentions Larry's community organizing [hopefully leaving out the part about community organizing's connection to the Crips, for Larry's sake], his desire for his kids to do well, and his aspirations as a parent. He sounds admiring and I ask him about this. He agrees, saying he thinks that

Larry is trying to do right by his kids and his community and that he's basically got good goals, but that sometimes "the gangster comes out."

As Area Captain, Himura had the final say over where, when, and how to deploy the division's resources. In directing his SLOs, he emphasized that they become "entrepreneurial" and take ownership over their BCA. They must become more personable, he told them, seek out more "face-to-face time," engage in foot patrols, and educate the public by participating in other community meetings or canvassing the neighborhoods and shopping centers. Sometimes he directed nonspecialized patrol units to assist SLOs in problem-solving operations. SLOs and CROs under the Captain's command also took charge of the juvenile boot camp and other youth-oriented programs, while Himura himself sometimes attended and spoke at their graduation (see Gascón and Roussell 2016). This style of public engagement was a key part of LAPD's post-1992 "Commitment to Action": "Patrol officers will be provided adequate training to serve as the first point of intervention on almost all problems. The rest of the Department's operations units will be a resource that patrol can call upon for support and expertise. Patrol will be designed around the basic car" (W. L. Williams 1995a).

Himura's SLOs and CROs are a policy throwback to the "territorial imperative" (Los Angeles Police Department 1992). Former LAPD administrator Roland Keller explained to us how the territorial imperative applied to patrol using the example of mountain lions: pushed out of their own territory by human development, mountain lions creep into public space instead of another lion's territory—their fear of territorial retaliation is stronger than their fear of humans. Jeff O'Malley, another former LAPD administrator, explained the SLO's role specifically as a "lone predator": "In LAPD, it was praised and expected that if a call comes out in your area, you better handle the call, handle your area. So that territorial imperative was pushed down to the peer pressure level. . . . That was very strong. If you were on a call long term or a child abuse or a shooting or something and you couldn't handle it, then everybody understood that, but if you were available then you better handle your area. So that territorial imperative was part of that culture early on." LAPD's revised and "flattened" police hierarchy is summarized in Figure

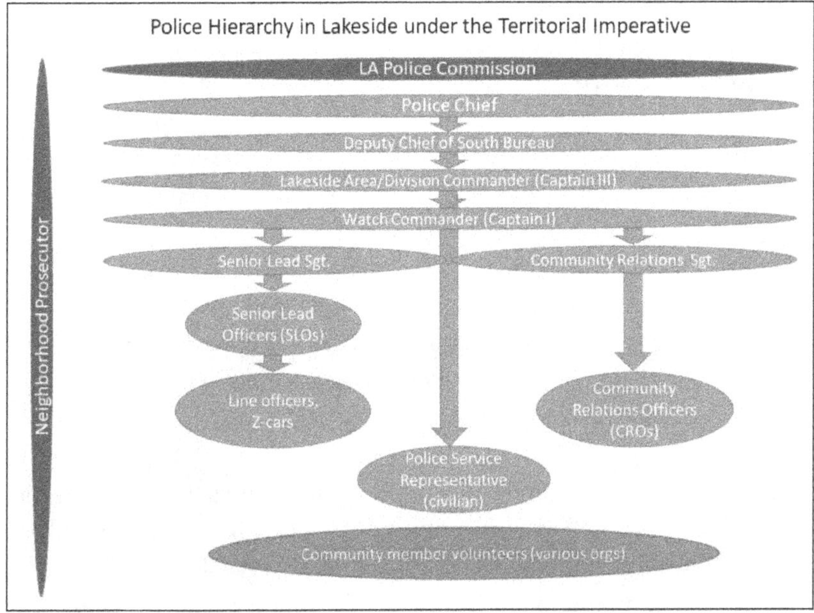

Figure 3.1. Community policing organizational chart.

3.1. Under Himura, Keller's mountain lions once again "own" their BCAs. LAPD has added to each division a Community Relations Office (CRO), run by a CRO Sergeant and supported by nine CRO officers, and more are available if a Captain requests them. The CRO is essentially LAPD's version of "Officer Friendly," and they typically run youth programs and make presentations at local schools and other public events. Although Herbert (1997) documents that LAPD's CROs generally were not seen as doing "real police work" by other officers in the 1990s, some individual CROs are highly regarded by the administration and believe the position can be a springboard for promotion.

SLOs are the archetypical community police officer envisioned in the Basic Car Plan revitalization. Himura's predecessor, Captain Patton, explained in his (hand-recorded) interview how we should interpret the role of SLOs.

> PATTON: The SLOs are the most important part of the LAPD's community policing model. They provide everyone in the BCA a name

> and a number to call. This way issues can be dealt with in a speedy, more personalized fashion. They are regular officers, but in addition to their normal duties, they are specifically charged with policing communities along with residents, in a manner of speaking. If SLOs are not responsive, Patton holds them accountable. Their role is to be the department's "face," address quality of life issues, and fix things before they become problems. If there's a burglary in the community, they do things like reach out to the victim or set up a block club. SLOs network with the community, which allows them to immediately react to complaints. Although budget cuts make overtime hard, they are supposed to attend CPAB meetings to interact, learn, be seen, and get information to the community.

Some SLOs avoided attending monthly meetings as much as possible, but Captain Himura had a habit of supplementing his officers' workload with additional administrative responsibilities regardless. Phil Hackett, for example, admitted to fabricating events occasionally during his SLO report out of irritation that CPAB cut into his job moonlighting as a security guard. Liz Fairbanks, on the other hand, attended nearly every CPAB meeting. One of Himura's most pronounced managerial strategies was to delegate responsibility to cops he found capable, often with little notice. Himura would do this especially when Compstat meetings came around. Upon being asked by the Captain to attend a Compstat meeting, CRO Robert Smith was startled to discover later that it was a management accountability meeting. One Watch Commander began his crime update one month by reporting, "I was just at a Compstat meeting yesterday. I got drilled for an hour and a half." Himura is typically a bit gentler with residents.

Himura's openness with residents reflected the general character of LAPD's approach to community policing. There was a willingness to regularly interact with residents and discuss problems affecting the community and work together to conduct outreach events. But it was also clear that while accountability to the public was the primary objective of the post-1992 reforms, in practice Lakeside privileged a traditional crime-fighting project outside the meeting room. Methods remained largely the same, while the data were augmented increasingly with community information (Domanick 2016). Treatment of marginalized populations, particularly undocumented Latin@s, complicated the community policing project as well, insofar as Lakeside relied upon community agents to supply participants for each meeting. Further, racial and cultural differences that created division within the community became exacerbated within meetings because police agents did not employ effective conflict resolution or coalition building. Revolving leadership also prohibited residents from building productive relationships with administrators or Spanish-speaking officials.

In spite of the deeply rooted mistrust that Captains said remained in Lakeside and other South Bureau divisions (and which we observed), there is survey evidence to suggest that citywide perceptions of police have vastly improved, particularly since the 2002 appointment of Bill Bratton as Chief. One *LA Times* poll of LA voters suggests that "Los Angeles police are riding a crest of goodwill that has pushed the department's popularity to levels not sustained since the late 1980s" (Rubin 2009).[2] The *LA Times* hailed these approval ratings as proof that Bratton's methods in the post-Rampart era—forging ties with leaders in communities of color, updating the training curriculum, hiring more cops of color, and implementing management accountability through Compstat— had "reinvented" the department's public image. Survey results from a Harvard study, which examined LAPD's progress toward fulfilling the federal consent decree mandates, showed similar improvements in the public's assessment of LAPD's performance with respect to their work and service (Stone, Foglesong, and Cole 2009). The study's focus group interviews, however, provide much more nuance to the public's positive evaluations.[3] While residents noted that LAPD "has come a long way," some remained "hopeful, but fearful" that the changes would not last beyond Bratton's departure in late 2009. Such methodologies, moreover, are likely to capture effectively those with less direct experience with LAPD tactics; undocumented immigrants, for example, are less likely to respond to official overtures.

Community Meetings

A key component of community policing, and a theme of the Christopher Commission Report, is to keep police "accountable to all segments of the community" (Independent Commission on the Los Angeles

Police Department 1991, 106). Proposals from concerned LA residents outlining strategies for community-police cogovernance and more general community-oriented rebuilding were rejected out of hand (Costa Vargas 2006; M. Davis 1993a, 1993b).[4] Instead, LAPD (1992) described its intent to "institute a 'new beginning' to build public safety confidence between the people of Los Angeles and their Police Department." The document, "Building Public Safety Confidence in Los Angeles," outlines a robust role for the community in shaping the city's police force by asserting their "legitimate right to participate in the design, implementation and assessment of public safety services."

LAPD's "Commitment to Action" announced that the department was using its territorial subdivisions to identify community concerns:

> Community Focus Groups—Consistent with the notion of partnership, direct community input into the decision-making process was critical. In order to maximize participation, community focus group meetings were conducted in each of the Department's 18 geographic Areas, with each group identifying its top 15 expectations of the Los Angeles Police Department. The results of each group were immediately provided to the participants, Department command staff, and the employees participating in the internal ad hoc task forces. (W. L. Williams 1995a)

The lesson from 1992 was that it is important to engage with residents and understand their concerns and motivations. Residents can be used collectively (as above) or individually: "By assigning officers specifically to interact with community leaders—ideally four people per city block—[Deputy Chief Mark] Kroeker said his department has a better chance of finding and fixing problems" (Pols 1995).

Residents are vital sources of information for ensuring the security of territory, and certain residents must be cultivated to serve as conduits. Individually, CPAB members provide intelligence to officers regarding trouble in their neighborhood; collectively, they represent their communities by communicating local priorities to law enforcement. Instead of building public concerns into the strategies that govern the everyday operations of the department, LAPD delineated two places to incorporate community involvement within the existing institutional structure: residents as information sources and as students to be educated.

In addition to community input and decentralization of command, flexibility to changing local conditions is also a cornerstone of community policing theory. Lakeside's contemporary community policing structure is a series of choices made by different Captains in response to perceived local conditions. The Captains in charge of Lakeside have responded to the division's decades-long Black-to-Latino transition by segregating community meetings by language.

Community-Police Advisory Board

Despite the demographic shift, CPAB mostly comprises older English-speaking Black residents, a very small contingency of middle-aged Latino residents with typically limited English abilities, and several local business owners of various ethnicities. Nearly all participants are over fifty years of age, and a considerable number are over seventy. Translation services are ostensibly available, but we observed the actual presence of translators only a handful of times, mainly at larger presentations occurring in CPAB's normal time slot. Meetings take place once a month in the Lakeside Station community room located down a short hallway past the front desk. The room comfortably holds about forty people, although it sometimes strains to hold more for various functions. The room is painted institutional white with florescent ceiling lighting and three large flat-screen TVs elevated over a seldom-used wooden podium; only the pictures that dot the walls—mostly dated depictions of friendly interactions between police and residents—enliven the room. A portrait of Donovan Butler, a beloved Black South Bureau Chief, adorns the wall to the right of the entrance. Immediately across from the entrance double doors is a set of glass windows and sliding doors that lead to the outside courtyard, where cadets from Lakeside's Explorer program can be heard doing jumping jacks and pushups during meetings. For the English meeting, the room's furniture is often arranged in a semicircular fashion, with the resident co-chair and Captain sitting up front and board members arranged along the curve. Guests and nonmembers tend to sit along the wall.

The Captains considered the English meeting Lakeside's official CPAB and structured it hierarchically. At the top was the LAPD Division Captain as permanent CPAB chair; in his rare absence, the Captain I, or Watch Commander (who often attended anyway), would be in charge.

The Captain's nominal equal was the resident co-chair, sometimes referred to as the CPAB President, although, as we have seen, the election process can be somewhat irregular. This duo, in conjunction with some of the more prominent residents, ostensibly steered the English CPAB through a loose adherence to *Robert's Rules of Order* and determined the meeting agendas, although the level of input and authority that the co-chair had depended largely on the personalities of the individuals. Both positions report annually to the public LA Police Commission forum on the activities of the Lakeside CPAB.

In Lakeside, the Captains led the monthly meetings directly, unlike some divisions where the task is delegated. Sometimes Himura shared this responsibility with the CPAB President. After calling the meeting to order, the Captain would open with a discussion of the monthly crime figures. His update would include a discussion of Compstat, where he would report on the crimes that occur with greatest frequency, increases or decreases in the frequency of those crimes, and crime control strategies that he or SLOs have employed.

Danny's fieldnotes

"We've been busy," Himura starts off. Though Part 1 crimes are down 1.3 percent from last year, several crimes remain persistent problems.[5] Up to July, the division's only seen eleven homicides. Half what it was this time last year. If this rate holds, Himura says, the division will see its lowest homicide rate ever. In the South Bureau, Lakeside has the lowest murder rate. "Even Northside has more," he goes on. Himura attributes these figures to the work done "in the community and by officers. . . . Those relationships are paying dividends right now."

Burglaries are down 15 percent from last year, but property crimes overall are up. GTAs [grand theft auto] east of the freeway in SLO Lilly Morgan's area are particularly high. But these figures are not without a "success story": in recent weeks officers discovered a chop shop [at a nearby intersection], where they found fifteen stolen cars. Patrol officers stopped a young man driving a stolen vehicle. When stopped, the suspect fled, but was later detained. Himura thinks this arrest will reflect in the coming crime figures, as he is believed to be the perpetrator of a number of car thefts in the immediate area. To protect against car thefts, Himura urges residents to take part in the station's "Club" program. Residents can purchase the antitheft devices at "cost" for fifteen dollars per unit (normally forty dollars, he says). Officers partnered with O'Reilly Auto to provide residents and members the discount. Vehicle break-ins are also a concern.

Residents continue to leave their personal items in plain sight inside their cars and trucks, many of which are unlocked. Perpetrators, mostly homeless the Captain suspects, then walk by in the middle of the night checking door handles in Phil and Lilly's areas. In SLO Chris Cordoba's area, "non-suppressible" thefts are on the rise. Loss prevention agents at Home Depot, El Superior, and other retailers along [a major thoroughfare] have been making up to thirty arrests a month recently, when the average is half that. Shoplifting is "driving up my numbers," says Himura. Most of the arrests involve thefts of food and hair care products. "As it heats up," the Captain says, residents can expect crime rates to spike.

This year's SNLs [Summer Night Lights—a gang prevention program] are being held at Mercer Park. They started last weekend and run from Wednesday to Saturday, 7 PM to midnight. Last Saturday night program volunteers fed four to five hundred people. Himura expects this will hold throughout the summer. SNL, the Captain says, is positive for the community because it gives gang members "and regular kids" a place to hang out.

With those successes in mind, Himura announces there was a shooting last Wednesday at Mercer Park once SNL volunteers had shut things down for the night. GRYD [Gang Reduction and Youth Development, a mayoral gang intervention effort] hires ex-gang members as volunteers to run the program, doubling as interventionists. One of these volunteers was shot when rival gang members saw the young man hanging out with other known gang members at the park. Two Hollywood actors were on a patrol ride-along at the time of the shooting in preparation for an upcoming film. They were among the first responders.

Gang issues: Currently there are "no big gang wars." But on July 4th a Blood gang member was shot after attending a house party thrown by members of the Crips. Twitter and Facebook notifications were sent out announcing the party and into the evening officers broke up the party. Some hours later the Blood member was shot and killed as he made for his car. Other than that, significant gang issues are "nonexistent right now."

Ending his update, Himura thanks CPAB members for their hard work in organizing the successful Emergency Preparedness Fair.

Himura's statistical exposition segues neatly into reminding and informing residents about local crime, but also community-building events. Nearly all meetings contain some combination of BCA reports from SLOs, presentations, short announcements, and often event planning. SLO reports, which contain area-specific information and discussion points for residents, are usually the first things cut from meetings that run long. SLOs take care to announce their specific territory by BCA number and boundary streets. Through SLO reports, new attendees learn and internalize LAPD's community definitions and can ask direct questions about their new understanding of community. SLOs also take this time to articulate publicly the crime fighting work they do by distributing fliers, meeting with businesses, filing civil injunction and regulatory paperwork, and conducting problem-solving task forces.

In some ways, Himura was a progressive thinker. The Captain theorized about how crime in South LA, and the government's ability to respond to it, was contingent upon broader socioeconomic factors. He also organized a workshop where residents identified problems in their neighborhoods and potential nontraditional/non-law-enforcement solutions. Himura usually had a soft touch with residents, but he expected a lot from them too. The Captain had the final say over patrol deployment decisions in the same way he created the menu at Officer Appreciation Day (OAD); all fell within the scope of his community policing authority. He was rule oriented and made sure to define his expectations of meeting decorum. Himura was usually considerate and grateful when asking for volunteers to staff tables at outreach events, canvass the neighborhood after a shooting, take on clerical duties during office furloughs, or donate money for CPAB programs. With CPAB volunteers, Himura coordinated numerous outreach events, including open houses and a job fair at the station, an Easter egg hunt, community sporting events, and OAD. They also took part in coordinating park initiatives, such as SNL and the National Night Out, and organized community service programs such as a youth choir and the health, safety, and emergency preparedness fairs, and created a "baby room" fully stocked with supplies at the station for neonatal and toddler emergencies.

Despite his progressive rhetoric, Himura saw everyone in Lakeside as his subordinate. Like he did with his law enforcement personnel, the Captain would unexpectedly shoulder community volunteers with responsibility, appointing community members to key positions without even so much as a discussion of the responsibilities. Under Himura's tenure, several residents carved out spaces for themselves as meeting authority figures in specific ways as well: Minerva Cooley, for example, founded and directed the area's domestic violence intervention program; Teresa Mayfield directed the preparations for OAD every year; Bruce Palmer served as the self-appointed neighborhood council liaison and the group's general emergency preparedness expert; and J. D. Evans, the unofficial sergeant-at-arms and time keeper, regularly interjected into heated exchanges or deviations from the meeting's agenda by rapping his nameplate on the table as a makeshift gavel.

It is difficult to overstate the level of control the Captain retained over CPAB operations. Because police designed and controlled the entire CPAB framework, it was nearly impossible for members to raise sustained challenges to police decisions. According to their own needs and perceptions, LAPD decided what the membership requirements and meeting format would be and when meetings would be scheduled or rescheduled. Some monthly meeting time slots were reappropriated for other public presentations to take advantage of residents' presence. To maximize attendance, for example, a public presentation and plea for information on the Grim Sleeper serial killer in 2009 pushed back CPAB for two hours. During the events surrounding ex-LAPD officer Chris Dorner's one-man war on police in 2013, CPAB was pushed back a week. This also allowed LAPD command extra time to formulate and standardize an official set of talking points. Contrary to LAPD's aspirational language, meetings are places neither intended for nor conducive to dissent.

In spite of the Captain's control, we found that meetings generally occurred within a convivial atmosphere. This was not surprising; one study found that elderly residents who attended CPAB meetings held the department in the highest esteem among all those surveyed (Stone, Foglesong, and Cole 2009). Some members are strongly loyal to LAPD, including specific officers, and seem not to engage with neighborhood criticisms that challenge police hegemony. April Umimoto, a Japanese American CPAB member in her seventies, is an extreme example, but her views are not uncommon: "When I was in LA Community College taking Spanish, one of the things the teacher asked was about police brutality. I thought that was so odd. The question came up about police brutality and I just said the police are doing a fine job, I don't see any police brutality—and there was a lot going around—but as far as I know, in my own little world, there wasn't any." Substantial meeting space is dedicated to the CPAB's and LAPD's expressions of mutual indebtedness for positive changes in the community. This dynamic is clear when CPAB members put time, effort, and their treasury toward such events as Officer Appreciation Day and National Night Out, but admiration also works its way into the institutional language used to present crime statistics and other mundane information. As Captain Macias summarized the crime update during one meeting: "We have the lowest crime in South Bureau, so keep it up. Whatever you're doing is working!"

Although Himura frequently mentioned alternative explanations for crime decreases, he regularly thanked the CPAB for the decrease and never blamed them when crime went up. CPAB could be easily and honestly thanked because they are a police creation, occupying a space that LAPD has created within its community policing designs. To give credit to CPAB is both a credit to police efforts and a reinforcement of CPAB members as true community representatives. One way to combat a rocky reputation is to remain in a constant process of improvement, thus forestalling critique. This put LAPD in the curious position of always caveating what it saw as its victories (e.g., declining crime rates), and such language represented a preemptive commitment to improvement as well as a way of creating empathy and solidarity with residents.

Hispanic Outreach

Rather than shifting to mirror its Latin@ majority, Lakeside's official CPAB has remained predominantly Black. The handful of Latin@ attendees nearly all speak limited English, and the Captain did not recruit translators consistently. Vera Fisher and several others didn't feel this was a worthwhile expense because so few Spanish speakers attended the English-language meeting, ignoring the circularity of the reasoning. To fill this void, Lakeside began a separate meeting for Spanish speakers with the help of local activist Hector Mendoza. Over the course of five years, the Spanish meeting took on a variety of forms, along with different purposes, names, and levels of official status.

Figure 3.2. Community room arranged in presentation style.

Like English meetings, Spanish meetings often occurred in the community room, but they were much more likely to be accidentally double-booked and relocated to the patrol roll call room at the last minute or co-scheduled with an outside program like SNL. Because meetings were not predicated on membership, anyone could attend, participate, and remain as anonymous as they chose. Attendees tended to be concerned Latin@ parents (often mothers) with their children and a few older men, mostly from Mexico, El Salvador, and Guatemala, together with a few representatives from local Latin@-oriented community organizations. The community room was usually arranged in a presentation style, sometimes without tables, only chairs assembled in rows (see Figure 3.2).

While English meetings commonly generated discussions about neighborhood concerns, strategic partnerships, and collaborative events, Spanish meetings combined outreach to the Latin@ immigrant community with orienting information on the US government and fear-reduction tactics. Many of those targeted by the meeting were fearful of the government from prior experiences in both the United States and their country of origin. Built along the lines of outreach and education, meetings were based less on deliberation and more on the presentation of information—there was no pretense of the *Robert's Rules of Order* that governs the English meeting. There were only three basic roles—police, who represented authority, no matter the officer's rank, and relayed information to participants; Hector Mendoza, the coordinator and translator who worked with a few others to recruit participants; and the Spanish-speaking residents who attended, listened, and raised their hands to ask questions or register complaints. As both translator and meeting leader, Mendoza was the linguistic broker, which granted him an enormous amount of control in not only filtering content, but also providing an audience. Although more than one Captain discussed hiring translators for the English meeting as well as hiring a permanent translator instead of Mendoza for the Spanish meeting, no sustained efforts along these lines were realized until late 2011.

Mendoza's unusual degree of control over the Spanish CPAB was short-lived, lasting only a few years before Patton officially retitled the meeting. Mendoza remained in charge, but this, practically speaking, amounted to a demotion—the meeting could no longer aspire to become the "official" CPAB of Lakeside, nor could it be coequal. As Captain Himura took control of Lakeside in 2010, what he called Hispanic Outreach (HO) became more of an auxiliary meeting. His feelings about the Spanish meeting were mixed. In theory, he understood the utility of such a meeting because his mother attended an Asian-focused police meeting in her LA neighborhood; still, the differences between an Asian immigrant experience and a Mexican or Central American one are vast. In Himura's mind, Lakeside's meetings could have eventually grown to be extensions of one another. The HO would be an educational meeting, a vehicle to grow Latin@ participation. Participants could learn the basics of law enforcement and build a relationship with cops before they eventually join the CPAB.

Himura's attempts to merge the two meetings, however, were both halfhearted and ill-fated. None of them withstood what he called Mendoza's "separatism," which became "an obstacle," as he explained it. Vera's resistance was less militant since her meeting occupied the official status, but equally resolute. Himura acknowledged that conflicts between Blacks and Latin@s are historically rooted and extended beyond the community room—"this is a problem I inherited," he told us. The Captain had Vera attend HO meetings to invite participants to the CPAB, an effort that Vera resented and which was stifled further by Hector's grudging translations. Himura then appointed one of the few HO members who spoke some English and did occasionally attend CPAB meetings, Aldo Peralta, to relay the details to the other group; while Peralta did attend, he either did not understand or did not perform his liaison duties. Thereafter the Captain spoke of merging meetings only theoretically and made no further efforts.

Unlike public opinion polling on the Latin@ perceptions of police (Rubin 2009; Stone, Foglesong, and Cole 2009), HO meeting participants are far less likely than either CPAB members or at-large Latin@ Angelenos to assess LAPD in a positive light. We dedicate considerable space in Chapters 4 and 6 to a discussion of the nature of the conflicts between police and HO participants. Yet the atmosphere of many meetings was somewhat similar to that of the CPAB—generally friendly and respectful, with some occasional challenges to police narratives. Given that there were far fewer regular attendees, it was not likely that residents and officers would be as familiar with one another as they were in the CPAB. Language issues might have also complicated personal relationships in HO meetings, as prior to Captain Macias's arrival few officers or administrators with whom residents regularly engaged spoke any Spanish, including most SLOs.

Captain Patton—Controlling the Partners

Rick Patton was a White man in his early fifties, well over six feet tall and whip thin. Together with his soft-spoken manner and bristly mustache, he radiated the quiet power of a veteran military officer, equally at ease both taking and giving orders. Although we only once saw him out of a blue uniform and utility/weapons belt, it seems likely that one could guess his profession even when he was dressed in jeans and a T-shirt. During the latter stages of our fieldwork, Patton shaved his mustache, to which residents responded with shock, joking that he'd ridded himself, Sampson-like, of the source of his power. Although Patton could be friendly, he generally maintained a very serious demeanor—indeed, we did not see him crack a smile for what felt like a year. The first time may have been when he mentioned in a meeting that he would be partnering with the local "prostitution school"—a sort of halfway house/recovery program—a curriculum he initially described, deadpanning, as, "We teach them to become better prostitutes." In another instance, a resident reported that her neighbors were selling gasoline out of their home, and Patton joked, "Well, how cheap is the gas?" Patton was well liked by HO as well as CPAB participants. He would push his Spanish-speaking abilities to the limit from the very beginning of meetings—"*Buenos noches*"—to general appreciation and amusement. HO participants Latinized him as "*Capitán Patón*" or showed their deference by calling him "*El Jefe* [the Boss]."

Patton's experience in law enforcement was extensive and multifaceted. He grew up in LA and "saw cops from the other side," but went on to join the department's Explorer program at fifteen. He saw his LA biography as conditioning him to listen to the community and empathize with their problems. His job required smooth interpersonal interactions and social awareness, but his exchanges sometimes came off as slightly canned—he may well have meant exactly what he said, but he also may have rehearsed it so that it came off exactly as he intended. When we met him, he had been with LAPD for nearly forty years, working first in Lakeside, one of the city's largest commands, as a Sergeant in the late 1980s and returning as Division Captain in the late 2000s.

Captain Patton set up much of the community policing command infrastructure that Himura managed, although their interpersonal styles and desired enforcement tactics differed somewhat. On the street, Patton wanted SLOs to identify a single "point of contact" in the community who could serve as a conduit for both soliciting and distributing crime information at the neighborhood level. Membership requirements under both Captains prohibited some community residents, such as felons and undocumented migrants, from participating, and police recruitment practices favored citizens they perceived as law-abiding and pro–law enforcement. After calling the meeting to order, the Captain followed a strict agenda. Crime updates, like the one discussed in the previous section, and guest speakers all proceeded in a preset order. The Captain countenanced breaks from this protocol but was mindful to keep proceedings from deviating too significantly. Patton and the SLOs promoted not only favorable views toward law enforcement, but also a crime-conscious sensibility that would shape everyday behavior and help reduce victimization.

Membership

In Administrative Order No. 10 (1993), Chief Williams gave Division Captains broad discretion in populating CPAB meetings. Captains are the arbiters of membership and set the size and purpose of the board. Advice from these bodies is rendered to the Captain for consideration. The following considerations guide Captains in choosing members:

> Selection should be made on the basis of a wide range of community input and not be restricted to those who openly support the Department. . . . Members should be respected in the community, knowledgeable about conditions of their community, and have the ability to work well in a group setting. Members should also have the ability and willingness to inform the public or their constituents of activities of the Board.
>
> Along with geographic concerns, commanding officers should consider the diversity of the Area, such as ethnic, religious, business, and community affiliations, when forming Advisory Boards. (W. L. Williams 1993)

LAPD's archetypical member is to be respectable, knowledgeable, collegial, independent, and willing to take on the role of unelected representative. In practice, however, power over membership lies directly in the hands of the Captain. Former LAPD administrator Roland Keller put such concerns in context in his (hand-recorded) phone interview: "There's a whole dynamic, Keller says, regarding those who want to be on the Boards: those who want to dictate to LAPD, those who want power, those who want inside info, and those who want to help their community. Some of these fell off pretty quickly." Keller went on to suggest that in the early 1990s there was some administrative worry that CPABs might become too confrontational. These concerns likely informed the decisions placing Division Captains in tight control of the meetings. The result was a body strongly supportive of LAPD and conspicuously lacking in autonomy or independent critique. It is difficult to imagine a true LAPD critic conforming to such a consensus-based structure as CPAB and remaining collegial while doing so—even the more cantankerous members ultimately labored in support of the institution.

There were a variety of more tangible barriers to overcome for CPAB membership as well. Members of CPAB must pass an LAPD background check and be "livescanned," or electronically fingerprinted. The application is several pages long and must be approved by the Captain before being fed through the FBI's National Crime Information Center database. The applications readily available were entirely in English in a division that is majority Latin@[6]—in 2010, Danny helped a Spanish-speaking aspirant fill out the English application form because no Spanish ones were available. These requirements screened out those who could not afford the time or transport to be livescanned downtown during business hours, spoke no English, had a past inconsistent with an LAPD background check, were immigrants concerned about their legal status, and/or were skittish of official biometric and surveillance efforts.

Announcements regarding the reapproval of CPAB membership by the Captain were made with some regularity. Over five years of fieldwork, there were three different Division Captains, each with the authority to reset membership requirements and at least one bureaucratic form change.

Aaron's fieldnotes

At some point during the announcements, the application requirements of CPAB membership come up. Apparently, the paperwork for several members who joined prior to my involvement is no longer valid—not because it expired, but because LAPD has gone (semi)digital and the old paperwork has been lost or is (now) incomplete. Yet the application, inexplicably, is still paper-based. Predictably, this is met with confusion from some and groans from those for whom it is clearly applicable, such as Mrs. Palmer, my very first interviewee in 2008, who is also a local neighborhood council chair.

Once a member jumped through these hoops, she was eligible for membership and Civilian Coordinator Jan Green would take a grainy headshot with her digital camera. CPAB member ID badges were laminated squares slightly larger than a business card that hung on an LAPD lanyard and contained the member's name and picture, division, annual expiration date, Captain's signature, and the official CPAB and LAPD seals. The roots of this practice went back to Deputy Chief Mark Kroeker in the mid-1990s: "We give them an ID card that looks like a police identification. . . . We have a swearing-in ceremony, I insist on it. We give them a little oath" (Pols 1995). Although the swearing-in ceremony and oath seem not to have survived the intervening decades in Lakeside, the cards remain.[7] Directives from downtown in 2012 informed members that they would have to attend various trainings to keep their membership valid. This was unpopular in Lakeside; even though many board members were formally retired, few wanted to attend lengthy trainings of questionable relevance for the privilege of volunteering their time at CPAB. Perhaps afraid of losing members, the requirement was subtly changed to the more flexible Community Emergency Response Team (CERT) training, which is useful in different organizational contexts and which many members had already undergone. Although the mandate continued as we exited the field, fewer than half of the membership had undergone the CERT training by 2013 and the requirement seemed likely to disappear through nonenforcement. Julie Coleman, the resident co-chair in 2013, announced officially that Lakeside CPAB comprised thirty-seven members, but there were more people involved on a regular basis who may have lapsed bureaucratically and a number of registered members who participated irregularly.

Board membership was a status used to demarcate community belonging and standing. In a concrete sense, CPAB membership confirmed one's standing as a community member for LAPD's purposes. When LAPD speaks of what "the community" thinks or having "consulted the community," CPAB members are often whom they mean. From this perspective, nonmember residents who attended CPAB (or a Spanish-speaking meeting) were not automatically considered part of the community. And as was occasionally noted wryly in meetings, the badge itself could also have tangible benefits should it be visible during a traffic stop.

Members had their names printed on yellow paper in clear plastic placards that sat on the tables in front of them. When the room was arranged in a horseshoe, members sat around the curve, while visitors and guests sat along the outside along the wall. Co-chair Vera Fisher, ever on the lookout for rules and regulations, made sure to ceremonialize this dynamic of belonging:

Aaron's fieldnotes

The meeting room is eventually packed, comprising by the end over forty people, not including us or the uniforms. I lose track eventually, but more than ten of these residents are Latino, which is unusual, some of whom have limited fluency in English. Fisher notes the new faces and has everyone who is not a "Board member" introduce themselves and who they "represent," although it's not always clear what this means. Most people name their neighborhood or their approximate address; one fellow names his neighborhood council, and another announces that he's an area resident who is here on behalf of the American Cancer Society. Board member Nicole Williams introduces most of the Latino newcomers as families involved with the after-school program Mission: Responsibility that she helps direct. She has invited them here to experience CPAB.

This has the effect of symbolically and ritually separating CPAB members from new attendees, insofar as newcomers must announce themselves for the edification of board members. I've noticed that Vera seldom misses an opportunity to do this and never makes current board members introduce themselves.

While visitors and guests in general were a mixed bag of race, gender, age, and profession, the dynamics of membership suggested that a significant contingency of Latin@ arrivals would almost certainly be located along the walls rather than at the tables. Fisher's efforts divided attendees in large part by race/ethnicity. Given the official requirements for full membership and immigration/legality dynamics of Lakeside, even if Latin@ residents were to attend English CPAB in large numbers, it is doubtful that many would apply for membership, thus maintaining the status difference. This dynamic has historical roots. In the post-uprising attempts to engage the community, LAPD excavated their social networks from team policing in the 1970s and reactivated those community points of contact who then formed the core of CPAB in 1993. To a large extent, recruitment then relied upon social networking, and the Black community, particularly the older generation of middle-class home owners and neighborhood old heads in their sixties, seventies, and even eighties, remained strongly represented in Lakeside's CPAB.

There is little question that Latin@ residents were tokenized at English meetings. Several Latin@ residents attended regularly but spoke little English and seldom were able to contribute—none were involved in titled positions. A few nonimmigrant Latin@s came as well, but the concerns of each meeting often reflected material concerns of citizenship status and naturalization, and this, as much as language, seems to have determined who attended which meeting. Carolina Zometa, a non-immigrant Latina, expressed such a belief in discussing her decreased Spanish meeting attendance in favor of the English CPAB: "They're [HO] always talking about immigration. I don't care about immigration. I gave up because they're always talking of immigration. I'm a United States citizen, I don't need to be involved with that. I don't need to be part of immigration classes." Zometa's response helps highlight the structural differences that surrounded the attendees of each meeting. Spanish-speaking Latin@s were outsiders to CPAB but were also often outsiders to legal status and mistrust a process that requires taking *huellas* (fingerprints). The Spanish-language meeting focus on problems faced by immigrants held little interest for Zometa, a security guard at Vernon High School and mother of American-born teenagers.

The Agenda and the Message

Meeting flow under Captain Patton was governed by an agenda. Collective rituals were important: A typical meeting (English or Spanish) began with the pledge of allegiance; occasionally the English meeting evoked a prayer as well. In one case, Captain Patton led the group in a somber prayer after an LAPD officer was killed in the line of duty. From there, Patton, like Himura, would recite crime trends and hot spots from his seat alongside Vera Fisher. The SLOs would follow in due course, speaking to the problems in their specific BCAs and their efforts to combat them. Most meetings also had one big-ticket item directly after the crime report. This was usually an informative presentation of about twenty minutes given by representatives of other governmental organizations. For example, in 2010 the US Census Bureau came to speak about the importance of accurately filling out census forms and to reassure residents that the process for gathering delinquent forms was unconnected to policing or immigration enforcement. Part awareness raising, part cajoling participation, and part fear reduction, the same talk was given at a variety of other neighborhood groups as well. An agent from the FBI came to speak in 2012 about the importance of database technology partnership for solving LA's unsolved homicide cases. The Inspector General for the LA

Police Commission also presented, discussing his job responsibilities and positioning himself (not CPAB) as LAPD's independent, external accountability.

As a vehicle for controlling perceptions and influencing behavior, CPAB pushed out LAPD messages in various ways. In keeping with Herbert's (2005, 2006) findings that community policing responsibilizes community rather than government, LAPD sought to cultivate self-regulating behavioral norms in its CPAB members. Methods were both written and verbal, but often standardized and repetitive. Next to the meeting attendance sheet (and also sent via mail and email) there were several stacks of flyers authored by LAPD and other government agencies discussing official policies, neighborhood problems, and sanctioned ways of correcting or reducing crime by regulating personal conduct. One document with the catchphrase "Lock It, Hide It, Keep It" induces personal behavioral change by depicting a thief lurking around an unattended vehicle and urging the readers to take precautions to guard themselves and their possessions (see Figure 3.3). Other prepackaged messages from downtown urged residents that if they "See Something, Say Something," promoting the police tip hotline for "suspicious behavior" and terrorism awareness. There were also copies of notices provided to public order offenders, such as the homeless, prostitutes, and illegal vendors (the latter are often in Spanish, providing an interesting counterpoint to the English-only membership applications). These verbal and visual messages directed residents to adapt their behavior to living in a high-crime environment. The overall message transmitted is that crime is a direct product of community negligence.

Similarly, discussions about rates for specific crimes often lead to archetypical stories about how such crimes occur. Patton refers often to the "door knockers," referencing an oft-repeated story of a set of burglars who knock systematically on doors to find unattended houses to burgle. Nearly identical stories with varying details are repeated in other LAPD divisions. Different meetings focus on different points, but the same general body of advice is accessed, focusing mainly on target hardening and awareness. A frequent reminder is to "keep your head on a swivel," or, in other words, be constantly suspicious of the potential for crime. New Captains and those running the meeting for the first time

Don't Become a Victim of an Auto Related Property Crime

Lock It !
A reminder to always lock your vehicle.

Hide It !!
If you have to leave your valuables in the vehicle, hide them from plain sight.

Keep It !!!
A positive reminder that personal responsibility and prevention can safeguard your valuables from theft.

For more Crime Prevention Information or to get involved in Neighborhood Watch, contact your local Los Angeles Police Station or visit our Web Site at www.lapdonline.org

Figure 3.3. "Lock It, Hide It, Keep It" flyer.

can be pedantic about repeating these points, and over time they become perfunctory.

Police also attempted to control the flow and interpretation of information regarding what police euphemistically call "officer-involved shootings" (OISs)—when police kill a resident. Not every police killing provoked such a response, but those that provoked neighborhood anger especially did. The following excerpt demonstrates the tight control over the facts and interpretations that LAPD can exert over such cases in their public CPAB performances:

Aaron's fieldnotes

Captain Patton discusses an OIS that took place this week. Apparently an officer chased down a suspect, a "second striker," who possessed a TEC-9 machine pistol. Patton highlights the fact that the magazine can hold fifty rounds. A little online research suggests that although this is possible, this requires special modifications and it is unlikely to have actually held fifty rounds. The varying possibilities are not discussed and the potentialities stand as fact. Also missing from his description is the fact that most people are unable to make the gun fully automatic, so it usually remains semiauto. Patton positions the weapon as a fully automatic piece. However, I am no weapons expert and am relying on Wikipedia and its sources, so perhaps it is exactly as Patton reports despite the verbal shading.

The officer "tried to disarm" the suspect and the suspect was shot to death in the ensuing tussle. As he speaks, Officer Liz Fairbanks circulates the room silently (and menacingly, in my opinion), inexplicably handing out Xeroxed pictures of a TEC-9 purported to be the one possessed by the slain man, photographed being held over a background of pine boughs by a gloved hand. There is no magazine present in the picture, fifty rounds or otherwise. Danny later tells me that Liz gives him a little gallows humor as she passes by: "This is the gun we planted on him." Understandably, she seems upset by the event—I wish that I would have been able to talk to her about it afterward, but that proves impossible.

Patton goes on to tell the meeting assembly that CPAB members were instrumental in helping calm down the neighborhood, telling everyone what happened, and trying to keep rumors from flying. That sort of feedback to the department is invaluable, he says, and we must keep that relationship strong. It's important to get facts and get the truth;

Figure 3.4. Image of the TEC-9 machine pistol belonging to a suspect shot by LAPD.

no matter what that truth is, he says, we want that truth. If you hear a rumor, trace it back, so we can find out what is really known, he says. There is no subsequent discussion and the OIS does not appear on the evening's agenda.

Although the monologue by Captain Patton seemed to be just an unscripted moment in the agenda, the prepared photocopies of the TEC-9 suggested otherwise (see Figure 3.4). Patton framed the event in very specific ways: He underlined the danger of the suspect by identifying him as a "second striker"—a two-time felon motivated to avoid the life term that awaits a third strike in California—and maximized the danger of the gun itself by presenting it in its deadliest incarnation. CPAB members were provided with portable photographic evidence to enable their explanations to neighborhood skeptics who may have questioned the police interpretation. Finally, the officer was depicted as trying heroically to disarm the suspect prior to the use of deadly force, presenting the resident's death as not only inevitable, but also within a strict and articulated adherence to the escalating use-of-force ladder.

The overall message was a tightly constructed set of talking points that rendered the suspect's death the result of the choices made by the suspect alone. The conclusion is inescapable and unambiguous: not only did the officer have no choice but to kill the man, but really the man killed himself.

Finally, some messaging was directed at the aspects of LAPD that remain baldly and institutionally oppressive. If community policing is the soft, friendly, community engagement piece of LAPD, Metro units are the unabashedly militarized and discriminatory LAPD of infamy.[8] Part of CPAB's job was to normalize and counterbalance this continuing aspect.

Aaron's fieldnotes

Himura continues with his crime update: "Every year around this time, we get extra Metro units. They are pure suppression. If you remember 'The Hammer' [Operation Hammer], it's like that, old-school LAPD tactics." Himura states this matter-of-factly. "So if your neighbors complain—Metro stops everyone, so tell them what's going on. That's why—suppression works."

Vera Fisher chimes in as well. "The new LAPD tactics are more about education. What Liz didn't say [in her SLO report] earlier is that crime drops after she does her flier campaign. And these fliers are specific to the problems going on in the specific Basic Car Area." In an apparent non sequitur, she continues to elaborate on such a strategy. "That's why we're all riding on buses tomorrow—we've had a lot of complaints about thefts, snatchings on buses so all the SLOs are going to ride tomorrow." Liz, sitting in the corner, looks surprised and mouths something to SLO Melvin Cantrell. She looks at me and rolls her eyes. Later, she informs me that this is the first she's heard of this bus campaign that apparently is kicking off tomorrow morning.

Captain Himura and co-chair Fisher's interplay resembled a scripted "good cop/bad cop" routine, an odd choice given Himura's general affability. Himura, playing the uncaring bad cop, blandly introduced the "old-school" suppression tactics of sweeping arrests and stop-and-frisks of Black and Latin@ youth, expecting members to justify these to their neighbors with the "it works" explanation (M. Davis 1993a,

2006). Fisher countered by underlining the educational component to Lakeside's policing strategy, which has the advantage of reminding critics that Lakeside pursued progressive community policing policies as well as distancing Lakeside's officers from the heavy-handed tactics of Metro. This strict dichotomy is betrayed by LAPD's own description of its Metropolitan Unit: "Today, the primary responsibility of Metro is to provide support to the Department's community-based policing efforts by deploying additional crime suppression resources throughout the City" (Los Angeles Police Department n.d.-b). Suppression was tightly interwoven into the community policing regime, despite Himura and Fisher's attempts to separate the two. Interestingly, in this instance, the balancing campaign, which may have been impromptu, took the SLOs by surprise.

Each Captain's impact extended into the broader Lakeside community as he formed partnerships with key area stakeholders. After tragic deaths occurred in Lakeside—a gang-involved shooting, a hit-and-run in front of a church—Patton sought out the mayoral gang task force manager and a local pastor to organize candlelight vigils. The Captain also solicited funds from local business boosters for equipment needs in the midst of the city's financial crunch. In one instance, Patton reported that such funds would help support the expansion of the division's surveillance capacity—the video feed from some private home security cameras (with the owners' permission) would be linked to the "Lakeside camera room." The residents burst into applause. "This is an exciting time for law enforcement—new technology," he explained. "The only damper is the economic crisis, which might dry up technology for law enforcement soon, but many of these things are already in the bag."

Captain Patton used meetings to shape external perceptions of the department, expecting CPAB members to disseminate and represent police viewpoints within their respective spheres of influence. Agendas sometimes eschewed outside organizations and instead scheduled big-ticket presentations by specialized police units, such as Traffic or Gangs, or local government agencies, including the Mayor's neighborhood prosecutors, the Department of Water and Power, the Police Commission, the Mayor's Gang Task Force, or the FBI. Detectives from Vice made a short presentation, where the Q&A covered prostitution, juvenile kidnapping/smuggling, *casitas* (party houses where prostitution and gambling occur), and abatement issues. Another detective discussed domestic violence but ended up spending even more time fielding questions about DNA evidence collection and processing compared to popular depictions on the forensic crime drama *CSI*. Guests were affable, informative, and no doubt evaluated on their performances, while residents learned about the police operations that the department chose to showcase. Presentations were nonthreatening and suggested transparency, insofar as residents walked away with shareable information about LAPD intertwined with positive messages about the police beneficence.

Some presentations were less friendly. Presentations in response to contemporary municipal or neighborhood events—such as the OIS above—could take on a darker character and were often run by higher level police administrators who controlled the messaging tightly. Under Captain Himura's tenure, Patton returned several times as a higher level administrator to personally shape messaging. Conversations in the Q&A (which was sometimes skipped) were stiff and truncated. Although they could take up significant meeting time, these presentations on current events remained unagendized and thus absent from the official meeting record. The script began by referencing the importance of community engagement. First, the Captain would praise the CPAB ("the community") for their work, even if the connection to the issue was murky; he would extend congratulations to SLOs for their efforts at community engagement; he would acknowledge that although LAPD has come a long way (presumably since 1992), everyone still has some ways to go, but, finally, that LAPD was committed to going the distance. Then the issue at hand would be brought forth.

These sessions addressed issues at the crossroads of policing and politics, most often related to racism and/or police brutality. In 2009, the federal consent decree imposed after the Rampart scandal ended. LAPD's release from a decade of federal oversight was a controversial moment, and Captain Patton, in a stilted tone during a Spanish CPAB meeting, followed the above script, highlighting LAPD's continuing efforts to extend its lessons forward. He carefully emphasized LAPD's internalization of the federally mandated changes, while downplaying the importance of the decree's complaint process, which LAPD had made a unilateral decision to drop. He name-checked the Police Commission and LAPD Inspector General (IG) as compliance managers, which both invested them with federal trust and distanced them from the department even though the IG and the commission are intimately involved in LAPD's affairs. While CPAB attendees generally supported law enforcement efforts, this announcement had explosive potential and Patton made a nearly identical presentation to the English CPAB later in the month.

Collaborative Governance

At the outset of this chapter, we demonstrated how much control the Captains have over the community policing apparatus. Both Himura and Patton imposed a community policing agenda on Lakeside that first and foremost served LAPD interests with respect to crime control. Though there were differences in their personalities and philosophies, they both yielded similar ends. Captains operated within an institutional setting and reproduced institutional norms that dictated the nature of the partnerships and their potential outcomes (Garland 2001; Herbert 2006). These dynamics are important for both theory and policy in police-led community governance in several ways.

Devolving responsibility for crime control to division Captains results in community-police activities that do not involve much community direction. LAPD's structure defines Captains as the primary problem solvers in the community—they coordinate all of the division's activities, including both SLOs and civilian participants. Captains Himura and Patton managed all specialized and localized crime control. They organized community meetings and enabled formalized interactions between civilians and officers to occur on a regular basis. Every meeting began with a run-down of the crime data. Rather than a listing of community complaints being addressed, the focus on crime data suggests that statistical crime goals are the official priority. When the Captains reported significant reductions in key crime categories, they would valorize the SLOs and the community for their hard work in bringing about these changes. (The inverse, of course, never occurred.)

LAPD directives prescribed that community policing reawaken the territorial imperative by devolving responsibility for everyday crime control to the SLOs. They patrolled their BCAs, "owned" their areas, and were held responsible for the crime in that area or subjected to sanctions. SLOs and CROs would act as Officer Friendly in these communities and bring a personalized brand of LAPD to the community and a trusted face to civilians. The SLOs, largely in isolation from CPAB input or activities, bore the brunt of the day-to-day crime-fighting responsibility. The bulk of their work involved engaging in problem solving in a variety of ways, from targeted patrols to foot beats, to address vending or prostitution or loitering hot spots. They also organized graffiti and alleyway cleanups and vending task forces as part of larger governmental collaborations.[9]

Delegating crime-prevention responsibility to the community involved teaching law-abiding civilians to begin "seeing like the state" (J. C. Scott 1998). Through their functions as eyes, ears, and mouths, these civilians become the "faces" of community policing. These faces most often include those who are pro–law enforcement and believe in the merits of crime control in a broad and uncritical sense. In many respects, the work of the community is disconnected from the crime-fighting work of SLOs. Instead, the community bears the brunt of the responsibility for CPAB's outreach programming. Police responsibilize the community by picking faces who share LAPD's crime control vision. The Captains are demanding; they command residents to take increasing ownership over the security of the neighborhood through community engagement and knowledge distribution. In this sense, the role of civilian partners becomes that of the "eyes and ears"—receivers and distributors of crime information—and the mouths, which pass on police messaging. Many of these messages seek to normalize the presence of law enforcement in the community and everyday life.

From a normative perspective, one key challenge to the community policing organization is the ever-present tension between professionalism and politics. There is not one community, but two (at least), separated by language abilities, which, given the Black and Latin@ makeup of the neighborhood, widens the existing racial, cultural, and ethnic divisions between them. Internal conflicts between community groups are, in some ways, inevitable—particularly when different leadership factions cannot identify sustainable solutions and are mutually antagonistic. Hector's and Vera's shared animosity was, in some ways, a reflection of views felt by members of the broader community, as others have documented (see, e.g., Costa Vargas 2006; Sides 2003; Vigil 2002). Two underlying issues remained unresolved: (1) CPAB's demographic mismatch and (2) Spanish-speaking residents no longer having even the pretense of community cogovernance. In 2013, incoming Lakeside Captain Victor Martín began once again to discuss these issues, and it remained unclear how—or if—they will eventually resolve. Chapter 4 elaborates on crime complaints—unplanned but crucial departures from the meeting agenda that otherwise tolerated little deviation. There we will see further evidence of the gatekeeping role played by officers in their responses to residents' complaints, the key component of community policing.

4

Complaint Encounters

Danny's fieldnotes

Ms. Carter asks Officer Hackett if she can ask a question and he jokes, "Okay, but I'm only taking three from the group today."

She tells him a man on her block has built an illegal attachment to his home and now he has a family living back there. The man owns three cars, and with the addition of that family, the total vehicle count has reached eight. The cars are all parked along her street, which has forced some residents to park on the next block or even a few blocks away. She asks what can be done about this.

"It's in our culture to see a space in front of our homes and to park our cars there. If he is parking his cars along the street, it may be inconvenient, but inconvenience is not illegal," Officer Hackett tells her.

From another angle, Captain Patton asks Ms. Carter if the cars are stationary. If the cars are never moved, they can be ticketed and towed because public streets are not for storage.

She replies that they do move the cars occasionally, but for the most part, the cars are parked.

Officer Fairbanks advises her to put together a petition and have the neighbors sign it and that way the city Building Services division can take care of it.

Negotiations over resident complaints like Ms. Carter's—what we call complaint encounters—occurred during most meetings. Meeting participants would report complaints about crime and disorder in a specific and detailed fashion. Each complaint could be part of a long series of discussions about recurrent problems over the course of months or years. Complaints seemed implicitly reserved for the "Other Business" section of the meeting agenda, but appeared during Captain's updates, SLO report, and in other places as well. Sometimes the Captain would announce, "Okay, no crime information?" requesting in an inverse fashion that meeting participants speak their concerns. Lakeside officials would never agendize Ms. Carter's parking issue, for instance, but this did not stop Ms. Carter and other residents from registering off-script complaints. Complaints are part of the implicit community policing bargain; they are a key mechanism through which to coproduce social order. And they take on added significance when moments of disunity emerge in an otherwise cooperative space.

Complaint encounters shape mutual understandings of police discretion and how police direct their considerable latitude. Chapter 1 demonstrated the sheer capacity of police discretion to occupy entire neighborhoods (e.g., Operation Hammer), suspending constitutional protections under the rubric of public safety. Although LAPD's approach has shifted somewhat in the intervening years, the legal architecture has grown even more lenient. This chapter examines the ways and directions in which that latitude is employed in a community policing context. Police discretion largely involves making decisions about whether and when to cite, arrest, or otherwise engage a civilian or to overlook a given behavior or situation. Reforms notwithstanding, workers on the ground tend to determine the most appropriate means of redistributing service. Public service workers, including police, teachers, and social workers, must employ discretion when delivering government services. This requires interacting with members of the public on a daily basis while rationing services based on the limits of the job. Public service work is limited by institutional goals and performance measures, high workload, and budgetary constraints.

Lipsky (2010) explains that public service workers have grown to be the largest and most visible workforce in the United States, and police are among the largest subgroups within it. In LA, for instance, the Mayor Antonio Villaraigosa's 2008–9 city budget report reads: "The proposed budgets for the Police Department and Fire Department represent the two largest expenditures in the City, accounting for 51.6% and 18.0% respectively of the City's unrestricted revenue of $3,780 million" (Villaraigosa 2009, 24). LAPD was by far the largest expenditure in the LA City budget, and while the Department was hit hard by cuts—up to $100 million in 2012, largely related to a new, more stringent overtime policy and a 20 percent salary reduction for new recruits—the Mayor supported increased recruitment between 2008 and 2013. LAPD deployed 9,700 sworn officers in 2008 and grew by two hundred within two years, with a goal of growing to ten thousand sworn personnel—the largest force in the Department's history (Villaraigosa 2009, 2010, 2011, 2012, 2013). Despite these expansions, police, as Lipsky (2010, 74) observes, "cannot possibly make arrests for all the infractions they observe during their work day." Indeed, overenforcement is one of the complaints that led to the 1992 uprisings.

Within a community policing framework, the ongoing collection of complaint encounters between police and civilians forms what we call a discourse of "policeability."[1] Policeability refers to the likelihood that a complaint will result in police action on behalf of the civilian. This is a major cornerstone upon which community policing's claim to coproduction rests. Within the larger set of practices that compose policework, community policing gathers its legitimacy from the maintenance of this policeable discourse and its successful satisfaction of resident concerns. How this discourse is produced thus becomes a crucial question. From an interactional perspective, community-police meetings are public performances in which the continued legitimacy of the forum depends on addressing the public's needs and working within LAPD's limits. As these exchanges and negotiations accrete over time, the parameters of policeability evolve into Lakeside Division's informal enforcement policy.

This chapter examines the complaints made by Ms. Carter and Mr. Palmer in the CPAB and by Sra. Santos in the HO and demonstrates how each conforms to one of three basic archetypes that characterize exchanges over policeability—cooperation, control, and resistance. Ms. Carter above complained about undesirable parking behavior in the hopes that police would solve her problem and sanction those responsible. Police have an institutional interest in community engagement but are also proprietary regarding their workload; as the institutional authority figures, they assume the role of "legal broker" in determining what issues are deemed policeable (Coutin 2003). Community-police meetings inherently presuppose the possibility of regular cooperation, but complaint encounters also manifest as control and resistance.

Determining the policeability of Ms. Carter's complaint first had to involve officers agreeing that the parking behavior did broadly constitute

Figure 4.1. Cars parked on Ms. Carter's street.

a violation. Although this was successful, in this instance officers then exerted control and deflected her concerns, reframing them as a non-policeable matter and directing her to other agencies. Captain Patton assessed the policeability of Ms. Carter's complaint by reframing it as a storage matter and improper usage of public space, which would not be policeable, rather than a parking violation, which would. The SLOs piled on, as Hackett asserted that she should simply endure the perceived offense, perhaps interpreting it as an overinflated neighbor dispute. Fairbanks, like Patton, agreed the offense could be read through the law, but suggested that regulatory action would be a more effective solution.

Residents and other stakeholders had a personal interest in social order as well as concern for the legitimacy of CPAB and valuable local knowledge to ensure that their concerns were heard. Some concerns must merit police investment. Residents could resist "controlled" outcomes in various ways and sometimes reached discursive agreement in ways that ensured their return, although this is not always the case. Residents did not always agree with certain police policies, practices, or viewpoints, and opposing opinions could directly challenge established narratives of what was policeable and what was not. But both sets of actors were interested in producing a continued policeable discourse. This chapter uses complaint encounters to examine how residents and officers actively discuss local crimes, problems, and resolutions. Some are collective problems and some are individual, but all invited response from LAPD. We break down the three archetypical categories of response below.

Mr. Palmer and Cooperation

Like most organizations involving regular state-civilian contact, CPAB and HO meetings required some level of cooperation to maintain themselves. The smoothest encounters involved interactions where police could easily act upon a given complaint and residents could engage in some simultaneous action to correct problematic conditions. In this section, we begin by highlighting forms of cooperation in those complaints that were easily policed. Definitions in those cases shifted very little or in ways that LAPD found comfortable.

Bruce Palmer, an elderly Black man, was one of the CPAB's most engaged and invested members, his involvement dating from the beginning of CPAB. He owned a local business and had lived in the neighborhood for decades. While normally speaking politely and gently in his deep bass, he was at times irascible. Mr. Palmer was a skilled operator of older technologies, such as shortwave radios, but would avoid communicating with police or other CPAB members if it required the internet, text messaging, or even an answering machine. This limited Mr. Palmer's ability to receive and disseminate information, but he nonetheless donated a lot of his time to the CPAB in other ways. Appropriately, Mr. Palmer was the CPAB's resident historian and gladly accepted the post. He led various community organizations, such as block clubs and his neighborhood council, and was the resident expert on disaster preparation in Lakeside. When calling the police to enforce a complaint, Mr. Palmer explained that "the officer on the scene needs faces that he knows in the crowd," and he intended to be one of those friendly faces at the scene who would assist; he even institutionalized this role by working intermittently as a crisis response counselor. Unlike some of his CPAB peers, Mr. Palmer made an effort to keep his Latin@ neighbors informed, making sure to invite them to Latin@-focused events, such as immigrants' rights seminars, or defending Latin@s against vendor complaints.

Palmer's complaint encounters demonstrate how cooperation between officers and residents occurs in small and large ways that reinforce institutional legitimacy. Cooperation, like resistance, inheres in the very structure of the meeting. CPAB is organized around cooperation. The resident co-chair, along with the heads of subcommittees, the secretary, and other members together with officers, form an organizational team whose official goal is to exchange information about local crime and disorder and to satisfy resident and police needs for addressing it. Conforming to this structure, Palmer organized his complaints in a specific and succinct fashion, and officers usually responded in kind, whether he reported traffic issues, illegal auto sales, or dilapidated houses—even if the complaint was resisted.

In the following situation, a prominent CPAB member requested enforcement over the issue of neighborhood car sales from unauthorized dealers. Car sales and informal mechanics concerned residents because the cars occupied many of the limited parking spaces on their block, similar to Ms. Carter's neighbor.

Danny's fieldnotes

Bruce Palmer asks what can be done about the illegal auto sales that take place in several areas throughout the division. SLO Chris Cordoba notes that without [Neighborhood Prosecutor] Dakari Hendricks's involvement, officers can go to the locations, run the VIN numbers, and check for proof of insurance. If none is found, they must impound the vehicles. If vehicles are registered, however, officers pass the information along to detectives who will organize a sting with the prosecutor. These detectives, Hendricks adds, are "very successful at filing cases and gaining prosecutions," but they have to catch the actual seller. "That's the tricky part."

It was easy for officers to recognize this complaint as policeable, and there was no conflict over enforcement mechanism. Mr. Palmer, as the complainant, identified local issues of disorder and relayed that information to police. From there, Officer Cordoba affirmed that this was a policeable concern and outlined the distinct role of each government official. SLOs could direct patrol officers to begin preliminary investigations with tips from community residents. They then passed that information over to station detectives who would determine tactical procedure, while working with the prosecutor to produce convictions. In partnerships like CPAB, the role of neighborhood prosecutors was to provide linkages between police and the courts to streamline prosecution—their commentary thus often spoke to method.[2] From start to finish, neither officers nor the prosecutor disputed the policeability of the residents' claim, only clarifying what must be done in the law enforcement process to ensure quick resolution. Both parties cooperated, agreeing on the issue as a legitimate local problem with a readily available solution. The issue was absorbed into the policeable discourse; it likely paved the way for similar issues in the future, affecting how they would be presented and executed.

Similarly, the following excerpt is another example where the issue was absorbed easily into policeable discourse. Officers required only the collection of pertinent information. In this case, the complainant is a newcomer to the meeting.

Danny and Aaron's fieldnotes

A resident who is here for her first meeting raises her hand. She tells us that she has two sons, twelve and sixteen. The older boy came home drunk the other day and she learned from the younger son that the liquor store near their home sells alcohol to minors.

Captain Himura responds. "I'm going to let you know what our strategy is. Businesses that sell liquor to minors get a five-thousand-dollar fine and can lose their liquor licenses. We have cadets [teenagers from an LAPD junior officers program] who go in undercover and make buys for us and catch them that way. You guys all remember the 'shoulder tap'? You know, the kid waiting outside the liquor store who taps you on the shoulder and has you buy him liquor? Those guys get a huge fine too. The Vice Unit can perform a sting using decoys and storeowners face a five-thousand-dollar fine if cited. So we will notify Vice."

Captain Himura immediately recognized the policeability of the resident's complaint, articulated an organizational response, and spelled out the penalty awaiting stores and individuals selling alcohol to minors. This sort of exchange was ideal for police, since it worked smoothly for them as institutional brokers. Policeability was achieved in this case in relation to a solution already within the arsenal of Vice responses. Situations like this rendered easily as policeable, and residents seemed comfortable in their role of complainant providing specific information.

CPAB members were integral in planning, organizing, and conducting police-sponsored activities throughout the Lakeside Division. Members planned and coordinated more than a half dozen major community events each year, from carnivals for kids to Officer Appreciation Day. Community events were an opportunity for the department to reach out to the community, expand its CPAB constituency, and become aware of further areas of community concern or interest as they relate to crime. While some, like OAD, had limited instrumental utility, others, like street carnivals and health/wellness fairs, could directly address needs within the Lakeside Division by mobilizing resources. These events served the institutional interests of the police, as they allowed noncoercive resident face time for officers and further fulfilled the "community engagement" mandate. These events were literally policeable as well, bringing youth and other residents into the regulable space of LAPD. CPAB was legitimated simultaneously through these events as a productive organization. A discussion of such an event illustrates of the cooperative potential of CPAB:

Danny's fieldnotes

Bruce Palmer notes that he will be involved in planning an amateur radio event during the last weekend in June. If youth want to participate, they can camp out for the three-day event, learn about and operate ham radios, and meet amateur operators. Palmer and Captain Himura decide that this potentially could merge with the upcoming Emergency Preparedness event. Himura says that he'll invite the cadets both for staffing purposes and for training. The LA County Sheriff's Office will be involved, donating radios for use during the event. In addition to the amateur radio training, the youth can also receive search and rescue training, and CERT [Community Emergency Response Team] training. The overall purpose of the event is to show the community the utility of amateur radios during emergency events—especially since we expect the "Big One" [earthquake] in the years to come.

Although originally an announcement of Palmer's ham radio event, the discussion quickly became a CPAB project through LA's municipal focus on emergency preparedness. The convergence of interests was clear: Palmer could amplify his event through might of CPAB, and LAPD could further their program of youth engagement and disaster preparedness. Encounters like this illustrated cooperation based on CPAB's understanding of itself as an organization capable of partnership. The interests of both Mr. Palmer's organization and community policing more generally were served in the planning of the event and the inclusion of other agencies that could potentially offer support and resources.

The issue here was less a problem of crime as of neighborhood security in the event of a disaster. LA's general mandate for emergency preparedness (as well as LAPD's own efforts) fitted this easily into the overarching discourse of policeability, yet Mr. Palmer also subtly inhabited a different role during this exchange—here he was a not a complainant but a resource partner. In this role, he was not dependent on LAPD for recognition and indeed had some leverage over resources of interest to police.

Ms. Carter and Control

Police officials in the CPAB context exerted their institutional control by denying service to residents who complained about issues they deemed unpoliceable. The context for interaction is important, and contestations over policeability were set almost exclusively within the walls of Lakeside Station. Although some long-term attendees were comfortable in the station and sometimes were recognized and greeted by officers as CPAB members even on non–meeting days, the setting is a place symbolically and literally regulated by LAPD. In this section, we discuss the exertion of control over complaint encounters by police authority. Control remained a significant product of police-community partnerships, despite its democratic rhetoric and espousal of cooperative aims.

Like Bruce Palmer, Ruby Carter is one of the original members of Lakeside's founding CPAB group. In her eighties, she is the group's eldest member but one of its most vocal and most energetic. Under her shock of white hair, she moves spryly, commanding the affection and respect of board members and police alike. Ms. Carter would smile widely as she cajoled meeting participants before the call to order, but she could be mischievous as well. Once, Captain Richard Lucas, a Black man with thick-framed glasses and a broad mustache, was reading the previous month's crime statistics aloud to the group. At one point he paused, lifted the frames above his eyes, and began squinting at the printed document. Before he could continue, Ms. Carter asked facetiously, "You want my reading glasses?" Months later an FBI agent from the LA Field Office visited the CPAB to discuss the bureau's community outreach programs and invite residents to participate. During his introduction, Agent Sylvester Harris, a portly, balding Black man, asked the group, "What do you know about the FBI?" Silence in the room broke when Ms. Carter pounced: "I heard FBI means fat, black, and intelligent!" The group erupted in laughter and struggled to recover their composure for some time, while Harris continued awkwardly at the front of the room. Ms. Carter could also be prickly. When meetings officially began, she took charge of lightly ribbing officers for their tardiness or their attempts to leave meetings early, catching them on their way out with a loud and officious, "Um, we did not excuse you."

Ms. Carter's high standards as an engaged community member enabled her to be playful. She volunteered for her neighborhood watch and domestic violence and crisis intervention groups. She participated in various community-building activities, such as the annual crab feed, helped coordinate CPAB's annual Officer Appreciation Day, and served on several CPAB subcommittees. She was well versed in the logics of community policing and espoused many of the same values that officers taught participants in meetings, reiterating lessons learned from police to the public. Her long tenure meant that she could identify gang territories just by a listing of intersections.

No matter how well regarded Ms. Carter may have been, her street vendor complaints began increasingly to fall outside the determined bounds of policeability. We began to think of these sorts of encounters as controlling the complainants.

Street vending was a common complaint at CPAB meetings. Ms. Carter was not the only board member to raise this issue, but she was often one of the most vocal. During one meeting involving a lengthy and heated exchange about the scope of the vending problem and the challenges to police enforcement, there was much debate about the appropriate solutions. Hector Mendoza, in a rare appearance at the English meeting, advocated that sellers could be brought into meetings, introduced to the group, and educated on relevant city laws to help bring them into compliance. Captain Himura equivocated, but SLO Liz Fairbanks, perhaps unhappy with the Captain's lack of force, broke in:

Aaron and Danny's fieldnotes

Liz (flatly, angrily): Sometimes education doesn't work. I've seen fliers in Spanish, I saw a guy selling oranges, I took him aside, and told him in English and in Spanish that I'd better not see him on that corner when I come back in a half hour. I come back thirty minutes later, he's still selling oranges, so I arrest him.

Ms. Carter (clearly wanting to refocus the issue on illegality): It really bothers me when they come down the street ringing the bells, yelling "hot tamales!" They're breaking the law! This is illegal. They are felons just by being here. They can "do work" or sell out of their homes. . . .

Himura (gently, but firmly challenging Ms. Carter's interpretation): I see this as a bigger problem. If no one buys their products, these people will go away. The community is clearly supporting vending and I have to take that seriously.

Vera: Some of these vendors are selling directly in front of restaurants. Not Italian restaurants—Spanish food. They told them they couldn't be on the street. They're selling the same things for a fourth of the price. Do I need to complain to a councilman?

Bruce Palmer: This seems like free enterprise to me, but still, people need to come together and solve this problem. Most people know that they're leaving their habitat and they're bringing their [vending] skills with them. It's the same with drugs, if there is demand, people will buy them. We need to have some dialogue with the [Latin@] community. We need a solution to make everybody happy, or at least a compromise that everyone can live with. I've been chickenscratch poor, I know, I understand. We need to get these vendors together and find out what will work. [Also, addresses officers:] I know how hard it can be—

Hector (cutting him off, but quietly and respectfully): Sometimes, we can practice tolerance. [Aaron expects an uproar about this, but instead there seems to be grudging assent, with the exception of Ms. Carter who is visibly displeased.]

Mendoza aside, the room was not generally supportive of street vending, but the meeting represented something of a turning point in LAPD practice. From her position as a respected elder, Ms. Carter continued to argue that the street vending law should be enforced, but Himura's quiet dissent and reference to the community outside the room was telling—the issue began to recede from prominence. While LA City laws prohibited vending during our research, the LA County Department of Health did grant vending licenses, which caused great and understandable confusion. Although anti-vending enforcement occurred with some regularity during the early years of our fieldwork, we began to hear less and less about this as time wore on. The issue of vending became embedded within a larger political economic move to regulate Latin@ labor in Lakeside.

Although both Blacks and Latinos vended in Lakeside, the issue was discussed almost exclusively as a Latin@ phenomenon at CPAB meetings. All kinds of things were sold on the streets of Lakeside (e.g., counterfeit jerseys, bootlegged movies, clothes), but illegal vending normatively referred to undocumented Latinos selling food items on the street. Participants used subtle race-neutral code words—discussing, for example, the sale of "*tamales*," "*carne asada*," and "*tacos*"—to signal both illegality and Latin@s as the culprits. During an interview, Teresa Mayfield explained: "We [CPAB members] can at least agree on the vendors. They come through with their little carts, with tamales, ice cones, and then they have—I don't know what it is in the bags, something like pork rinds or whatever—that come through and down the quarters [streets] to sell at the school corner. They put their pots up on the fence. It drives me crazy!" Ms. Carter and other CPAB members complained that vendors walked down the street honking horns and causing noise pollution, forced pedestrians into traffic by setting up carts and tables on sidewalks, sold fruit and meat (sometimes as much as three hundred pounds) held in unrefrigerated storage units, and harmed the local economy by avoiding the taxes imposed on legitimate business or by sending remittances outside of the United States rather than circulating money locally.

LAPD cooperated with CPAB complaints about vending for a time. Patrol cops wrote tickets on the street or coordinated with the Health Department to confiscate vendors' bikes, carts, and other belongings. As SLO Fairbanks mentioned above, they also canvassed vending hot spots with fliers in English and Spanish detailing relevant laws and penalties.

Figures 4.2 and 4.3. Street vendors at the local shopping center.

Partnerships with the neighborhood prosecutor and the LA County Department of Health on task forces known as "vendor sweeps" occurred infrequently during our fieldwork, but one such incident resulted in the arrest of thirty-one vendors, twenty-three of whom were undocumented immigrants. Such operations were "resource-intensive," but in other

LOS ANGELES POLICE DEPARTMENT

Attention Street Vendors:

The Los Angeles Police Department has received numerous complaints from business owners and area residents regarding illegal street sales in this community. Due to these complaints, the Los Angeles Police Department will strictly enforce laws related to illegal street vending. This letter is to inform you that you are in violation of section 42.00 of the Los Angeles City Municipal Code. If you do not stop your actions, your merchandise will be confiscated, your vehicle or cart will be impounded and you may be subject to arrest.

REGULATION OF SOLICITING AND SALES IN STREETS.

"Street" shall mean all that area dedicated to public use for public street purposes and shall include, but not be limited to roadways, parkways, alleys and sidewalks.

"Roadway" shall mean that portion of a street improved, designed, or ordinarily used for vehicular travel.

"Parkway" shall mean that area between the edge of the roadway and the adjacent property line excluding that area occupied by the sidewalks. Parkway shall also include any area within a roadway which is not open to vehicular travel.

"Sidewalk" shall mean any surface provided for the exclusive use of pedestrians.

(b) **Street Sale of Goods Prohibited. (Amended by Ord. No. 169,319, Eff. 2/18/94.)** No person, except as otherwise permitted by this section, shall on any sidewalk or street offer for sale, solicit the sale of, announce by any means the availability of, or have in his or her possession, control or custody, whether upon his or her person or upon some other animate or inanimate object, any goods, wares or merchandise which the public may purchase at any time.

(c) **Street-Soliciting Employment of Services Prohibited. (Amended by Ord. No. 145,691, Eff. 5/2/74.)**

(1) No person, except as otherwise permitted by this section, shall on any street offer for sale, solicit the employment of, or announce by any means the availability of, any goods, wares, merchandise, services or facilities, or solicit patrons for or advertise any show, exhibition, entertainment, tour, excursion, sight-seeing trip, or real estate viewing or inspection trip. **(Amended by Ord. No. 169,319, Eff. 2/18/94.)**

(2) No person who is visible or audible to any person on any street shall, in a loud, boisterous, raucous, offensive or insulting manner, offer for sale, solicit the purchase of, announce the availability of, or solicit the employment of any goods, wares, merchandise, services or facilities, or solicit patronage for or advertise any show, exhibition, entertainment tour, excursion sight-seeing trip, real estate, or oil well viewing or inspection trip.

(3) Nothing in Paragraph (1) of this subsection shall be so construed as to apply to a sight-seeing tour operating under and by virtue of a permit from and regulations of the Public Utilities Commission of the State of California and for which tour a fixed charge is made to the person carried.

(d) **Street-Sidewalk – Advertising on.** No person shall except as otherwise provided in Subsection (j) of this section have, bear, wear or carry upon any street, any advertising banner, flag, board, sign, transparency, wearing apparel or other device advertising, publicity announcing or calling attention to any goods, wares, merchandise, or commodities, or to any place of business, occupation, show, exhibition, event or entertainment. The provisions of this subsection shall not apply to the wearing of apparel without remuneration for doing so or business identification on wearing apparel. **(Amended by Ord. No. 145,691, Eff. 5/2/74.)**

Please respect the laws of our City and cease your illegal activity. Thank you for your cooperation.

Figure 4.4. A warning notice to street vendors.

situations this has not proved to be an obstacle. Chapter 1, for example, recalls the Operation Hammer dragnets and other neighborhood-level mobilizations that yielded mainly parking violators.

Unafraid to hold officers accountable, however, Ms. Carter pressed on this issue some time later when the Captain explained the limits to enforcement.

Danny and Aaron's fieldnotes

Citation or no, vendors continue to sell because it's profitable, Himura says. Tickets are the cost of doing business, no matter how many are given out. Offenses on public property are easily policed, but some business owners allow vendors to sell on their property so they're protected. "The railroad track," which is privately owned, Himura explains, "is like restaurant row on Sundays" and vendors are pretty much untouchable. Officers know about it, but according to the law they can't act unless the railroad property owners complain. Even the graffiti on site was a battle to clean up because railroad authorities were at first hesitant, refusing to foot the bill. Eventually, the tagging was removed.

What about my neighborhood, Ms. Carter says, "What about venders riding through ringing bells?"

"Ice cream?" asks Himura.

Yes, she returns, but "tamales too, on the weekends." She reminds us that we talked about this a year ago too.

"Yes, I remember talking about that," Himura admits. Much of the problem with vendors is that "they're on the move" throughout the neighborhoods. And when stopped, some vendors have county-issued licenses, even though what's required are city licenses. We're looking at it, Himura says. "We're also trying to prevent and solve murders, but it's a balance, which is why we have the Business Car. We don't want the Home Depot to get up and leave, either."

Phil Hackett interjects that vendors are selling because people are buying—just like those dealers and their drugs.

In any case, Nicole Williams adds, many judges refuse to seek prosecution for vendors. The officers in the room don't deny that this is true.

At the time, we got the sense that Himura was struggling with two things—first, that judges were frustrated with vending complaints and would negate police efforts and, second, that carrying county-issued licenses did seem to grant vendors some legitimacy, since city inspectors accepted them on the street. Himura also assured Ms. Carter that in addition to her interests, he also had those of the business community in mind. This was almost to suggest that these were mutually reinforcing interests: an orderly community is an economically vibrant community. With that, Himura began neutralizing vending complaints. While she and other members saw both vendors and their customers as undesirable, it was a relatively low priority offense compared to more serious threats to public safety. As the issue grew in importance, however, it became clear that organizing efforts on the part of Latin@ street vendors were complicating enforcement and that enforcement efforts were doomed politically—perhaps Himura and other Captains had been told to back off. Vending would become legal in Los Angeles. As this book goes to press, this has become the case—what CPAB members referred to as "legitimate businesses" would get a voice in the process, but not a veto (*Los Angeles Times* and Friel 2018; Reyes 2018). Although police could likely continue to harass vendors if they chose, this issue, officially at least, is now outside the bounds of policeable discourse.

Sometimes LAPD manifested control over the boundaries of policeability by deflecting resident requests entirely. Officers deflected many complaints and questions back to residents because they simply did not believe the complaints were within the scope of their job. To incentivize attendance, officers and community leaders made explicit and implicit promises that they could help solve problems, even in light of fiscal and temporal constraints. The promise of such problem solving means that officers received complaints that they saw as outside their definitions of policeability.

In exerting control over these requests, officers sometimes made use of strategies that intersected with other municipal departments or regulatory systems, as we've seen above. At other times, officers saw in these requests a failure of residents in their role as complainant. This strategy deflected the concern back to the resident. Complaints about police inaction became recast as failures of residents as partners. By suggesting that residents must improve reporting before coproduction could be possible, officers positioned themselves as upholding their roles and the residents as failing in theirs.

In the example below, a man broached an issue he has been negotiating with a "sober living community" in his neighborhood:

Aaron's fieldnotes

Resident (late middle-aged Black man with white streaks in his hair sitting behind me): First I want to express my gratitude for the job that you do. I live right in the vicinity of three sober living houses and not a week—sometimes even a day—goes by without those residents driving my nieces out from playing in the front yard because of their profanity and their craziness. I've made a lot of complaints and I've gotten a lot of lip service, but they continue to use drugs right on my street, sell drugs right on my street, and smoke their drugs right on my street. I confront them about it and they say "I know where you live." I know the [sober living] owner is in violation, and I know your hands might be tied, but. . . .

Captain Himura: Dwayne Glover is your SLO over there. Everything we do is tracked by statistics, so I know you aren't the first to complain about the sober living residents. Keep complaining, because for the neighborhood prosecutor to take action, there needs to be a demonstrated history of complaints and calls for service at that house, SLO action, and other testimonials. So keep calling and complaining.

SLO Phil Hackett: When you call 911, make sure that you call in their address, not yours, and then tell them to contact you.

Himura: —or call 311 [nonemergency complaints], but make sure it's that address and that house and in the notes, make sure that you say, please contact me only by phone.

Collectively, LAPD officers informed the resident that he and his neighbors (1) must generate more of the same responses that drove him to CPAB in the first place and (2) were failing to report the problems correctly. The concern was safely deflected, in other words, because the problem would have been solved had residents reported correctly and/or more often. Although this seems like particularly fertile community policing ground, officers deflected the whole issue and we did not see that resident at a meeting again.

In a twist on such a partnership deflection, Ms. Carter sometimes spoke nostalgically about the closer relationship she once had with the department and complained that SLOs had become estranged from the neighborhood. At previous meetings she lamented how SLOs were not as involved in meetings as they once had been and how previous Captains would bring new SLOs around to meet her so she could acquaint them with the community's expectations. When Captain Himura took charge, one of his first undertakings was to build closer ties between officers and participants. As he laid out his plans, Ms. Carter jumped to make these points, only to be swept aside:

Danny's fieldnotes

"The face of Lakeside has only been my SLOs," he says, but he wants board members to reach out to officers more frequently, getting them involved in community activities. Himura asks that board members notify him when neighborhood watches or block clubs are holding events, so officers can attend. Even if it's a community cleanup, he's open to sending a black-and-white out for support. Officers and residents only bond three days a week during officers' shifts, before they drive back out to their homes outside the city. Himura emphasizes, "I want to force that interaction with my younger officers."

Ms. Carter speaks up, mentioning that she used to meet new officers personally and insists that *they* make an effort to get to know the community.

Officer Margie Sierra invites Ms. Carter and the others to speak with the Watch Commander about attending roll call, which is held throughout the day—6 AM, 11 AM, 4:45 PM, and 6:30 PM. "And if you bring cookies, they'll love you!"

Although we can read this invitation as a cooperative gesture, SLO Sierra's "cookie" comment deflected Ms. Carter's criticism as the failure of residents to cultivate sustained communal relations with officers—and to bake for them(!). When Ms. Carter complained about this issue in previous meetings, other Captains cited a variety of limitations, mainly referring to the stringent county budget that prevented officers from taking the necessary overtime to attend meetings. Police deflections that established the importance of institutional priorities placed additional pressure on participants to fulfill their expected role. By suggesting that meeting participants should put forth additional efforts, officers situated themselves as having upheld the partnership and the community as having failed.

Sra. Santos and Resistance

Residents sometimes expressed resistance to determinations of policeability, particularly regarding decisions with which they disagreed. Police-civilian conflict is not an anomaly in the larger context of public service worker-client relations. Although CPAB and HO were both organized as relatively cooperative spaces, some residents did buck the trend, participating in meetings only insofar as they could directly confront police, and by extension the justice system, a decision that was not without risk. As Lipsky (2010, 59) explains, "In some circumstances clients can effectively express anger or demand their rights, but these strategies appear useful only in certain circumstances and not for long." Señora Santos was the rare participant who maintained her confrontational stance.

Georgina Santos was a frequent Hispanic Outreach participant. A short, stocky Latina in her sixties who wore brightly colored velour tracksuits with her hair slicked back into a ponytail, she said little to others before meetings and did not usually stay long after. Although we would attempt to engage her in conversation, she was often standoffish. When Sra. Santos was upset, the group knew it. She would raise her hand and voice to ask questions and would press officers relentlessly until she received a satisfactory response or until they decided to move on.

CPAB members like Ms. Carter questioned Sra. Santos's status within the community. By her own admission Sra. Santos is undocumented, like many Latin@ residents in Lakeside, and is fearful as a result. Contact with immigration enforcement made her uneasy, despite her regular involvement in meetings and honesty about her undocumented status. She did not take part in the planning or coordinating of other community policing activities and did not attempt to integrate into the English CPAB meeting and thus, in the eyes of many, the community. Her undocumented status prohibited her from directly participating in some civic organizations.

Sra. Santos repeatedly questioned the operation of the US criminal justice system, and police would educate her on the normal practices and procedures of various agencies. Feeling trapped by government rules, she resisted police by avoiding volunteer applications and making a scene during meetings. She wondered aloud whether checkpoints around the neighborhood were immigration stops even after officers explained that they were sobriety stops. Sra. Santos also wondered whether tow trucks steal cars, how police investigations unfold, and what normal court procedures involved. Police often chose to manage Sra. Santos's complaints by clarifying misunderstandings to assuage what they saw as misplaced fears.

Danny's fieldnotes

From the back of the room, Georgina Santos raises her hand to speak. Her husband was arrested on a DUI about ten years ago. Apparently the driver of the vehicle, when pulled over by the black-and-white, jumped into the back seat after tossing his keys at the feet of Sr. Santos, who was the front passenger. Sra. Santos is emphatic that the fault was not her husband's.

"*¿Le tomaron las huellas?* [Did they take his fingerprints?]" Macias asks.

"*Si*," says Santos.

"*¿Fue a la corte en frente del juizio?* [Did he go in front of the judge?]"

"*Si*."

Having little to say once the Captain explains the criminal justice process from arrest to sentencing, Sra. Santos remains visibly unsatisfied. "*Si eran un grupo de borrachos* [Yes they were a bunch of drunks]," Sra. Santos concedes, but the driver had a warrant and did what he had to do to avoid rearrest.

Rather than address her concerns directly, the Captain defends the officers involved after Sra. Santos implies they mishandled her husband's case.

In the last few years, Macias tells her, patrols cars have been affixed with dashboard cameras and officers now carry microphones in their utility belts to record civilian interactions, saying "*todos somos ser humanos y hacemos errores* [we're all human beings and we make mistakes]." As a general comment, Macias says that as the department's tools and culture have changed, so has the department itself.

Moving from evasive actions inside the car to abusive encounters with police, Sra. Santos painted an erratic picture of her concerns. She questioned the motivation behind what officers saw as normal law enforcement practices. Without actually speaking to her complaint, Captain Macias eschewed the possibility of wrongdoing by officers in light of the proliferation of regulatory technologies. The Captain exerted control over the encounter and deflected her complaint, while reassuring her not only that police were safe because of their surveillance technology, but also that mistakes could be recognized and rectified. If her husband had been wronged, Macias suggested, it would have been addressed; therefore, he had not been wronged. It is crucial for police to reassure Latin@s that law enforcement contact is normative, while at the same time distancing themselves from immigration law enforcement.

Sra. Santos complained about police inaction, about feeling vulnerable and unprotected as a result, and police often deflected those concerns too. On several occasions she claimed that complaints during meetings had not resulted in even one of her problems being resolved. Vice Unit Detective Mario Montes joined Captain Richard Lucas in facilitating a Hispanic Outreach meeting one month. Lucas opened the meeting, introduced himself, gave his crime update, and then introduced Montes, who discussed Vice's role within the department. In the midst of this discussion, several participants interrupted:

Danny's fieldnotes

Sra. Santos explains that she works at a laundromat where people buy and sell drugs, and where prostitutes frequent. She explains how most recently she called police because the drug dealers and prostitutes have been verbally assaulting her, but no officers arrived on the scene. [No officers taking notes.]

On Peltason and Seventh there is a school where, again, prostitution seems to thrive, Niccolo Nazario says. It starts at 4 PM and goes all night. On several occasions he's seen a black four-door there, the driver has a ponytail and usually rides with a bald guy, "*un moreno*" [a dark-skinned man]. They pick girls up and stay five minutes at a time. And at the new school near the station the same thing starts at 5 PM.

Marvella Quito, one of Hector's assistants in coordinating HO meetings, tells Lucas that she wants help from the next division over because she lives outside of Lakeside, but she's found it difficult to partner with them because the other division does not have an HO meeting.

What are those issues? Lucas asks.

Quito insists she's already given the information to Captain Patton, but nothing's been done.

"Ellos quieren ayuda y todo se queda en la basura [They want help and everything winds up in the trash]," Niccolo tells me, referring to the information residents provide officers.

Becoming defensive as the agitation in the room grows, Lucas states that crime in LA is way down. And while there's still a lot of crime, a lot of time goes to calls for service. "What we try and do is look at violent crime," Lucas says. "Those are number one." Further, officers can't take overtime any longer, given the current city budget. It's not like before, he says. There are no extra officers anymore. Which is why he maintains that it's important for residents to prioritize their problems. "Have you seen SLOs in the community?" Lucas asks.

"Si, pero nunca se nos han presentado [Yes, but we've never been introduced]," Niccolo returns.

"Who's been here a year or more?" the Captain asks, and about fifteen people their raise hands. "That's most of your people," he says, scratching his head. "Number one," Lucas continues, "we're gonna deal with it for the next couple weeks. And we'll tell you if we make arrests."

Several girls were just arrested at a nearby intersection, Montes says, as if to reassure residents that police are still active in enforcing crime in the community. Prostitutes, he jokes, are like cucarachas, when we turn the lights on (organize a sting) they scatter (are displaced to other areas temporarily).

Amid the hail of complaints, officers did not respond directly to Sra. Santos's concern and continued discussing Vice Unit activity. They generally sympathized with Sra. Santos's complaints, but officers shrugged off the responsibility for order maintenance due to budget concerns. In spite of his characteristic flippant and dismissive tone, Captain Lucas committed to act on prostitution in the neighborhood, but also scolded residents for not prioritizing their problems for officers in a time of reduced resources. Later in the same meeting, Sra. Santos and others returned to the issue:

Danny's fieldnotes

Again Sra. Santos speaks up and asks why officers never show up.

"No es emergencia [It's not an emergency]," Hector returns without translating for Lucas.

"*Ni cuando me insultan o me hacen desmadre* [Not even when they insult me or cause chaos]!?"

That's a "low-grade radio call," Lucas responds once Hector clues him in. Violent crimes are the priority. "If we respond to calls that were just potentially violent we couldn't respond to anything," Lucas explains. In the event of low-grade radio calls, officers do drive-bys and if they see no activity, they take off.

"So what do you want the people to do?" Hector asks for the group. "They get frustrated."

Montes explains a scenario, saying that sometimes drug sale calls require time for investigation, but patrol just doesn't have that time [Lucas yawns loudly].

But, Hector explains to Montes, Niccolo's been doing this ten years and hasn't had one of his problems resolved. Santos too says she has called the station and spoken to officers at these meetings and has yet to see one of her problems resolved.

"We haven't resolved one problem?" Lucas asks.

Several return with a rhythm of "Nos!"

Reiterating, Lucas says, "Well, we'll start with this problem here [prostitution] and we'll have an answer next month."

Exchanges involving actors as forceful as Sra. Santos and as dismissive as Captain Lucas revealed cracks in the veneer of CPAB legitimacy. As Watch Commander, Lucas saw his prioritizing of serious crimes as a reasonable boundary to set in narrowing the discourse on policeability, but this undermined Sra. Santos's trust in police. To regain the trust—of other residents, if not Santos—Captain Lucas restated his commitment to address prostitution in the future. But he alone set the agenda, the method, and the timeline, while residents had no recourse but to sit and wait until the next month. Surely irritating to officers interpersonally, Sra. Santos acted as a conduit for her community, destabilizing the usually peaceful and cooperative community-police relationship by demanding that police fulfill their promises of partnership. She would later accuse Captain Himura of being a "bad Captain" and questioned his dedication to the Latin@ community when he failed to attend a regularly scheduled meeting.

Some months after the above exchange occurred, while the newly minted Captain Macias discussed his plans to improve the group's capacity to prevent crime, Sra. Santos again forced the issue, having gotten no satisfaction from Lucas in the interim:

Danny and Aaron's fieldnotes

Next time, says the Captain, "*quiero obtener el crimen en una area para que residents le hechan el ojo* [I want to get crime information for an area so residents will keep an eye out]." In passing, Macias recommends that residents use the Club to protect against vehicle theft.

Sra. Santos charges in; something has to be done: "*No nomas hablar y hablar. No resolvemos nada* [Not just talking and talking. We don't resolve anything]."

That's why, "*como grupo tienen que enfocar esfuerzos para atackar esas problemas* [as a group you have to focus energy on attacking those problems]," the Captain says. Everyone has individual problems, he goes on, so residents should come together as a group to be on the same page. Noting the difficulty in building such a coalition, Macias reminds residents that "*Roma no se hizo en un dia* [Rome wasn't built in a day]."

Although she began as a complainant, Sra. Santos eventually positioned herself in opposition to law enforcement, questioning the meeting itself to spur police into action. Santos expected that officers put forth effort in fulfilling their end of the partnership, which would begin with taking an active and responsive role in partnership meetings, rather than simply providing a forum and considering the job finished. Sra. Santos claimed that police inaction violated the promise of meeting partnership. Monthly meetings turned out to be little more than idle chatter to Sra. Santos, and she saw police as failing to reciprocate their efforts. As in previous instances, officials attempted to control and reframe complaints as the group's deficiency rather than that of the police. Yet Sra. Santos continued her resistance.

Volunteer requests were a constant source of frustration for Sra. Santos and other meeting participants. Erika Dominguez, a volunteer of the city's Crisis Response Team (CRT), visited an HO meeting and explained that the city needed participants' help. The program involved acting as a facilitator or liaison for emergency services and the community. Following emergency situations, families have numerous questions about the support and services available, whether they ought to go to the hospital or the morgue to find their loved ones, and CRT volunteers are key to explaining certain procedures and directing them toward psychiatric services and other avenues available depending on the circumstances. As Erika discussed the logistics of the program, Sra. Santos and others took exception to the fact that undocumented participants were ineligible.

Danny's fieldnotes

The volunteers go through eight weeks of training and, once finished, will be asked to commit to a window of active availability twice a week. For Erika, her window is on Tuesdays and Thursdays between 4:30 PM and 4:30 AM. Volunteers should be bilingual, fluent in both English and Spanish, with enough familiarity to fill out official documents and write reports. She notes that this program is important because emergency services in the US are much more sophisticated than they are in Mexico and Central America and Latino residents living in the US should be aware of these processes.

"*No es un trabajo bonito. Van a ver la gente a su peor* [It's not a glamorous job. You'll see people are their worst]," Erika warns. Only those residents who are mentally prepared to deal with the tragedy should go. Erika explains that on her first trip, she was asked to visit the city morgue. There she saw a number of corpses in the freezer after which, she says, she didn't sleep for three days. In cases like these though, she says, the city makes arrangements for the volunteers to speak to counselors. The catch is that volunteers have to be residents of South LA and must be legal residents of the US.

At this point several residents counter, angrily in some instances, that this is simply unfair. How could the Mayor be asking for volunteers from the Spanish-speaking community without considering that this might involve hiring undocumented people to do the work?

Erika attempts to sell the job as a valorous duty to one's community, but residents are unconvinced:

"*Discrimina, ¿verdad?* [He discriminates, doesn't he?]," Hector fires referring to Mayor Villaraigosa.

"*¿Cual es la ventaja?* [What's the advantage?]," Sra. Santos asks suspiciously.

And before Erika could respond another resident declares, "*Dile al señor alcalde que aunque mucha gente quiere ser voluntarios, no llegan a los requi-*

sitos [Tell Mr. Mayor that though many people would like to volunteer, they don't meet the requirements]."

Sra. Santos agrees: "*No son nada de inteligentes* [They aren't intelligent at all]" because what the Mayor is asking for is simply unrealistic. The workers in the Mayor's office haven't appreciated the reality of the situation. "*¿Quien de los ciudadanos estan siendo voluntarios?* [Who among the citizens is volunteering?]."

Erika, in an attempt to assuage residents' concerns, notes that she came to the US as an immigrant, and so shares in their experiences. "*Yo quiero acerlo para servirlos a ustedes* [I want to do this to serve all of you]," Erika explains.

"*Graaaacias*," Sra. Santos says, sarcastically elongating her response.

While the first issue Mendoza raised is that undocumented immigrants were barred from participating, several participants, including Santos, also seemed convinced that this was a ploy to take advantage of a vulnerable community. Sra. Santos was particularly disturbed by what she felt was a deliberate attempt to both alienate and exploit the labor of the undocumented. When she and others heard that the volunteer forms were in English, it was the last straw—they threw their heads back in frustration at further proof of the city government's insensitivity and prejudice.

The Boundaries of Policeability

In this chapter, we have described a major element of community-police coproduction as the process of producing "policeability." The development of such a discourse is an interactive process that revolves around police response to public complaints and attempts to partner over problems solving. Envisioned as "direct community input into the decision making process" (W. L. Williams 1995a), such encounters are supposed to allow the public to help shape police actions. These encounters are a key mechanism of the coproduction of social order, which itself is the cornerstone community policing (J. D. Scott, Duffee, and Renauer 2003; Skolnick and Bayley 1988). Our observations suggest that police take on the role of "broker" within the partnership, sometimes cooperating, sometimes controlling the discourse. Residents arrive both to partner and to complain, but can become frustrated at being excluded from decision making. Police tout the accessibility of the platform, but retain the keys to accessing the discourse of policeability.

The legal landscape of police power grants police wide latitude in discretion—LAPD's history attests to this—which has only broadened in the past decades. Police choose to classify and categorize residents' concerns as either policeable or not. Mr. Palmer's encounters with police in this chapter reveal the importance of institutional and public interest convergence. Based on institutional priorities, officers place a greater emphasis on serious and violent crimes, for instance, or privilege issues such as prostitution, which lend themselves to traditional enforcement strategies within the existing Vice Unit arsenal. Incorporating such issues into policeable discourse requires only explaining the efforts already under way or reanimating past efforts toward similar purposes. Each and every issue deemed policeable loops back into the larger discourse, shifting it and building a growing history and understanding surrounding what ought to be policed under a community policing regime.

Ms. Carter's experience of being controlled shows how tightly LAPD brokers policeability. Police exert control over these exchanges both situationally and discursively, making it clear that LAPD alone has the power to define policeability. LAPD services in our observations leaned toward crime control and enforcement measures and only secondarily toward situational crime prevention (e.g., encouraging the use of the Club) and public cooperation. City-imposed budgetary cutbacks beginning halfway through our fieldwork were touted as a problem, but these next few budgets saw increases in personnel. Officers tended to deflect or rearticulate those issues they believed were outside the boundaries of policeability. Ms. Carter and other seasoned and engaged board members found that their complaints ran against the shifting political currents regarding vending. Such rationing can alienate meeting participants and challenge the legitimacy of collaborative meetings.

Sra. Santos's aggressive resistance (and Niccolo Nazario's low-key observations) demonstrate the danger in unfulfilled partnerships, but in such a controlled setting, this sort of resistance is difficult to maintain. Over time Sra. Santos escalated her resistance from questioning the partnership to accusing police of shirking their partnership responsibilities. Several conclusions can be drawn from this. It seems likely that police did not respond well to Sra. Santos's aggressive stance, although the packaging did not change the contents. As well, in general, it seemed that police were more responsive to CPAB members than to HO participants, likely because the CPAB had more residents like Mr. Palmer who knew not only what complaints they could report but also how to package them for police approval. Yet police are charged with helping not just the polite. With little further recourse, residents who feel unheard adopt resistance strategies and make their displeasure known in direct and public ways.

Coproduction implies a partnership, a word that occurs often in LAPD's own characterization of community policing (e.g., Parks 1999) as well as in the academic literature (e.g., Skolnick and Bayley 1988). Much as it designs the setting and controls the electoral process, LAPD also designs a role—CPAB member, HO participant—that institutionalizes residents as local experts and provides a platform for complaint. Residents need LAPD services, but LAPD does not systematically rely on CPAB members to define patrol allocations or enforcement policy. In an impoverished area like Lakeside Division, resources like those of Bruce Palmer cannot back every complaint. To the extent residents are relegated to supplicatory positions, entreating for intervention, community policing scholars (Herbert 2005; Manning 1997) may be right in suggesting that residents are excluded from having definitional power with respect to law enforcement policy. Our next chapter extends this focus on the police role in social order maintenance and follows SLOs and CROs as they respond to the unique needs of Lakeside's business community—a community with substantially more resources.

5

No Place for the Mom-and-Pops

We don't want the Home Depot to get up and leave.
—Captain Himura

One of the first challenges Captain Himura set for himself upon his arrival was to reduce Part 1 crime in the division by 5 percent. Focusing particularly on property crime, Himura decided to make strategic use of his community policing tools, strengthening the division's crime-prevention capacity by increasing the size of the Community Relations Office and emphasizing the "Business Car." Officers assigned to this car would liaise specifically with local business interests to learn about and service their "separate concerns," as Himura put it. At the same time, he began organizing meetings with several corporate boosters, including Chase Bank, Bank of America, McDonald's, Rite Aid, Ralphs, and Walgreens, to support the Lakeside Boosters, a nonprofit charitable organization sponsoring juvenile programs, college scholarships, and community events supporting LAPD crime-prevention operations, which acquired 501(c)(3) status.[1] Although he invited neither the CPAB nor HO volunteers (nor us) to attend, Himura explained later that 80 percent of the proceeds from such closed-door meetings would go to support youth programming. Himura's administration generally preferred to engage with and solicit Boosters funds from major corporations to the exclusion of mom-and-pop shops—smaller Black-owned businesses. This preference reflected LAPD's view that the gradual disappearance of mom-and-pops and the influx of newer, brand-name, or "known" businesses—along with concurrent racial and demographic shifts—signaled that the community was moving in a positive, more secure direction, away from Lakeside's disorderly and economically insolvent past.

Municipal redevelopment—sometimes called "urban renewal"—in LA was a key post-disturbance reform alongside community policing.

LA Mayor Tom Bradley, formerly an LAPD Sergeant, helped set up the structure of both the Community Redevelopment Agency (CRA) in 1965 and Rebuild Los Angeles (RLA) in 1992. Both agencies aimed to address the social and economic needs of the areas most affected by the disturbances, but they did so in divergent ways. CRA was a city agency that favored activist social policies, welfare, public housing, and block grants to invest in the local community. RLA, on the other hand, was a private agency that focused on retail and commercial enterprise and generating consumption rather than revitalizing flagging production. Zilberg (2002) discusses these as emblematic of their respective political-economic eras—RLA had become hostile to CRA-era policies as undermining consumer capitalism by the mid-1990s. Community as a vehicle of political empowerment was replaced with an image of community as a hospitable environment for capital growth. RLA masked this shift by adopting War on Poverty–era language to frame the spaces they sought to target for redevelopment—the "neglected areas" and "zones of need." Pico-Union, for example, the heart of Rampart Division, became "Cluster No. 1" in RLA's redevelopment plans, beginning with the redevelopment of a mini-mall attacked in the city uprising. This site was also in the heart of 18th Street gang territory. Police and business partnerships at that time helped to bring together public images of the looter (threat to businesses) and the gang member (threat to public safety), positioning these toward RLA's goals of redevelopment and LAPD's goals of crime prevention. LAPD's CRASH Unit took charge of enforcing the 18th Street gang injunction in order to create a hospitable atmosphere for local businesses (Zilberg 2011). Rampart's CRASH unit itself, of course, operated as a street gang, running drugs, implementing extortion and kidnapping schemes, and assaulting, torturing, and even murdering Rampart residents (Kaplan 2009; Rampart Independent Review Panel 2000).

As Cluster No. 1 suggests, a defining feature of postindustrial government is the creation of collaborative problem-solving structures that seek to maintain a hospitable environment for business investment (Beckett and Herbert 2009; Loader 2000). Anointed as "knowledge-risk-security" experts on matters of crime and urban affairs, police shape "urban spaces and behaviour at the same time" (Raco 2003, 1872) within urban planning and social engineering agendas. Police play a key role of municipal knowledge consultant as both public and private urban space becomes increasingly involved in "urban regeneration" (Raco 2003). In this vein, Lynch and her colleagues (2013) found that economic and political pressures from gentrification and tourism largely drove aggressive drug policing tactics and the removal of Black residents in San Francisco's Bayview/Hunter's Point "ghetto" and "tough love" surveillance for "skid row" occupants in the Tenderloin. Several miles from Lakeside in downtown LA, Stuart (2011) similarly found that the "tough love" special task forces in Skid Row swept up the homeless from "prime" commodified urban spaces and coerced them into subpoverty wage positions (Stuart 2014). In the struggling postindustrial city of Racine, Wisconsin, bar owners of color won a $1.3 million racial discrimination settlement against the city where testimony suggests that police targeted minority-owned and -patronized bars in an attempt to "clean up" the downtown in preparation for waterfront development investment (Roussell 2015a). Similarly, Beckett and Herbert (2009) trace how saturation patrols around Seattle parks and businesses create "no-go" areas from which police bar the homeless, drug users, and other perceived undesirables.

Like Ms. Mayfield in a previous chapter, police also have particular ways of reading historical space. Business regulation is channeled through officers' particular historical narrative regarding the Lakeside community. Officers interpret contemporary events and enact future-oriented strategies based on historical interpretations and a hierarchy of racial desirability. Greenhouse, Yngvesson, and Engel (1994) argue that localized history is more than simply a timeline of events; rather, it is an interpretive schema regarding not only what has come before but what it suggests about the contemporary moment. As part of their expertise on community, crime, and safety, officers tell a specific story of the historical transition of Lakeside from a high-crime Black community to a Latinizing community where the crime rate is much lower. This historical narrative comes with a vocabulary of racial coding, using evidence of community transformation to pathologize Black residents and valorize the Latinization of the space. Over time, cops came to see mom-and-pop shops as synonymous with "Black-owned"—which is to say that the fewer there are of them, the better for the community. Police deploy this racialized story, tying together the national crime decline, ethnoracial transition, and business investment in the service of corporate investment at the expense of local business. In terms of labor, this means that space is made for exploitable Latin@ labor, while Blacks are slowly pushed out of the job market.

We begin this chapter by introducing the Business Car, run by CRO Robert Smith at the behest of Captain Himura. Smith was empowered by Himura for his savvy business acumen and brought a capitalistic ethos to the police force. We then shadow two SLOs—Phil Hackett and Marge Sierra—as they wield their enforcement authority and elevation as experts to reshape Lakeside's demography and business community. We argue that police business expertise in Lakeside manifests in two basic orientations. The first, regulation, is a push for a controlled, predictable marketplace. Police prefer businesses that respond to a larger corporate hierarchy, produce market-standardized and easily regulable products, and generally correspond to a recognizable US retail landscape. Franchises of famous brands are preferable to local or niche efforts—famous brands signal the relative safety of the community, useful to enticing external dollars. Second, advocacy is another instance of police gatekeeping where businesses are induced to conform to police-specified security requirements. This not only embeds businesses within a surveillance network, but also allows police leverage in designing and executing local security apparatuses that are funded on the private dime. We show that community policing practices are reinterpreted as expertise as the business community becomes a neighborhood stakeholder to be both commemorated and regulated according to principles of capitalization and racial preference.

CRO Smith and the Business Car

The Business Car (BC) did not begin under Captain Himura, but he certainly breathed life into the effort. Referring to the Lakeside business community as "underserved," Himura directed the BC to provide a general interface with business, a direct line to officers sympathetic to business concerns, and greater resources for responding to crime and disorder in those locations. The BC targeted businesses to ensure that their licenses were up to date and to interface with security efforts. BC officers, always CROs, contacted new businesses to get to know the owners and operators, and potentially to enlist them as Lakeside Boosters sponsors, although this had to be done delicately. Many business owners seemed to like BC officer visits for the effect of their presence and would be even happier to have officers park a black-and-white in front of their store. Both officers whom Himura eventually hired to work the BC were non-White. One of them was CRO Robert Smith, a Southeast Asian man with a medium frame and round face. Over time we came to know him well.

Himura brought CRO Smith into the unit because "I was able to deal with people," Smith explained to us. He was charming and cracked wise with board members during meetings, helping to generate a good-natured atmosphere. When asked to perform for the department publicly, he was sharp and prepared with information and packets of Xeroxed handouts. The CPAB leadership in particular liked Smith and respected his work. Julie Coleman, the CPAB president at the time, reflected after one meeting, "Robert put together a nice packet, and that's why the Captain has him on the project—he knows how to communicate, the value of it, you just see it."

Aaron's fieldnotes

I walk up [to the BC meeting] with Ms. Carter and CRO Robert Smith bows us in, handing us a packet of info. We sit together in the front and make jokes the whole time. The room is arranged presentation style with room (Smith tells me later) for sixty-five people. We get almost exactly that and there's a lot of folks left standing, although they're mostly cops and other official people. The crowd is mostly mixed Latino and White with a few Black people, although not many after Ms. Carter and Julie Coleman are factored out; a few Asian folks. It's a quarterly meeting, which must correspond neatly for such a business oriented audience.

Smith's official-looking folder contains crime information and handouts, including a welcome letter, a quarter-page Xerox on target-hardening, a sheet of SLO, CRO, and Sergeant phone numbers, a color copy of the Lakeside map with delineated BCAs, a pamphlet for juvenile boot camp, and a half dozen full-page "crime alert" notifications, complete with pictures and video stills. Himura later tells me that they tried BC meetings before and got nowhere because it was seen as an opportunity to fund-raise. This went over poorly—people told SLOs that they didn't want to show up just to be shaken down for money. Himura now has a strict "no fund-raising" policy at this meeting, and he has separated out his Lakeside Booster efforts explicitly from this meeting.

Smith plays emcee. He is funny and affable, an excellent host who keeps the crowd entertained. Himura also speaks early and often, but time is made for Gus Fernandez as well as two business community members to speak and Ms. Carter rounds it out at the end. Overall, a collection of hyper-competent public speakers—particularly Fernandez and Smith, although the Auto detective is a drag.

Himura kicks things off by discussing his vision for the business community of Lakeside. Business has "different needs," he says, and he wants to offer this "opportunity to speak to the police department," because if the area businesses are successful, it will lead to a "better community." In fact, he maps the "changes in the community"—by which I think he means crime declines—directly onto the growth in both larger and smaller (mom-and-pop) businesses. I note that the mom-and-pop businesses, with the exception of Paul's liquor store, tend to be Black, while the franchises (Subway, El Pollo Loco, etc.) tend to be run by a more diverse array of folks. I also note that Himura is very clever at impression management—he never misses an opportunity to thank whoever is in front of him for the crime declines.

Smith's approach to policing was very much influenced by his immigrant and business background. Never shy about self-promotion, Smith aligned his personal trajectory within the classic immigrant discourse of rags to riches through unrelenting personal effort. "We literally lived in the projects, in Baltimore, where the projects don't have palm trees like they do out here," he told us, while attributing his business experience to the small cleaning and accounting corporations his parents owned and operated. "I mean, hard work doesn't scare me," Smith said, reeling off his weeks working eighty to ninety hours while earning his bachelor's degree, his successful career as an electronics salesman, and the eventual establishment of his own small business. Smith felt that his status as a second-generation Indian immigrant positioned him uniquely to engage with the racial dynamics of both the community and the department. In his interview, he discussed that people on the street made a lot of assumptions about his skin color and place him as either Latino or Black depending upon the context and the relative length of his hair: "'Don't you like Mexican food? I saw you eating a burrito!' [laughter] Because I like Mexican food. Most of the time in the summer, they assume I'm Black. Constantly. And I just crack up at it."

It was perhaps the combination of his business experience, racial liminality, and self-aggrandizement that motivated Himura to assign Smith, as well as Officer Simon Chung, to the BC. "Without tooting my own horn," Smith explained, supervisors valued his entrepreneurship and regularly handed him the authority to implement his own problem-solving strategies. When thefts increased at a local shopping center, Smith drafted an action plan with targeted enforcement strategies, coordinating SLO activities and a patrol schedules to deter and more quickly respond to property crime. Captain Himura and later Captain Martín gave Smith's plans only cursory oversight. Pleased with his progress, Himura eventually began asking Smith to coordinate CPAB meetings and at one point he represented Lakeside at an LAPD-wide Compstat meeting. When Himura asked him to report his successes to the top brass at the high-pressure Compstat meetings downtown, Smith was taken aback by the vote of confidence: "I said, 'Excuse me, sir?'" The Captain used Smith not only to liaise with businesses for the regulation of licensing, implementation of problem-solving strategies, and crime deterrence, but also to recruit local businesses to donate to the Lakeside Boosters. From the fledgling efforts of Captain Patton, Himura branched out and diversified his approaches to business using Smith and the SLOs to help coordinate his efforts.

SLO Hackett—The Regulator

Phil Hackett was a burly, gray-haired White male SLO in his early fifties. Early on, Danny described him as a "hard-ass" who sat rigidly and quietly in meetings until his SLO report, whereupon he scowled a lot and seemed generally annoyed. As we spent more time in the field, however, a more rounded image appeared. With some residents, Hackett could be warm and attentive, smiling as they talked, reassuring them they could count on him to address their problems. He could be a supportive colleague too—for instance, he took time out of his SLO report during one meeting to recognize SLO Fairbanks for the recent alleyway cleanup she organized, which he boasted resulted in significant crime reductions in the area. At other times Hackett could be sarcastic, passive-aggressive, dismissive, and intimidating, emotions he sometimes directed toward us as well (see the Methodological Appendix). In one Spanish-language meeting, other officers asked Hackett about the potential fallout after police shot and killed a Central American migrant in the Westlake neighborhood near downtown. Hackett turned to the residents, and in a serious and admonishing tone said, "We're not going to have that [public backlash], are we?"

Hackett organized community meetings at a church in his BCA, where he played emcee. He could be comical and cartoonish, jutting up his hand to excitedly ask rhetorical questions of other officers to give residents information he thought they needed. Tomás de la Garza, a younger resident, told us that Hackett really "cares" about the residents in his patrol area and called him "Tío Hackett." Niccolo Nazario, an elderly Mexican American HO participant, explained that Hackett was much more responsive than the Captain—he could see the steps that Hackett took to resolve problems in the neighborhood. Yet we began to notice that Hackett's warmth was colored by his racial attitudes. He openly expressed negative feelings toward his two Black male colleagues for using sick leave, remarking suggestively, "Some officers just don't do shit" and that they "get sick a lot." As one meeting where CPAB members discussed an upcoming potluck came to a close, Hackett asked what we planned to bring. We told him we hadn't decided yet. "Well," Hackett told us smirking, "you can't go wrong with fried chicken," gesturing at the largely Black group. He made similar remarks on several occasions, questioning the intelligence and capacity of Black residents. At the time, Aaron wondered whether he also whispered these asides to us on purpose to make us feel uncomfortable.

Although Hackett was a solid "union man" usually present and on time at most CPAB meetings, he resented the time away from his moonlighting job as a security guard and saw CPAB as a waste of time. He found his own meeting to be much more effective. By the time we met him, Hackett was already a thirteen-year veteran of the same patrol assignment. Affectionately referring to his squad car as his "chariot of justice," Hackett dedicated his patrols to the enforcement of the moral, economic, and racial order. He enforced against vagrancy around schools, churches, and parks, creating his own exclusion zones, as Beckett and Herbert (2009) describe them. Other officers recognized Hackett as a specialist in prostitution enforcement. SLOs Liz Fairbanks and Lilly Morgan mocked some of the male SLOs for their approaches, but particularly Hackett, who they said spent most of his time on patrol "fuckin' with the hookers on First [Street]."

Patrolling the spaces around liquor stores and other such businesses involved SLOs enforcing both racial and economic boundaries. This took the everyday form of issuing traffic tickets but also "ped stopping" people (stopping pedestrians), usually homeless individuals (often Black), unauthorized vendors (both Black and Latin@), and whoever else roused an officer's suspicions. Unemployment was a widespread problem. Many of those whom police stopped were unemployed but also, at least under the current economic practices, unemployable. Community organizer Rick Rinaldi asserted that many fast-food joints have racialized hiring practices: "You know, you're here, you go to El Pollo Loco, you go to McDonald's, you go to any place and you'll see it more populated with Latinos than you do Afro-Americans. But where there's Afro-American managers you'll see Blacks hired." Indeed, many Black residents were not convinced that even McDonald's wanted to hire them, and Hackett used their skepticism to fuel his perspectives on the laziness of Black people:

Aaron's fieldnotes

We pull up beside a skinny Black man with lots of tattoos in front of the Library on Main. Hackett asks about his crimes, his job, his charges—"What did they *say* you did?" He responds, "Robbery's not my MO." Hackett asks him what he does for a living, tells him McDonald's is hiring today. He's a felon, he says, and so McDonald's wants nothing to do with him. How does he support himself?, Hackett asks. "I just sell a bit of weed," he says, turning out pockets as he says this, letting Hackett see that he's got nothing on him. He's glowering at being stopped and never looks directly at Hackett, staring straight ahead. Hackett drives on, making snide remarks to me about his lack of employment. . . .

We pull over and Hackett shouts down two Black women on First Street. Hackett identifies them as prostitutes and they confirm this, although Hackett seems to prefer the term "ho." He tells them repeatedly that he's only interested in getting them across the freeway into a different division, but the conversation extends for probably fifteen to twenty minutes, mostly with the older one. She asks him why she has to leave and he responds angrily that the neighbors hate it and that it's illegal. She looks around as if to say, "No one's complaining," and then shoots back that he's illegally parked, and why doesn't he give himself a ticket for breaking the law? He tells her that McDonald's is hiring today, maybe she should think about getting a job and turning her life around. She responds that they don't want her [no doubt true] and that she'll make more money today than she would during a week at McDonald's [also no doubt true].

Hackett's approach to field interrogations like this involved adopting a "tough love" approach with those Blacks Hackett perceived as lazy, and thus undesirable, to coerce them into the low-wage labor market. SLOs positioned themselves as experts for planning purposes and sometimes as interlocutors for low-wage hiring. Similar to its role in the early twentieth century, LAPD continues to reinforce the racial segmentation of the labor force. LAPD officers also enforce the neighborhood's racial hierarchy by moralizing about the promising future given the community's increasing Latinization and diminishing Blackness.

Later, Aaron learned that Hackett's business regulation while on patrol often involved reinforcing racialized boundaries. Apart from trying to push the Black underclass into the low-wage labor market, Hackett generally engaged and hassled Blacks on the street in the hopes of removing them. Like other SLOs, Hackett characterized Blacks in Lakeside as undesirable and Latin@s as desirable, entrenching perceptions of positive changes in Lakeside as the result of demographic change. He particularly enjoyed disparaging what he saw as Black culture:

Aaron's fieldnotes

We circle by the liquor store parking lot once more, and disperse the people in front of it, including the skinny Black guy we harassed earlier. "If you're not washing clothes, get out." Hackett points out a guy walking away, and tells me that he walks to the store every few hours, buying one can of beer each time, which he drinks on his front porch. "It's his socialization," Hackett tells me, but I think he means "socializing." Or maybe not. He says the guy's daily routine consists of this and gossiping, to know everything that's going on in the neighborhood.

It's a Black culture thing, he says, dismissing it. Just like BBQing in their front lawns—you can't drive through this area in the summer without seeing BBQ everywhere and people talking about their BBQ methods and process. "Smells good though," he admits.

This culture is the same reason that Black people have pit bulls: so they can fight them. These dogs all look tough and have huge chains around their necks tied to enormous stakes in their front yards. The "Spanish population" has much smaller dogs, chihuahuas, which he much prefers, although he does tell the story of [SLO] Adrian Nilo getting his crotch bitten by a chihuahua during a dog roundup.

During ride-alongs, other SLOs also engaged in business enforcement by seeking to clear the streets of undesirable Blacks near businesses. Part of SLOs' normal patrol routine involves shooing perceived loiterers or troublemakers away from these sites. While there are no formal injunctions prohibiting those that police perceive as undesirable from frequenting local liquor stores, Hackett, Fairbanks, and others focus their patrols on creating de facto "no-go" areas around liquor and convenience stores in order to maintain an orderly marketplace:

Aaron's fieldnotes

We pull up to a convenience store, out front of which two Black people, a man and a woman, are talking. Liz thinks it's two men, but she immediately realizes that she knows one of them and she's female, but that she didn't recognize her at first "because of the condom on her head," referring to her white hat, styled in a shape that curls up at the sides. She is tiny, probably under five feet. Liz has arrested her before. The man is considerably larger and on a bike—Liz and Lilly shoo him away, although he clearly wants to stay, and he goes away grumbling. The woman is not particularly cooperative, trying to move away several times once Liz and Lilly's attention wanders, but they keep her there for more than a half hour, trying to run her file and find some warrants, but the glacial computer connection foils them again.

Either because they summoned them, or because they happened to be driving by, two officers with faster computers pull up. They run her name, which has multiple capital letters, like LaRae, or something—these letters cause some back and forth between Officer Moreno and the woman, who is missing a few teeth. I am instructed to go with Moreno and see how it's done, which I do. Her name is linked to her DMV file and her rap sheet. Nothing particularly interesting comes up, although Liz repeatedly refers disparagingly to the alcohol on her breath. Eventually, they let her go.

In addition to regulating the desirability of the clientele surrounding liquor stores and the division's shopping centers, Hackett and other SLOs also regulated the businesses themselves. Hackett made multiple attempts to shut down a particular liquor store. To his frustration, the owners resisted his attempts and he used the opportunity to explain to Aaron his historical understanding regarding the relative positions of Blacks and Latin@s in the community. Liquor stores with cinder blocks where the windows used to be he characterized as Black-owned, stemming from memories of the 1992 violence. Liquor stores with windows, on the other hand, were owned by Latin@s and non-Blacks with no memory of those days. He continued to note the desirability of South LA's increasing Latinization:

Aaron's fieldnotes

We drive by the liquor store that so irritates Hackett. I'm never quite sure what his specific problem is with the store although he intimates that drugs are sold out front. Mostly he seems bothered that there's a lot of loitering going on—we drive by it three times, eventually running off the people who are in front of it the third time, announcing that if they're not buying or doing laundry next door, they need to leave. They do—I get the feeling that this is fairly commonplace for them.

He tried to get it closed, but the legal battle has been complicated and I can't follow all the twists and turns. Hackett got the courts (or maybe the licensing agency?) to revoke the license, but the owners fought it. The courts subsequently issued an injunction allowing them to remain open. The prosecutor and Hackett fought that in turn, and there have been several subsequent hearings. It will be open another three years at least he says, and at the most recent hearing, the judge wanted recent reports of the trouble that's been caused there. As soon as he managed to get legal action brought against the store though, he thought the problem would be taken care of and gave up on enforcement. This is also frustrating for Hackett because the courts have interpreted his lack of enforcement as good behavior from the store's owner.

SLO Hackett also assumed the mantle of regulator in investment and development efforts at large and small levels. On one ride-along, he stopped by several businesses to raise money for a police fund-raiser while discussing his partnership with a local construction site to protect the copper piping from vagrants. Thieves like to strip copper piping from the site, he said, which they sell, no questions asked, at copper recycling plants. As much as you can carry might net you fifty dollars. He understood such observations as contributing to his expertise, which he deployed in a municipal planning context to enact a racial hierarchy of desirability:

Aaron's fieldnotes

Hackett laughs as we drive past where the new school is being built. "This," he says, pointing toward a dilapidated housing complex, "is where the 'I Hate Phil Hackett Club' lives." Due to his long tenure in his BCA, Hackett tells me that city planners consulted him on where they ought to put the new middle school. Since they were going to "eminent domain" the site and the housing therein regardless of location, they asked him which of three locations would have the best impact on crime. Hackett didn't hesitate to pick the multidwelling, low-income, predominantly Black housing complex. The city has since razed it, relocated many of the residents to the dilapidated complex that we drive past, and is building the school, as well as some new housing, where "many Mexicans have moved in," which he likes. The people he helped displace, however, aren't fond of him, he chuckles.

In addition to maintaining order by controlling community desirability, Hackett also engaged in enforcement practices that sought to "clean up" the streets of delinquent establishments to promote business investment and development at the local level. For a community policing officer, Hackett's approach resembled a modified version of Herbert's (2001a) "hard-charger," focusing his energies on fighting crime by chasing off prostitutes, strategically deterritorializing his least favorite residents, and aggressively pursuing businesses that displeased his sense of order.

SLO Sierra—The Advocate

SLO Marge Sierra, by contrast, preferred to facilitate business investment and development through advocacy work. Sierra was a short, stout, dark-haired Mexican American Senior Lead Officer in her mid-fifties. Her tenure in her Lakeside BCA was even longer than Hackett's, rounding out nearly three decades. Aaron noticed during one meeting that she carried an absolutely enormous gun. Residents spoke highly of SLO Sierra, saying that she was "devoted" and "responsive" and did a "great job" of working with residents to reduce crime. She was an avid college football fan and bantered with residents about recent games. Off duty, the officers joked that Sierra had a different reputation entirely; she, like some others, liked to party. Captain Himura referred to her partying alter ego as "Large Marge."

On CPAB meeting nights, SLO Sierra was often present with a cheerful affect. In her reports, she emphasized the importance of community awareness, encouraging residents to adopt the victimization prevention strategies referenced in Chapter 2 to improve their informal control capacities. Unlike Hackett, Sierra placed a much greater emphasis on community involvement in crime control, claiming that "it is a proven fact that involvement from the community brings down crime." She understood that some people would be reluctant: "In the past, people didn't want to get involved." LAPD Chief Charlie Beck, she says, has asked officers to grow their community-building efforts instead of "hookin' and bookin'." She encouraged residents to become better acquainted with new officers, regularly inviting them both to attend the weekly roll call meetings and to curry favor by bringing cookies as she did with Ms. Carter in the previous chapter. Building these sorts of connections and strengthening police-community partnerships, Sierra believed, would help reduce crime. Resident involvement was indispensable; the cookies were nice too.

On the street, one way that Sierra implemented her community partnership goals was through her business advocacy. In the latter years of our fieldwork, the owner of a proposed 7-Eleven in Sierra's area sought the department's official endorsement. She and several other officers worked with the storeowner, Dan Venkatesh, to negotiate the details that would satisfy local zoning ordinances for liquor-selling establishments but also the necessary security measures for new businesses in such a high-crime area. Despite her belief in community engagement, Sierra's advocacy worked against those Lakeside residents attempting to block the city from authorizing Venkatesh's new 7-Eleven store. Her reasoning was that Venkatesh, unlike the owners of mom-and-pop shops—Black-owned businesses—promised to bring the community a new legitimate business, jobs, and a safe shopping environment. To those residents who attended the zoning hearing and opposed its sanctioning and construction, Sierra explained that although they will sell alcohol, the 7-Eleven should inspire confidence, not fear. She, like Hackett, argued that as more businesses like this enter, and as the division became increasingly Latin@ and less Black, the community would improve.

The sale of alcohol in poor communities is controversial in a number of ways and for a number of different interest groups. Some residents condemn it for religious reasons, others as part of the set of commodities (including fast food and convenience stores) that generally contribute to ill health, while yet others contrast the ubiquity of alcohol with the dearth of fresh produce and grocery stores—a situation that has generated the term "food desert." LAPD's relationship with alcohol distributors was complex. At one meeting in the spring of 2012, SLO Gus Fernandez leaped at the opportunity to build closer ties with a Vietnamese liquor store owner who now runs one of the establishments that was looted and burned during the 1992 uprising:

Aaron's fieldnotes

As the BC meeting winds down, liquor store owner Mr. Nguyen is asked to come up and speak. Paul Nguyen is one of the smallest men I've ever come across. He is five feet or under and slightly built. He speaks very quickly with a severely limited English vocabulary and a thick Vietnamese accent, but he gets his points across through a very athletic presentation and much repetition. [To transcribe his speech would be impossible, so I'm going to present it in a slightly more linear form, without the little epiphanies that I had throughout in comparing his words to previous points in the speech.]

Mr. Nguyen is here because of Officer Fernandez. Gus was asked by the media to discuss the twentieth anniversary of the riots, but instead he directed them to various community members for interviews. Paul was one of those people and he ended up on featured prominently on the local news. He owns a liquor store right near where the riots started. He is quick to define it as a "community store" because you can go in and also buy some limited grocery items. He is very proud of the exposure and had relatives in New York and Florida call him up because they'd seen it in their media outlets as well. Jokingly, he says he now greets customers by saying "Welcome to celebrity store!" Over retirement age, Mr. Nguyen was a soldier and fought in Vietnam and then again in Desert Storm as a mine sweeper. He has pictures from his service hanging up around his community store.

His philosophy on business ownership, being a good community member, and community relations is to greet every person coming into his shop. "I talk to everyone—businessman, gangster—bring it on!" He has a sense of humor, he says. He doesn't need cameras, because he checks everyone out himself. A kid comes in, what do you need? How can I help? You need energy, he says, a positive attitude. Otherwise, word spreads by mouth—that store's negative. He has a sticker out front that says "Responsible ABC Retailer."

Mr. Nguyen seems perfectly content to repeat and recombine the above set of ideas long beyond the audience's patience, but his appeal is undeniable and there are many murmurs of agreement. Fernandez interjects to remind us that "even the gang culture is going to shop at your place." He introduced the local gang leader to Mr. Nguyen when all three were in the shop together so Mr. Nguyen could get to know who his "regular" was. It displaces behavior—they won't create havoc here, because of Paul himself, but also because they all know each other now. Smith takes over for the last time, asking us, "Did you all learn something?" like a satisfied teacher.

Liquor stores, bars, and other alcohol-selling venues are not often favorites of officers, as Hackett's long-running court battles attest. He and SLO Melvin Cantrell, among others, regularly pressured liquor stores and began adding cannabis dispensaries to their list of problematic locations. Police, however, seemed to see Paul as an exception because he enthusiastically embraced collaboration with LAPD and even profited from their presence. His racial and immigrant background combined with his military experience to render his business fertile ground for partnership. Although he preferred active engagement with customers to cameras, his close relationship with SLO Gus Fernandez lent him protection against potential threats.

Far more productive than grafting onto existing businesses was growing relationships from the ground up. Dan Venkatesh proposed that his

7-Eleven "convenience market" franchise would break ground in Lakeside by the summer of 2012. Venkatesh, an immigrant with the cut of a businessman—short hair, clean shaven, conservative suits—was the owner/operator of several Quiznos restaurants and mini-markets. His businesses were barely breaking even however, and he admitted to us that if his 7-Eleven failed, he would have to pack up his family and go back to India. Consequently, he carefully scoped the area—literally watching the space from his car for days at a time—found a site he liked, and proceeded cautiously.

Before he could break ground, Venkatesh met with City Council, a group he described as "not very open to the idea of a 7-Eleven . . . because of the alcohol sales." Their advice was to seek out LAPD and gain their approval, which involved negotiating a security agreement that would be attached to his liquor license. He proceeded to communicate with Lakeside's officers, who told him to attend CPAB and get "community support." With CRO Smith literally standing by his side in encouragement, Venkatesh presented his business plan to CPAB, ending by praising the community involvement of the attendees and saying that he looked forward to being a part of the community. Venkatesh attended several more meetings that year, bringing sandwiches, donuts, and other snacks for the group and making a similar speech each time.

Venkatesh was required to sit in a public zoning hearing with a city planning department administrator to determine his compliance with state regulations and overall benefit to the area. To prepare for this meeting, he hired legal representation and consulted with Smith and Sierra to further negotiate the terms of his license. "Lots of cops didn't know about business, but Robert knew," said Venkatesh. "So he kind of put his input, like [hiring] the twenty-four-hour security guard. I talked to him, and he said 'Let's call different security companies.'" Lakeside SLOs linked Venkatesh to various community groups (including CPAB), which he canvassed for support and took advice.

> Venkatesh: So I came to different CPABs. Basically, we have been trying to go to a number of council meetings, which we haven't been successful at. And then there's two local churches in the area. We outreached to them and we gave them the conditions that the LAPD is going to include, and they were okay with that. They were

> not too happy but they were not protesting. They were not out here saying okay we don't want 7-Eleven. They are neutral, which is good. Because the church is not going to come out and say we support beer and wine! They're not going to do that . . . I told them . . . I'm going to be there, you have my cell number. And we worked it out. I'm not saying there's not going to be any violations, like somebody's loitering, and I'm not the employees so there's going to be some issues, but we'll work on them.

Police decided that since Venkatesh was willing to not only come to them but also follow their directives and implement their regulations, they would support his efforts. Although he knew that churches were not going to be wholly supportive, Venkatesh canvassed them anyway. Here, he used his initial relationship with LAPD to supersede concerns about direct crime effects, relegating the terrain of complaint for churches to basic morality, arguments that would gain little traction with the municipal government. By canvassing local CPABs and neighborhood councils, he embedded himself within the public safety institutional network at the behest of LAPD, solidifying his business's legal standing and his security credentials. When the day of the hearing arrived, Venkatesh was prepared and organized with a lineup of witnesses on his behalf, equipped to combat the objections of the administrator and community residents regarding the health and safety implications of a twenty-four-hour operation hocking beer, wine, and fatty foods:

Danny's fieldnotes

After passing through the security gates, we head to the tenth floor of City Hall, to a room composed of several lines of tethered plastic chairs, two tables facing each other at the front of the room, and microphones sitting on top. Dan Venkatesh, and his representative from a firm specializing in zoning law, are seated at the table facing away from the crowd, speaking to Carlos Escobar, Associate Zoning Administrator, who faces us. There are about twelve people in the room when we arrive, and maybe six or seven more enter as the hearing wears on.

As we settle in, Venkatesh explains deviations from the original agreement with LAPD. The store will operate twenty-four hours a day. Daily deliveries, in a "thirty- or forty-footer," will take place between 2 AM and 5 AM.

Clarifying for Escobar, who asks semi-facetiously if he could call for a few cases of beer and have them delivered to his home, Venkatesh says the store will not make deliveries, but will receive stock from the 7-Eleven Distribution Center, consisting of fresh items—fruit, milk, donuts, and sandwiches. Other, less frequent, deliveries will come between 8 PM and 7 AM. Continuing with his request for a "deviation" from the original contract, Venkatesh's representative allows that these deliveries may be unconventional, but are integral to store operation. And after meeting with the LAPD, the Vice unit, members of the Religious Roundup, and SLO Marge Sierra all support the proposed 7-Eleven franchise. Sierra even wrote a formal letter of support.

Despite Venkatesh's "deviations" from his agreement with LAPD, he managed to get police to double down on their support. Sensing in him a biddable ally facing some level of desperation, officers waved away his violations of standard hours, deliveries, and liquor sale exemptions, and Sierra submitted a signed letter expressing her approval. Following the agreement precisely was less important than willingness to work together with LAPD on such things as cameras, security, floodlights, and defensible space. Venkatesh's tight relationship with police was not only foundational to his business, but now contractual.

When Escobar opened the floor for public comment, some community members expressed their concerns about such "convenience markets." Evidence included in-person as well as written testimony explaining that convenience stores enable all sorts of ills in the community, from alcoholism through liquor sales to obesity through the sale of salty and fatty treats and gang crime and violence due to lax security measures, notwithstanding police efforts. One by one, citizens stood behind the podium facing Escobar and spoke into the microphone:

Danny's fieldnotes

Carla Lewis, a white woman in her fifties and living half a block from the proposed 7-Eleven, opens, "Let me take you on a walk down Main Street." Her first "stop" is at Liquor Store 6 on H Street and Main, across the street on H Street, she says, is another. And down the street another. She goes on like this a few times suggesting that "it's like there's one on every block." These businesses, she says, are "detrimental to our community," contributing to the presence of alcoholism, prostitution, gang crime, and obesity.

The latter is one of her more pressing concerns, saying that [then First Lady] Michelle Obama is speaking at a local middle school today to address the issue in LA. What's more, the LA City Council has an ordinance against fast food, bringing 7-Eleven under the same umbrella. Her evidence: sodas for $2.50 a bottle and fresh fruit at $3 per pound. This is not "convenient," she says. [I'm confused as to her opposition; is it the price or nutritional value?]. Donuts and other "snacks," she says, also contribute to the obesity phenomenon, high among "Hispanics."

Lewis was unable to gauge local residents' feelings on the matter, as her health issues and disability prohibited her from going door to door as she normally would have. Alcoholism is a significant problem in Lakeside, otherwise the LAPD wouldn't have an ordinance against certain alcohol sales, she says. The 7-Eleven will also invite transients. In the windows, ads read "EBT/Lottery/ATM," which is the wrong message for local businesses to send. All this indicates that the 7-Eleven is not "beneficial to the health" of the community, where the focus should be on diabetes among Hispanics and African Americans, and on supporting surrounding churches and schools. Were people in the audience today to look up sex offenders, Lewis says, they'd see a large concentration of "red dots" around Main. And with sex offenders comes alcoholism.

Ms. Lewis's son also spoke, echoing his mother's sentiments, as did Pedro Chacon, a middle-aged Latino who spoke only Spanish through an interpreter. Chacon, however, added an alternative viewpoint on the nature of the problem and potential next steps:

Danny's fieldnotes

The community doesn't need more alcohol, Chacon insists. Instead it needs more education. The 7-Eleven will only bring more *delinquentes*. Because of the dearth of police resources, they can do little to abate the alcohol problem, he insists, saying this sort of business should come only when the department has funds for more patrols. Since the beginning of the year, there have been four to five shooting deaths, so why not build more schools or churches or a community center for the Latino youth?

Although a current of contemporary scholarship points to the ways that police use zoning laws to facilitate the banishment of populations they find undesirable (see Beckett and Herbert 2009), LAPD in this instance helped Mr. Venkatesh negotiate zoning requirements, seeing his stewardship and the 7-Eleven brand as a welcome addition to the community. LAPD assisted Venkatesh with their underlying goal of keeping undesirable people and businesses out of Lakeside. SLOs deemed Venkatesh and his 7-Eleven a controllable ally, so they helped him rather than let an undesirable business and/or business owner fill the space. This is not an altruistic move, but the enforcement of desirability. Despite his merchandise and deviations from the agreement, police at the hearing endorsed Venkatesh as a moral and legitimate businessman, committed to enacting LAPD's suggested security measures and hiring area residents:

Danny's fieldnotes

Officer Sierra speaks next. Somewhat antagonistically, she counters residents' claims about the level of crime at the intersection. At first Sierra addresses her comments to Lewis, standing off to one side of the room and apologizing sarcastically for not having met Lewis earlier in the twenty-eight years she spent as the area's SLO. Escobar asks that Sierra sit at the mic and address her comments to him. Alcoholism, gangs, prostitution, and obesity are not the result of businesses or the environment, Sierra says. "We don't make those people go to these locations and buy alcohol." And neither does Mr. Venkatesh. People drink, join gangs, hook, and use drugs "because they want to." In almost three decades as a SLO, Sierra has seen the area go from "a ghetto to a nicer area," noting that in that time, it's also gone from mostly Black to 75 percent Latin@.

Businesses like 7-Eleven give the area "a different look," by which she means brand-name stores, or national chains, signaling a sense of economic well-being that's been absent for many years. All stores there now are mom-and-pop shops. People want to see "known names" and won't stop at mom-and-pops out of fear. Unlike those establishments, Mr. Venkatesh's store is offering a security guard and cameras. The department wants businesses of this sort because familiarity with brands equates with feelings of safety. Again contesting Lewis, Sierra adds that while it may be true that there's a liquor store on every block, it's important to consider that the blocks along Main are not normal city blocks, but are three times the size/length.

How true is it that the sale of beer and wine contributes to local crime? Escobar asks. Do those stores become magnets for nuisance?

"No," Sierra returns.

Reiterating her point, Escobar says, okay, brand-name stores evoke a sense of familiarity, and therefore safety, for patrons. But that's only one issue. How concerned are officers for the surrounding area given the store will be open twenty-four hours?

There are no problems with a twenty-four-hour operation, Sierra tells Escobar. There won't be issues, she insists. "Bad guys don't want to be seen" she says, referring to the proposed lighting improvements. Venkatesh's "offerings will allow people to be good witnesses," in fact. People can take comfort in knowing they can buy milk, if needed, "safely" at 3 AM.

The testimony of police officers is given great weight in official settings. Here, Sierra took on the mantle of expert criminologist, geographer, and historian to dismantle the testimony of concerned citizens on a number of issues (including matters of criminological theory and opinion) using the authority of her position. Curiously, the speakers who most emphasized concerns of law and order were not police but community members. Sierra's testimony in many ways sounded less like that which one would expect from a cop—concern with safety and reducing intoxicant use, prostitution, and gang activity—and more like a business executive pitching a client.

The key to making sense of SLO Sierra's testimony rests on the historical and racial narrative since 1992 that guided officer thinking. Like Teresa Mayfield, Cynthia Stacy, and Hector Mendoza, officers saw the historical and demographic changes in the neighborhood in a certain light. Rather than anchoring it to a notion of community solidarity, however, officers presented the historical narrative as a temporal comparison—the "bad old days" of Black dominance in comparison to the days before Latin@s began to move in. Sierra accessed this meaning when she referenced the change in neighborhood quality from "a ghetto" to "a nicer area." Moreover, the demographic shifts also co-occurred with a consolidation of capital and the spread of retail and restaurant chains, displacing local Black mom-and-pop businesses. Officers see stores that respond to a massive centralized hierarchy and sport a recognizable, class-signaling brand as safe and encouraging. These institutions are interested in lower liability and standardizing security, rather than organizing directly with the community—they also have corporate money to donate to police booster programs in search of image enhancement. Hackett's beliefs about the differential security measures taken by liquor store owners similarly reflected this schema. Cinder blocks for Blacks symbolized the bad old days, whereas Latin@s represented a sort of naïveté about the past, and a more desirable present that he worked actively to effectuate. Elevated to the status of area experts and consultants, SLOs enforced against Black residents and encouraged the in-migration of Latin@s at both the personal and institutional levels.

In her testimony, Sierra baldly contradicted Lewis's concerns regarding alcohol, health, and crime as baseless, asserting well-worn tropes of personal responsibility to explain crime and disorder. The idea that crime is solely a function of individual pathology is not an idea that Sierra espoused when commending community involvement—her explanation in that moment was opportunistic. Indeed, this discourse of crime as purely a function of individual pathology is often deployed in the service of racist ideologies and the disenfranchisement of the impoverished, undergirding the gutting of the US welfare state in the 1980s and 1990s (Taylor 2016). Under the officers' historical narrative, "convenience markets" and "community stores" are less the purveyors of vice and ill health and more a clear sign of a healthy community changing for the better. The officer's concern was never about an abundance of predatory liquor stores but rather one related directly to neighborhood racial composition. Sierra directly contrasted Venkatesh's 7-Eleven with mom-and-pop stores, things of the past that linked the community to crime and disorder from which it was just now beginning to move away.

Serving the Business Community

For Captain Himura, supporting and enticing corporate investment was a law enforcement imperative that worked neatly within the turn to community policing, as the organization and logic of Rampart's RLA experience suggests. Police work to maintain a hospitable market environment, and businesses reshape neighborhood aesthetics and social order, facilitate racial demographic change, and may perhaps show their appreciation to police through charitable donations.

Business engagement is probably not the first thing people consider when thinking about police, be it in the figure of regulator, advocate, or fund-raiser. Yet police increasingly adopt the role of area expert to aid business and municipal planning and to carry out development schemes. Police both assert and are tapped for their expertise on crime and geography in ways that interact with economic interests. Indeed, this was only the latest iteration of the police relationship with business. Recalling Chapter 1, we can find police in cozy relationships with business, yielding labor for strikebreaking, spying on and disrupting union activity, and accepting generous institutional remuneration for these services outside of the normal tax allocations. We also find the police-business relationship in the impetus to form LAPD in the first place—capitalist interests preferred stable labor repression to the chaotic low-level war approach of the LA Rangers. And as we move from industrial capitalism through neoliberalism and into austerity politics, we will no doubt see the police role continue to change; a thing apart from a change in ethos.

Intervening in the business community to influence the composition of area retail and employment structures was an important part of the historical narrative that police created in Lakeside. Greenhouse, Yngvesson, and Engel (1994, 149) suggest that "the link between 'community' and 'place' is similar to the link between 'community' and 'history.'" Residents in their studies crafted historical narratives of social importance for defining their community that corresponded much more closely to their cultural and social understandings than a strict chronology of events. In comparison to Chapter 3, where the Black and Latin@ communities of Lakeside articulate communities of affect, resilience, and activism, LAPD officers construct their own narratives of Lakeside that revolve around their key areas of concern.

Under such an umbrella, police-business intervention in Lakeside tended to reflect two core missions: a push for a controlled, predictable marketplace and the installation of a security network schema promulgated and anchored by police. Throughout our fieldwork and Venkatesh's process in particular, officers disdained mom-and-pop stores as unfriendly to their interests and worked to bring various franchises into their BC meetings. The payoff for attendance was enhanced patrols and responsivity coordinated by the unctuous Smith who served as a crucial conduit to the larger business community. Some SLOs took a hard-nosed route through enforcement and regulation, deterritorializing undesirable characters by physically running them off or influencing municipal governance. Others were more encouraging, helping the desirable Venkatesh, a community outsider representing an international franchise, in his quest to sell in Lakeside things that police might normally find objectionable—alcohol, fast food, and twenty-four-hour access. They pushed him to sign an agreement, which he broke; yet he also proved willing to invest heavily in security, while LAPD held hostage his license with the city to ensure his compliance. Unlike other studies that have documented resident partnership with police in efforts toward neighborhood "collective self-regulation" (e.g., Carr 2005), the officers in Lakeside worked against the active residents who attempted to mobilize against the 7-Eleven. With the institutional might of LAPD behind Venkatesh, the community members who resisted his 7-Eleven plans appeared as myopic and disconnected activists with an ax to grind.

All of these things are consistent with the historical police narrative regarding the Lakeside community. This narrative revolves around three major transitional elements—race/ethnicity, crime, and external respectability. First, the Black-to-Latin@ transition of Lakeside over the past four decades has been aided and abetted by a restricted labor market hostile to unionized blue-collar jobs that pay citizens a living wage and a carceral state that has displaced about 14 percent of the Black population of LA in a "forced migration" of incarceration and deterritorialization (Costa Vargas 2006; Marcelli, Pastor, and Jossart 1999; Soja 2014). While capital has shifted needs for labor, LAPD has helped direct the population shift. Simultaneously, there has occurred a dramatic nationwide crime decline between the mid-1990s and the present day (e.g., Zimring 2007), for which LAPD takes personal responsibility within its territory. Crime declined throughout the United States, as well as in Canada and parts of Europe, but police feel as though they deserve the credit for initiating the decline, an attitude fed by NYPD and LAPD Chief Bill Bratton in particular (Bratton and Knobler 1998). Finally, LAPD has also taken a direct hand in exchanging mom-and-pop businesses for nationally recognized corporate investment to make newcomers and visitors feel safer and more comfortable in Lakeside. In contrast to the community's visions of Black and Latin@ residents in Lakeside, the department manipulates municipal power to, seemingly inevitably, realize its own vision of the community.

6

The Politics of Partnership

Vera Fisher and Hector Mendoza led CPAB and HO, their respective community-police meetings, for several years. Contemporaries who lead meetings that could work at cross-purposes, they spent a great deal of time complaining about one another, sometimes involving us in their arguments. The two excerpts below, collected early in our fieldwork, detail Vera and Hector's reactions to a phone call they shared as meeting leaders:

Aaron's fieldnotes

When I open the community room door, Danny has already engaged Vera in a discussion about the new Captain (Albert Himura) and how the meetings are now going to be more integrated. This quickly transitions into a discussion about Hector where Vera is indignant the entire time. We've heard much of it before from various folks, but Vera apparently had a three-hour phone call with Hector during which they shouted at each other quite a bit—each one separately maintains that they have an effect on other people whereby they "lose it" and spill how they really feel—about the purposes and futures of the separate meetings. Vera is convinced that Hector is on a power trip due partially to the fact that Latino CPAB was convened with the eventual goal of merging with the English meeting, not staying separate—that was five years ago.

She takes issue with the fact that Hector continually refers to how things were back in his country—"You're here now, and none of your people are going back!" She also claims that Hector keeps "his people" in the dark, telling them not to merge, not to engage except through him, and then tells the police exactly what they need to hear to keep the status quo. I ask about his attempts to segregate the Lakeside High School PTA, but she does me one better, saying that he's taking it "citywide." I'm no longer sure whether she means the PTA segregation thing specifically or something else.

To make things even more interesting, then Hector walks in. We're seated by this point, with Danny helping Elder Figueroa fill out his membership form. Hector sits by them and I mosey over after Vera finishes. I feel vaguely awkward—each has confided in us their dislike for the other, so being on good terms with the opposite number has its disadvantages. Hector is friendly, but a little distant.

Danny's fieldnotes

[W]hat's the CPAB doing? Hector asks.

I'm not sure what he's fishing for. "*No mucho ha cambiado* [not much has changed]," I tell him.

Hector rants a bit about Vera and other CPAB members. He feels no need for a badge, but for them, "it makes you feel good to have a badge," he says, referencing the official membership cards. All it is is a symbol that says nothing about their actual activity. The CPAB doesn't go outside of the station, he says. They don't want to go to churches [for Latino outreach]. Whenever he asks they say, "*Domingos no* [Not Sundays]." Vera, he says, "*rechaso mi oferta* [refused my offer]" to take CPAB meetings outside the station.

What about Himura and the SLOs? I ask.

They're all too busy tending to the CPAB, he says. But for Deputy Chief Buchanan, he has "*mucho admiracion*." Hector describes him as honorable and aware and interested in making "real" changes. He's interested in helping the community. "*Puede ser blanco, pero es de linda corazon* [He may be White, but he has a beautiful heart]."

I ask about the nature of their conversations versus his working partnership with the Captain, but he tells me he can't talk about it because much of it is "*confidenciál*."

People like Vera, on the other hand, are biased. Prejudiced. He reminds me again of a conversation they both had where each says the other revealed themselves to be racist. Hector says, "*la pele como una naranja* [I peeled her like an orange]." He claims she said, "People here illegally are felons." When CPAB members discuss the vending issue, he says, "*No usan el sentido de tolerancia* [They don't practice tolerance]."

Both Hector and Vera considered themselves to be racial interrogators, strategically pressing just the right buttons to reveal the true feelings of the other. The investigations of each confirmed that the other's underlying racial attitude was the reason that their opposite was incapable of collaborating. Vera expressed her antipathy toward Hector by refusing to acknowledge his comments in open meetings. As we discuss later, Hector at times played his own games in meetings. It seemed he also had strong feelings toward Vera, the CPAB, and some police officials for doing a disservice to Latin@s by not putting their full efforts into outreach where it would be, to Hector's mind, most effective. Vera's and Hector's mutual dislike typified the larger set of antagonisms between Blacks and Latin@s in Lakeside's community policing regime.

At a theoretical level, community policing is supposed to involve coproduction where police and residents share responsibility, strategy, and assessment over local crime problems (Pino 2001; Renauer, Duffee, and Scott 2003; J. D. Scott, Duffee, and Renauer 2003). Residents should also take on a wide range of activities, actively engaging in the law enforcement project alongside officers (Greene 2000a). As discussed in Chapter 3, LAPD's internal documents define the purpose of the community groups it generates as facilitating direct community input, identifying local priorities and expectations and decision making about how police resources should be used to address crime and disorder (W. L. Williams 1995a, 1995b). In Chapter 4, however, we suggested that police remain in a position of power in terms of the major pillar of coproduction—complaint encounters. We turn more directly now to the internal politics of community policing, examining the distribution and exercise of power.

As we have intimated, the discussion of a community policing "power struggle" between Blacks and Latin@s takes place within defined boundaries, premised on the idea that police devolve authority to the community. Herbert (2005) similarly argues that in resolving police-community tensions, the turn to neoliberal community governance is a political "trapdoor" that swings open under the weight of the responsibilities that police place upon the community. Moves to responsibilize community members often confront a disunited and ill-equipped community, particularly in disadvantaged neighborhoods devoid of political clout. Although we take some issue with the idea that real authority is ever devolved, the recognition by scholars that contextual factors can undermine the community policing project is well-taken. The point is not peripheral—it is exactly the political complaints of these neighborhoods to which community policing is offered as a solution. Indeed, Grinc (1994) found that historically bad police-community relations, racial/ethnic heterogeneity, and intragroup conflicts are some of the most significant impediments to sustained public involvement in community partnerships. Contrary to community policing rhetoric, Martinez's (2016) thoughtful ethnography on South LA's community capacity to prevent Black/Latin@ violence found that uneasy tensions lie under the surface of Latinizing neighborhoods. Yet through what he calls "alternative governance" strategies, conflict is managed (mainly) nonviolently by the efforts of organic leadership from gangs, schools, and churches. Given the complex tapestry revealed by Martinez, the capacity of Lakeside police—feared, hated, and mistrusted more here than in the average neighborhood—to lead such a project in the first place is questionable.

This chapter explores how power struggles with police and racial antagonisms between Blacks and Latin@s problematize the goals of community policing and diminish the influence community leaders could build to shape police action. The first sections of this chapter are framed around Vera Fisher and Hector Mendoza respectively, while the final section revisits the limitations of CPAB through the figure of Julie Coleman, Vera's activist-oriented successor as co-chair. Vera was responsible for a wide range of CPAB tasks, yet even in her elevated role as CPAB president, her powers were contingent upon police assent. Like Vera, Hector Mendoza was responsible for accomplishing a wide range of tasks for HO, but his role as HO community liaison was more restricted than Vera's. Captains valued Hector's abilities to fill a room, but his leadership position was weak and police began to define him as an "obstacle" in shifting the Latin@ meetings to conform to police goals. Finally, Julie Coleman attempted to use her position to hold LAPD accountable for their personnel decisions, but quickly became disillusioned with the distance between the promise of community engagement and the actuality of her contingent authority. As a counterpoint, we provide CRO Robert Smith's explanation of the situation, a "bad apple" defense that highlights LAPD's bedrock interest in "voluntary compliance" over organizing solidarity or community partnership.

Mrs. Fisher—Contingent Authority

Vera Fisher was named the CPAB president/co-chair just as we began fieldwork. In her mid-fifties, she described herself repeatedly as "mixed race," while mainly aligning herself as a light-skinned Black woman. A longtime South LA resident who claimed the community as her own, Vera never considered herself a native because she had lived all around the world while her husband served in the military. Vera was warm and greeted people with an excited smile—"Hiiiii Daaaanny!"—and a hug as they entered the community room. She was also strongly opinionated and quick to express her dis/approval verbally or in some other manner. Her body language was always informative—sometimes animated and whimsical, while at other times assertive. Informed during a CPAB meeting that her grandchild's car seat was beyond its warranty and needed to be replaced, she mock-collapsed her head into her arms on the table with an audible groan, drawing a laugh from the room. More subtly, during an exchange about street vending, her disagreement with another resident's statements took the form of a rhythmic shaking of her head and a defiant swig of water. To those on her good side, Vera could be loving and playful. She joked with the neighborhood prosecutor Dakari Hendricks that he couldn't take his allotted vacation despite his exhaustion and overwork—"He has to wait." When SLO Marcus Beasley, whom Vera affectionately called "the little brown one," lost a close family member to terminal illness, Vera took a card around for everyone to sign. Her frustration with Latin@s made it difficult to accompany her to Spanish language meetings, as she would get so worked up that she would constantly pester Aaron for translations and then interject her own commentary in a loud voice.

In many ways, Vera Fisher was an ideal choice to co-chair the CPAB from LAPD's perspective. She was active in several neighborhood public safety and community service groups for which she acted as a quasi-LAPD/CPAB representative.[1] A SLO recruited her from her neighborhood council in 2003 to be the representative for "younger folks"—a commentary on the relative age of the CPAB. A true believer in the LAPD (and the CPAB by extension), Vera always rushed to defend police even when serious questions arose regarding departmental anti-Black discrimination. As the co-chair, Fisher was responsible for a wide range of tasks. These included parliamentary responsibilities such as calling the meeting to order, checking the meeting's progress against the agenda, and making announcements about upcoming events, as well as tasks that positioned her as CPAB's representative, such as reporting back on her experiences at leadership conferences, civilian police academies, or addressing the LA Police Commission. She invested in CPAB's growth by reminding participants to "become official" or to keep up their membership paperwork and by soliciting volunteers to take part in community fairs and carnivals. On different occasions, we found Fisher handing out fliers and canvassing the neighborhood alongside the police-supported clergy group (the Religious Roundup), passing out foil-wrapped hot dogs to kids during park events, making tea and coffee for monthly meetings, and wagging her finger at volunteers to serve no more than two pieces of meat during OAD, no matter how much officers protested.

Vera Fisher channeled LAPD's authority in her position, but this was a complicated strength. It didn't take long for Fisher to arrogate to herself the ability to deflect complaints from CPAB members or guests. Sometimes she would beat officers to the punch if she could predict the response, such as crime complaints that could be left to other government agencies. Yet despite her position and great reverence for law enforcement, this was a power with strict limits. Below, on one of the rare occasions that officers stepped out of the meeting room, Vera tried to leverage the Captain's authority, but board members were resistant:

Aaron's fieldnotes

Vera begins the planning for Officer Appreciation Day (OAD) by noting that this will be a simpler affair than in years past. The menu will comprise only meat, various salads, desserts, and drinks. "We'll have Board members bring salads, we don't need a zillion dollars for this. We used to have CPAB dues that cost sixty dollars, but we haven't been doing that and so this will simplify things."

She also attempts to define how this will be advertised, nixing last year's idea of sending out letters: "We can send out letters, but most of them will come back, because our community has become very transitory over the last few years."

If Fisher and Himura thought that these changes would be easy to push past the group, they miscalculated. These pronouncements receive significant pushback, particularly from Ms. Carter and Foster Gill. (These comments are as near to verbatim as I can manage given the crosstalk):

"What about mac 'n cheese, beans, and potato salad?!"

"We used to have collard greens, mustard greens. . . ."

"We always have food left over!" Vera responds.

"So? Better to have too much than too little!"

"One at a time! *One at a time*!" hisses J. D. Evans.

Vera continues: "This is supposed to simply things, you don't have to worry—"

Bernadette attempts to calm things down. "I think Vera means that you can bring any type of salad that you want, and we'll do different kinds of meat. . . ."

Foster Gill pipes up. "No grape drink? What about beans?" Given Foster's aggressive assertion of his Whiteness, I suspect that he is being mocking with his grape drink comment, since he drops the food issue almost immediately when his mailing labels are jeopardized.

Ms. Carter: "Who decided this?"

Vera responds sharply, "I *suggested* this to make things simpler." Through the cross-talk, it becomes clear that Himura is also a co-conspirator in this decision.

"Make it simple," suggests Cynthia Stacy. "Have a menu and have people bring specific things."

Foster, the group's list keeper, protects his turf: "If you want to do letters, I cleaned the list, Jan sent me all the rejected letters from the post office."

"You don't have all the letters. There's a lot that you didn't get." Vera is getting defensive now and Foster is easy to provoke.

"No letters, okay." Foster says, trying not to show his anger, while Ms. Carter starts muttering loudly about "these changes."

Foster won't let it go. "I cleaned out the list, why not use it?"

"Send letters to who? No one responds!" Cross talk: "*One at a time*!"

Cynthia is tired of the bickering and wants to be the voice of reason. "What's the response rate? If no one responds, the list doesn't matter. Do we have a good read on that, the response rate?"

Foster ignores her and continues protesting, "I have the labels if you want—"

Nicole Williams: "We *should* be sending letters to businesses and churches."

At this point I realize that there isn't a single cop in the room. Officer Fernandez has been poking his head in every now and again, but it's pretty clear that he doesn't relish getting in the middle of this. Vera attempts to assert her authority, slapping the table. She's almost shouting, but still in control of herself.

As the argument wore on, Ms. Carter continued to press Ms. Fisher, "Who—other than *you*—decided this?" Vera, flustered but never at a loss for words, returned, "Captain Himura asked me about it, and we talked about it and decided to make it simple, easier on us as a community."

She managed to sufficiently leverage Captain Himura's absent authority to regain control of the room. To close the conversation, Ms. Fisher asked residents to volunteer for the committee that would take charge of the meals. Himura and LAPD would be forced to take furloughs, so they could not commit time to coordinating OAD.

Himura and Fisher made decisions about OAD behind closed doors. Though Himura was rarely absent, this instance highlights Fisher's reliance on him to maintain her authority. Attempting to casually push through a backroom decision, Fisher received pushback and disrespect that Himura would never have received. Such a reaction may have been foreclosed if even a single officer had been present, but Fisher was essentially left to manage the situation on her own and the room quickly erupted into dissent and conflict. Despite the title, the co-chair role does not carry weight equal to that of the Captain's, even among the membership and in as minor a matter as the OAD menu. One reason for this may be that the process of elevation is appointment by police rather than election by her peers. The little authority that Fisher possessed was entirely contingent on the presence of LAPD to exercise—in its absence, the result is public debate. CPAB is a group invested in the idea of democracy, except for the presence of police, from whom they take direction.

On the other hand, Fisher's attempts to speak on behalf of the Lakeside community were also foreclosed:

Aaron's fieldnotes

Vera, as usual, speaks with us at length before the meeting. She's prepared to fight the good fight for all those who have lost their jobs in the recession and are now homeless. It's unclear as to whether it's on the official agenda or not, but she has a head full of steam. They aren't the *homeless* homeless, she tells us—you know, those that *like* being homeless—rather, these are former community members who have lost their houses and are camping in and around their former communities or even in front of their former houses. She is scandalized by the fact that housing prices are still "market value" and repeatedly references a house she is familiar with that is three hundred square feet and going for eight hundred a month. Nobody can afford that. So there's all this empty housing and a whole lot of homeless people, some of whom squat in them. . . .

[Later in the meeting] Vera Fisher addresses the CPAB about the homeless problem. "What do we want the police to do? Other communities have these problems too, given the economic crisis. Some have opted to allow motor homes, grant permits, park in lots at night, but there are still some in the street. At the neighborhood council meeting, this was a big issue—we had our highest turnout ever because it was on the ballot. These are folks from the neighborhood. They just want to get it together. What should we have them do? We've got the second highest homeless problem in the city." [Skid Row is number one.] This provokes a quick response from Captain Patton.

"There are two kinds of transients. Some want to be on the street, because the help that we provide them requires abstinence from sex and drugs and alcohol. They're frustrating because officers book them and they're back out again the next night. The other type is from the economy."

After some cross-talk, Fisher continues addressing Patton's second type of homeless person. "All those places they rented for nothing [SROs and Section 8 housing], now they're [the homeless are] getting pushed out, losing their jobs. My question to the city is, this thing with the market-value housing, Section 8 [federally subsidized housing] can't take care of those people in the margins."

But there is no assent from Patton or the other officers and it soon becomes clear that the battle over the course of this discussion is over and that Fisher lost. The authorities present in the room push on and begin focusing on how to police "transients"—the "voluntary homeless"—and basically ignore the issue Fisher raised about the "economic homeless." Fisher anchors her concern over the homeless in the tanking of the economy. Conversely, to hear LAPD tell it, the economy may have increased the absolute numbers of homeless, but they are easily dealt with, weren't a problem to begin with, and to discuss them is to merely postpone the discussion of the real issue—those who like being homeless.

Dakari Hendricks, the neighborhood prosecutor, heatedly outlines the steps that he and police have taken to curtail the problem. "I would not agree that officers don't care for the homeless. Cops have not been heavy-handed, we've even been generous, running task forces until our ears turn blue. People who are interested in assistance get it and are not arrested. Most of them simply aren't interested."

The issue itself—homelessness—seems a suitable topic for a deliberative body like CPAB. Yet the authorities in the room, the Captain and neighborhood prosecutor, casually rejected Fisher's argument and reasserted law enforcement priorities. Fisher overestimated the capacity of the co-chair in this direction as well. The two sides of the role of co-chair entail representing community interests to the police and representing police interests to the community. Yet she was resisted by residents in the latter and dismissed by police in the former, both of which limited her effectiveness.

Fisher was most effectual when making demands of the CPAB body itself, rather than attempting to extract concessions from police. In meetings, Fisher periodically positioned CPAB as a historical body to be valorized and eventually managed to get a committee formed for the purpose of concretizing that history.

Aaron's fieldnotes

Fisher: One thing that we looked at was getting someone to take a picture of the CPAB board members. We need to get a historian, write up our history.

Himura: There's a lot of history here, Lakeside is known for it. There are old officer's photos downstairs, but there are no CPAB members' photos. There's a strong story here.

Fisher: We should get a committee together and get the really old people out—well, maybe in the summertime when it's not so cold outside—get together and take pictures, find old documents, PAL [Police Athletic League] pictures, make a history of this CPAB.

Bruce Palmer: How are you going to store it?

Fisher: On CD.

Palmer: You know, Captain Santiago started CPAB here in Lakeside, and I think now he's Chief of Police in Seashore.

Bernadette Ayers: Mr. Gill would be a real asset here.

[Unknown member]: Bruce should head the committee!

Palmer: You volunteering me?

Fisher: This is a big deal—CPAB is still here.

Ayers: Maybe we should all do our own research, reconvene, see what we have, and then form a committee?

Fisher: Yes, see what you have and then let Jan [Green] know.

Palmer: I got boxes of stuff, Jan!

The dual sides of Fisher's role as liaison between the community and police was emblematic of the larger constraints under which community representatives find themselves within CPAB spaces. That Fisher was able to articulate, gather support for, and eventually establish a subcommittee on CPAB history provided an unusual moment of independent strength in her leadership. Himura was immediately on board; outlining the CPAB's history promoted LAPD interests without detracting from other police priorities.[2] Police can favor the self-efficacy of CPAB activities, so long as residents concentrate their energy within the confines of the organization and make moves to strengthen it as a police appendage. There was genuine energy from the group toward the project, although police did not take a direct hand in the organizing and few LAPD resources were reallocated to assist.

The unqualified support that Fisher garnered for preserving the CPAB's history was also notable within the realm of its racial politics. When LAPD chartered CPAB in 1994, Lakeside's CPAB, as now, was almost entirely Black. The broader discussion on CPAB's history extends back to the community groups of the 1970s and 1980s, when proto-CPAB bodies and individual community leaders began engaging with police at the behest of then-Chief Reddin—or back even further to meetings during the Watts Rebellion. Undertaking such a history project would crystallize Lakeside's CPAB as a historically Black organization—whether its viability depended on the maintenance of or threat to that dominance is an open question, given the Latin@ population's parity during the 1990s. Either way, HO was not consulted. LAPD's provision of support for this boundary marking moment could be seen as one of Fisher's racializing moves and could continue to reinforce the Latin@ community as one of outsiders.

Conflict with her Latin@ neighbors over parking spaces on her street motivated Vera to accept recruitment into CPAB in the first place. Vera and her Black neighbors saw her Latin@ neighbors as playing by a different set of rules and laws than everyone else, and her solution was to get involved in neighborhood governance:

FISHER: My neighbor don't like the people across the street from us because they used to park all they cars in front of our places and would leave them the whole week. but they didn't want nobody to park on they side of the street, literally.

AARON: And who lives across the street from you?

FISHER: It's a combination now but there was this gentleman, he still lives there, he would bring his parents' car from up the street and park it right there on our side of the street and he would take his car out of the driveway on Friday he would take his car out of his parking, out of his driveway and park them here and nobody could park and then if you went and parked over there he would tell you, you can't park there. Literally.

AARON: Latino guy?

FISHER: [My neighbor] didn't talk to the Latinos on this side of the street, and I didn't know that when I first moved here. I am pissed at this guy taking up all the parking and parking all around the block and everything. And so, one day I seen going down the street and we was watching him, and I go, "What the heck?" And the lady next door to me, a Black lady, she told me, "Well, you know, they have special rules."

AARON: Who has special rules?

FISHER: The Latinos! You know? That Special Order 40. Well everybody was under the impression that they had the right to do whatever they please. Literally. And that's what [the guy across the street] thought.

AARON: Interesting, but he didn't get away with that.

FISHER: No, no, no, no! And see, no one ever told him anything because he told them that he was a property owner and they wasn't. Well, this guy was, but the other [Latin@s] weren't. But still, he could park in front of his place and then nobody could come over there and park.

AARON: And what happened?

FISHER: Well, this [got me] involved in this and the CPAB. Because I'm like, when she told me, I'm like, "Excuse me, you mean they have

> separate laws?" She says, "They have separate laws. They don't have to go by the same laws as we do." No. I'm like—that didn't go well with me. My husband had just got out the military for twenty-seven years. That did not go well with me. That's why I went to the CPAB and got involved. It was basically the things that was going on in my block that got me involved with these two groups because I'm like, "What the hell has happened in the city of Los Angeles?"

As discussed in Chapter 2, Special Order 40 was meant only to reassure undocumented immigrants that police would not make inquiries into their legal status during routine and misdemeanor encounters, although the word "special" seems to have convinced more than one person that it means preferential treatment.

Sensitized to the issue, Vera continued to react negatively to what she perceived as Latin@ separatism and their "special status" throughout our time in the field. In addition to her specific problems with remittances, taxes, and street vending, much of Vera's frustration came from her belief that they were opposed to integrating into the South LA community. At her annual presentation to the Police Commissioners, Fisher used her last five minutes of speaking time to call out the "Latino Outreach" as a significant problem for her CPAB as an answer to a Commissioner's question:

Aaron's fieldnotes

Due to my own tardiness (I always underestimate the time it takes to get downtown), I make it to the Police Commission Board meeting about twenty-five minutes late. Vera is wrapping up her prepared comments and Himura has said his piece already, although he remains seated beside her, facing the ten-person Commission, who are elevated on the dais with nameplates facing outward.

After Vera's scripted presentation, a Commissioner asks her about "challenges to the CPAB" and she is off, beginning a diatribe about the "Latino Outreach [HO]," the Latin@ community, and, by implication, Hector Mendoza, that lasts for the full five minutes that she has remaining. I reproduce faithfully below the notes of what I could get down. [I have added grammar to make my notes intelligible. Vera has a habit of not finishing thoughts that have clear conclusions/implications before moving on. I therefore sometimes also finish her logical conclusions to make her written representation as clear as her oral one.]

Vera: Our big challenge is youth on the board, which is one reason that I'm disappointed in the Latino Outreach. We have lots of volunteers, but it's not required. Our board was told that the Latino Outreach was started because of trust issues on the part of the Latino community, such as fear of police, but it's been five years since it began. "How long will it take them to adapt?"

The few Latino members that we have were recruited from that meeting, she says, but somehow the rest of them feel that they can't join that main group. Latino Outreach is about "separatism, not about promoting community, and it promotes a you-against-us atmosphere." She has been to those meetings, she says, and we have a few come to our meetings and she's talked to some of the members of that group and they say that "they aren't being invited to join our group. And a lot of them do speak English." Because "crime has no race," she says, they're all victimized. She asks rhetorically: What is their part in the community? How will they contribute? "So, yes, I'm a little disappointed in my CPAB, I mean, it's not my CPAB, but when I go to Outreach, I get told that 'I don't have to come to your meeting.'"

For a time, Himura tasked Fisher with attending HO meetings to remind attendees that they could also participate in the official body. She made her required announcements, but was also disruptive and dismissive, shaming Latin@s under her breath for being afraid of government procedures: "If they filled out the *form*, nobody would knock on their *door*, and we wouldn't need to *talk* about this!" Vera whispered loudly to Aaron during one meeting about census visits. In summer 2011, Vera took the initiative to organize an information session on immigration law—what she later calls an "Integration Seminar." She got the idea after attending an immigrant rights workshop, but did not care for the information they presented. Irritated, she reached out to an agent from the US Citizenship and Immigration Services, the nonenforcement federal immigration agency, to organize a seminar for CPAB. Though on the surface the meeting was a noble effort—an organized public meeting *for* immigrants—her explanation gave the sense that this meeting may have been aimed *at* undocumented Latin@s instead:

Aaron's fieldnotes

Vera introduces Andres Peralta, whispering to him to get his name right, and still gets it very wrong. She laughs about this. He chuckles too, but for a person who considers herself a seasoned world traveler, Vera routinely gets names wrong. Particularly Spanish ones.

Vera reminds us that we can't address the law if we don't know the law. Although we had a seminar with an immigration lawyer, but "I felt that a lot of people didn't know . . . I was leery of what the man said, so I went right to the source," she says with a nod to Peralta.

Vera basically tells us that she didn't like what the immigration lawyer said, so she went to find answers that she liked more. From what I know of both Vera and immigration law, I'm guessing that the lawyer was telling undocumented migrants what their rights are, even as non-US citizens without papers. This would not sit well with her, so she went to find the "official source" and sure enough, he discusses mainly legal immigration and purposely sidesteps issues of the undocumented. At some point he also makes the statement that the US is a very generous nation when it comes to granting citizenship—debatable surely, and just as surely a political point that Vera would echo.

Peralta introduces himself as a non-sworn officer of the US Citizenship and Immigration Services Department. He's a smooth, unruffled public speaker with a booming inflection. I'm impressed by his delivery. He tells us that he will soon put on a whole forty-five minutes to an hour presentation where he gets in depth about immigration issues, but "I came here tonight to judge the level of knowledge and find out what questions you will want answers to."

He hands around several fliers, mostly about green cards, although one is targeted toward those who might get scammed by people in their quest to jumpstart, or hasten, their immigration process. [I have to think that this one is strongly relevant for undocumented folks.] "There is no 'Obama visa,'" he informs us, and the "thousand dollars that the con men and bad lawyers want to help you out is wasted money," referencing predatory immigration law practices. He wants to partner with the CPAB and the LAPD—"This is the first time that anyone from my office has been inside an LAPD division, let alone the Sheriff's office." For this partnership, he wants to route things through Himura and Fisher.

Captain Himura noted that the meeting was for CPAB members only, responsibilizing members in their role as "mouths" for disseminating information from official sources. Much like the idea of merging meetings, Captain Himura's strategy of getting CPAB members to disseminate immigration information to their Latin@ neighbors seemed a bit farfetched if Vera was any indication.

Sr. Mendoza—Undocumented and Unofficial

Hector Mendoza was a stout Salvadoran man in his late forties whom police already recognized as Lakeside's Latin@ "community liaison" when we began observations. This was an unofficial designation, but nonetheless reflected his meeting leadership. Mendoza was a resident of South LA for nearly thirty years and a documented citizen for the last ten. When not presiding over meetings, Hector worked full-time as a PTA liaison at Vernon High School. New participants at Spanish-language meetings were personally welcomed by Hector with a smile, handshake, and deep but booming "*¡Buenas noches!*" as they entered the community room. Hector darted about the room doling out commands, particularly to the two women—Abril Solis and Marvella Quito—whom Hector described as his "*mano derecho y izquierdo* [right and left hand]" of organizing. Hector tried to use his patriarchal style to project HO as a big family united under his direction through language, since attendees' countries of origin included Mexico, Guatemala, Honduras, and El Salvador. For certain, when meal time rolled around at the end of each month's meeting, everyone ate together—even the researchers, no matter our polite refusals.

Though commanding and patriarchal, Hector also brought levity, giving officers nicknames, which residents adopted. When Vice detective Mario Pesci, for instance, came to speak to HO participants, he left the room known as "*Detective Pescado* [Fish]." Hector also offered jokes and commentary while translating between the Captains and residents. When meeting time rolled around and attendees were still trickling in, he would joke, "*Pues en estilo Latino, lluegan tarde* [Well, in Latino fashion, they arrive late]." Consistent with his style, he also behaved in a fatherly fashion at times. Tomás De La Garza, a regular HO participant, several times suffered epileptic seizures during meetings, and Hector would often be the first to come to his aid, holding his head up or rubbing his back, telling officers, "*Asi se pone cuando se emociona* [That's how he gets when he's excited]."

At first Captains valued the work that Hector did in keeping the HO meeting together. Hector called meetings to order, adjourned them, and directed participants to the potluck dinner that Abril and Marvella organized in the meeting room. He made announcements about recent notable crimes, notified participants of upcoming outreach events, and served as the general facilitator and translator in meetings. Captain Patton expressly recognized Hector's ability to get "bodies into the room." Collapsing his efforts with those of Solis and Quito, Hector boasted of making more than a hundred phone calls every month to notify participants of upcoming meetings and changes in the location. Like Vera, Hector was deferential to police definitions and was knowledgeable about crime hot spots, specific officers, and LAPD's special units. He was particularly critical of what he saw as the failures of Latin@ culture that contributed to crime and disorder. Hector, for instance, told Danny that "*nuestra gente* [our people]" scam the welfare system "*cuando tienen hijos, hijos, hijos* [when they have kids, kids, kids]" for the monthly checks. When HO participants complained about what were widely thought to be LAPD-led immigration checkpoints, Hector reassured them these were sobriety checkpoints, which were needed because "*nacemos tomando* [we're born drinking]."[3] His tenure as community liaison extended over the terms of at least three Captains—he was particularly close to Dan Buchanan, who had Captained Lakeside before promoting, and shared Hector's enthusiasm for HO. Toward the latter stages of our fieldwork, Hector leveraged this relationship, which came with an increased proximity to Chief Beck, to work around the Lakeside CPAB to achieve his own goals.

When we entered the field, the "Spanish CPAB" was a Lakeside meeting without an official charter from downtown. Spanish CPAB began as a separate meeting to meet the language needs of Lakeside Spanish speakers, but also to address the feeling (articulated by Mendoza) that Latin@s, particularly immigrants, were neglected and vilified at CPAB. In 2008, Captain Patton presented Spanish CPAB to us as a separate but coequal meeting to the English one. Mendoza's leadership arose from his activist efforts to extract practical resources and build networks with legal actors to benefit undocumented Latin@ residents. In an interview that Danny translated from Spanish, Mendoza said he was dedicated to Spanish-language government engagement, which grew out of his own experiences as a recent migrant:

> MENDOZA: Personally, I think things have changed because I speak English now and I know how to defend myself. I am an American citizen. I know the laws and my rights. It's not as easy to walk all over me, but in reference to other people that don't have the luxury of speaking the language or can exhibit that they know their rights, it's easy to dismiss them.

Spanish CPAB underwent a series of transformations as Lakeside leadership changed. Hector's tenure as Latin@ community liaison, which began under Captain Buchanan, predated Captain Patton. Both Captains were largely content to let the meeting continue with few alterations to its structure or administration. In 2009, however, the LAPD Office of Operations directed that there could be only one official CPAB meeting per division. Patton interpreted this as a direct rebuke, and the Spanish meeting became the "Spanish-Speaking Community-Police Meeting," an ungainly title that always seemed temporary. By this time, Patton was on the way out (and up), and the goals, purpose, and personnel of the Spanish meeting began a near-constant shift under Captain Himura, despite Mendoza's objections. Himura listened to the complaints and advice of many people, including Fisher and Mendoza, but kept his own council. It took him nearly the entirety of his two-year tenure to decide what to do. His first plan was to integrate the meetings, although it was never quite clear how this would be accomplished.

Aaron's fieldnotes

Captain Himura and I turn the conversation toward the CPAB meetings. Particularly on his mind is Hector Mendoza, who he describes as "an obstacle." He tries to avoid casting Hector as a problem inherited from Patton, but this is the undertone I read. He says, somewhat apologetically (since I think this is all secondhand information), that Hector's past track record has been very good—Buchanan claims that Mendoza [and, invisibly, Solis and Quito] used to "produce two hundred people for large meetings." But

Himura backs off this statement immediately, first by sheepishly admitting that maybe some of them weren't actually area residents and then by walking back the entire idea that community policing is best characterized by counting people at meetings. Overall, Himura confesses he is frustrated by Hector's determined separatism. He says he is trying to integrate the CPABs, but that Hector is opposing him at every turn.

Although perhaps not clear in his own mind about what he wanted the meeting to accomplish, Himura noted that Lakeside had squeezed a good deal of mileage out of the ever-growing private contact list and phone tree operation coordinated by Solis and Quito. Although Himura quickly acknowledged that having more bodies was not the same as better community policing, given the lack of communication with the Latin@ public in general, he found it important to maintain and grow this participant base to build credibility within the Spanish-speaking community.

Mendoza's power and control over Spanish language meetings would take a significant blow once Captain Himura set his plan to integrate the English and Spanish meetings into motion. Himura's plan, although never well articulated, was encapsulated in the new name he bestowed: Hispanic Outreach (HO). Outreach, a mandate from downtown, was key, but it was not clear whether HO would be a "feeder" meeting, where new Latin@ attendees would be trained for (English) CPAB, or whether Himura intended to dissolve HO entirely once a critical mass of Latin@s joined the CPAB. Both formulations were discussed at different times. Although we never got clarity from Himura, his subordinate, civilian coordinator Jan Green, indicated her understanding as the latter:

> GREEN: [T]hey are a subcommittee of the CPAB of which they are supposed to attend the meetings, most of the regular meetings, the CPAB, the English ones. [Mendoza] kind of understood that, and so I expressed that to the members of the [HO] meeting as well and invited them to attend. . . . So that is how I feel about the Hispanic subcommittee [HO], and initially I'm thinking that it was started so we can see what the response would be and then gradually and eventually combine the two.

Himura roped Vera Fisher, who spoke no Spanish, into the "feeder" approach and for a few months served as a Spanish meeting liaison. She browbeat several HO attendees—Niccolo Nazario, Aldo Peralta, Elder Figueroa, and Fabricio Alcala—into attending the CPAB, even though they spoke little English and a translator was almost never present. They attended faithfully for a similar time period, spoke little, and took no leadership positions.

Mendoza felt differently about unification under either option. Although he supported the idea of unity in theory, in practice he felt strongly that Himura's plan would not address the issues of Latin@ marginalization that had led to the creation of HO in the first place. Fisher, on the other hand, described her fear that Mendoza ultimately desired a single meeting with himself as the co-chair. For Mendoza, this seemed like a simple matter of having the official CPAB meeting reflect the actual neighborhood demographics: Latin@s and their concerns should be foregrounded in a neighborhood that was majority Latin@. Spanish CPAB, in his eyes, was the first step in making Latin@s the official face of Lakeside's community policing efforts. For Fisher, continued control by the Black community made sense, since the demographic shift comprised a good number of people who lacked legal standing, compared with English speakers who were eligible, able, and knowledgeable citizens who had cut their teeth during an earlier movement era. Through Fisher's lens, Latin@s could not represent the "community" as LAPD understood it.

Officiality was important to Fisher, who drew her arguments in part from the documentation process necessary to become a CPAB official member. Second, while she saw the idea of Black citizens representing the views of Latin@s (documented or not) as natural, she had difficulty with the idea that undocumented immigrants—seen baldly as felons by many CPAB members—could participate meaningfully in CPAB without significant guidance from the existing members. Mendoza was a US citizen, but for Fisher, Latin@s were racialized as undocumented, and thus illegal. His accent, national origins, and Spanish language preference mark him as "other" in Fisher's eyes, and Hector's naturalization seemed almost provisional.

Mendoza was keenly aware of this dynamic. He articulated his desire to keep his distance from Blacks as the result of his experiences and perceptions of the relationship between the two communities, although anti-Blackness among Latin@s in the United States is well documented in LA and elsewhere (Bobo et al. 2000; Wilson and Taub 2006). Hector was the victim of what he perceived as Black criminality. His son's car was stolen by what he reported as "*un Afro-Americano*." His mother was robbed and injured at a bus stop by what he reported as "*un moreno* [a dark-skinned man]." Hector claimed that when he visited government offices, the Black clerks were often the rudest. And even when he was reading the newspaper or watching the news at night, most of the coverage, he said, dealt with Black victimization by Latin@ criminals, and never the other way around. In a twist on the White racial frame described by Feagin and Cobas (2014; Feagin 2009), for Hector, Black criminality and Latin@ victimization were actively suppressed from public consciousness. Understanding Hector's attitudes helps put his antagonistic relationship with Vera into perspective. Upon our first observation at the HO, we notified Hector of the subject of our study. He responded with his perspective on the strained relationship between Blacks and Latin@s, which strongly resembled the White racial frame in centering neighborhood change as a matter of choice between similarly situated individuals:

Danny's fieldnotes

Hector tells me that "*los negros* [the Blacks]" harbor some resentment toward the Latino community as they feel displaced and invaded by the recent heavy influx of migrants into the South Los Angeles area, where many of their families have been residents for over forty years. Offering a brief history, Hector explains that there has been a competition between Blacks and Latinos with regard to purchasing homes. "*¿Si quieren que sean puros negros que viven aqui, porque no venden a su propia gente?* [If they want only Black people to live here, why don't they sell to their own people?]"

Hector and Vera's mutual antagonism, and its reflection of the broader relationship between Black and Latin@ communities, forced Himura to shift his plans. The halfhearted attempts by police and board members to have Latin@s transition to the English CPAB en masse had not yielded the desired results, although the Latin@ recruits from HO faithfully attended CPAB for months and Vera did the same in reverse. No positions of authority were taken by Latin@s, and it seems unlikely that the existing CPAB membership would have taken it well should it have occurred.

Perhaps beginning to feel slighted by Captain Himura, Hector became strident about holding police directly accountable for missteps, at least in the community policing context. When Captain Himura failed to turn up at an HO meeting, Hector and HO participants turned on Jan Green in his absence. Himura was forced to apologize at the next meeting, admitting that Hector had yelled at him. Later, Hector explained to Danny privately, "*El sabe que la cagó* [He knows he fucked up]." On other occasions, Hector would dart accusatory questions at officials, forcing them to answer for instances of law enforcement misconduct in other places.

Lakeside leadership began to see Mendoza as less and less useful and began phasing him out. Over time, Captains took notice of Hector's more problematic translations. While Danny can attest that most of his translations were clear and accurate, there were times when Hector, an untrained translator, made mistakes, and produced inaccurate or incomplete translations. Some of the blame certainly belongs to police for providing confusing information.[4] There were also occasions in which Hector would simply change, omit, summarize, or decline to translate information to residents, particularly for guest speakers with whom Hector disagreed or disliked. When the Captain would ask Vera to speak, for instance, Hector would suddenly fall silent and shoot Danny a mischievous smirk as others stepped in to translate. Captains eventually began to bring in Spanish-speaking officers, at first to discuss their work in Lakeside, but later to assist in translation. Thrust into a position of redundancy, Hector would respond by dominating the Q&A sessions. When the officer was a woman, as in the case of the Homicide unit commander who came to speak, Hector would become notably grouchy and restless.

Whether they viewed Mendoza as an impediment or because of simple negligence, Himura and the Watch Commander, Captain Carlos Macias, began to regularly fail to inform Hector (and thus HO attendees) of upcoming events and excluded him from planning alternative outreach. They actively considered other potential Latin@ community liaisons for HO, provoking Hector's competitiveness. Captain Macias, himself a Spanish speaker, invited Ricardo Diaz, the head of a local Latin@-focused organization, to help transition Lakeside's HO into a new meeting style. Although Diaz was willing to help, it quickly became obvious that no one had told Mendoza. One of the last HO meetings in the Lakeside Station occurred in the roll call room because the community room was double-booked. Without a clear structure, the Captains set up Mendoza and Diaz as coleaders and let the two spar verbally for control:

Aaron's fieldnotes

Public introductions are Ricardo Diaz's idea and he greets each attendee. Most are from Mexico, but a couple are from El Salvador and one is from Guatemala. At the end, however, Hector Mendoza is the one to call for applause. He then discusses the plans to spread the good word of community/police engagement to different places throughout the division, such as schools and churches. He reminds us that this group's mission in doing these things is to combat gangs and drugs through education of youth.

Hector then does something he's never done before: he begins *reading* the minutes that Danny had prepared from last time [which had itself become a recent practice]. Although not his fieldnotes, what Danny gave to Hector is fairly long, and sure enough, it takes an awfully long time to read it all aloud. Ricardo eventually sits down in the face of the monologue after a failed attempt to shut off the flow of words. . . .

[Later on,] Roberto is now up front, having assumed the floor completely, explaining the ramifications of calling the police on your unruly teens—a conundrum where parents and kids often fight over legitimacy in terms of parental authority versus citizenship. He assures them that although the system isn't perfect, they try hard not to penalize parents for using it (i.e., by not referring them to CPS, and potentially, ICE).

Captain Macias tries to provide continuity by referencing the accumulating list of issues to discuss at the next meeting. Next time, he says, we'll have more SLOs who speak Spanish here to help (or any—there are none here, only CROs). He continues in this theme, suggesting that since now they know what the meeting's about, next time they can tell him/the SLOs what their issues are and what about LAPD they need to know—K9 units, Vice, etc. I'm always caught by surprise when things like this happen: for some reason, this meeting suddenly seems to have "reset"—we're at Meeting #1 again. What happened to all those previous meetings, issues, concerns, discussions, and attendees? Hispanic Outreach often seems to have a goldfish's memory—brand new each time, no continuity.

Hector, presented with an opportunity to reassert control, does so, by summarizing the thrust of the meeting: do the things we've talked about, report people, report crimes, report when the *niños no están en la escuela* [truant children], and together we can build a cleaner, healthier community. Ricardo, not to be outdone, tells everyone it was good to have them, thanks for coming, please come back, thanks to the Captain. Himura, suddenly acknowledged, looks up from his phone in the back of the room and awkwardly says, "Thanks, yep." Jim Washburn, a White man who has been acting as Ricardo's assistant, calls for applause for Ricardo, saying he is very dedicated to the Latino community.

Hector announces that the meeting used to have a communal food style feel. He wants to bring that back, but he claims to have forgotten to bring *vasos*, so next time bring something to share. Abril Solis gives me a puzzled look, since the cups are right in the bag behind me. Perhaps he realizes that the hour is late, thanks to all the additions.

Ricardo points out in the back the two recent graduates of Vernon High School who "want to give back to the community" and everyone claps. They look uncomfortable. Hector takes it a step further by seizing the two other high school students who have come in to be with their parents now that Explorers class is over and having them come up and talk. They speak very slow Spanish. The officers are strict, they say, but we learn things. Right from wrong, for instance. Macias whispers in one of their ears, and that Explorer quickly mentions that their training is both mental and physical.

Wrong-footed, Mendoza appealed to formalism as a reaction to Diaz's challenge, but in truth there was little formal structure to apply. By reading of the minutes, he established himself as a historical presence, but the history of HO is contingent and brief and stands apart from the CPAB history that Fisher began separately and institutionally valorizing. He appealed to the attendees' affection for the old family style, but this did not produce the necessary enthusiasm. The more confident Diaz introduced new elements, such as the personal introductions and presentations by Latin@ youth Explorers, but LAPD did not back his plays in any formal way. Himura instead lurked near the back with his phone, allowing the meeting to turn into a struggle for control and direction.

As was emblematic of the entire Spanish meeting trajectory, however, disagreements between Latin@ leaders regarding how participation should unfold were eclipsed by LAPD. The Mendoza/Diaz tension, though dramatic, was short-lived: after the next round of promotions, Macias promoted to Captain III in command of a neighboring division and Diaz followed him over. Mendoza concentrated his activism on Chief Beck directly as part of a small circle of Latin@ advisors and eventually ceased his CPAB activism entirely. Himura, meanwhile, shifted the Spanish meeting to be under direct LAPD control. He assigned Juanito Ruiz, a Spanish-speaking CRO, to coordinate HO at churches, schools, and other public venues within Lakeside, sidelining a cooperative meeting structure completely.

Ms. Coleman—"Voluntary Compliance"

It is crucial to note that while the Hector-Vera dynamic reflected the politics that govern Latin@-Black community tensions, these tensions occurred under the political umbrella of community policing itself. Meeting leaders made choices within their domains and strove to represent the interests their communities, but did so within a particular opportunity structure. Sparring over the politics of representation absorbed energy that could possibly have gone toward expanding the community's role in decision making. Vera and Hector's conflict raised as many questions as it answered regarding the ultimate limits of their political power. Did Vera "win," given Hector's ouster? Was Vera's replacement as co-chair a response to her combativeness? Or was the power struggle incidental to police plans? What are the limits of a resident's political authority?

We take up the last question as it relates to the co-chair's ability to affect community policing personnel, by considering the third leadership figure in the realm of Lakeside community policing meetings—Julie Coleman, Vera's brief replacement. About a year after HO became completely CRO-run, Vera was also sidelined as CPAB co-chair. Although Captain Himura had found Bruce Palmer insufficient as a replacement for Vera Fisher in Chapter 3, he recruited Julie Coleman into the Lakeside CPAB co-chair position independently of the meeting, much like Macias's recruitment of Diaz. Himura used Coleman's preconceptions regarding the agenda-setting capacity of CPAB to recruit her, despite the lack of due process which might ordinarily have bothered her. This foreshadowed what was to come. Unlike Palmer's public candidacy, there was no pretense at nomination or voting; at the next CPAB meeting Himura simply announced that Vera's two-year term was over and that Julie was the new co-chair.

Julie Coleman, a social worker in her early fifties, was quiet until you got to know her, then at turns funny and forceful. Coleman's family was very active in the Civil Rights Movement. She was proud of their activism and showed us several pictures of her family at various well-known movement events, although she was cautious and reserved regarding the details with police. Her concerns about policing brought her to CPAB. She channeled her personal activism through her service to her neighborhood council, the Lakeside Crisis Response Team, and her job. As a professional social service provider and manager who supervised dozens of employees and volunteers, Coleman was in many respects uniquely qualified for the position of co-chair. She was a wily veteran of the vagaries of public service provision, including underfunding, bureaucratic gridlock, and supervisor careerism. In addition to her energy and sense of justice, she also had a propensity toward taking the initiative and a concern for police leaders' accountability.

Community policing work is not always well regarded by police officers. Various sources suggest that it is denigrated as "chicken shit" and "social work" as opposed to real police work, particularly within the LAPD (Herbert 1997; Kroeker 1994; Skogan and Hartnett 1997). Choosing officers who will work effectively and smoothly with volunteers is an important concern for an organization with a spotty record on community engagement. One CPAB meeting contained a spirited discussion regarding the hiring of a new SLO for a vacant BCA. CPAB members spoke out strongly in favor a particular officer who had been brought in on a trial basis. After absorbing the feedback, Captain Patton hired a different officer who had not been discussed. To assuage the grumbling that arose, Patton reassured the group that he was open to reports on the new SLO's progress and to "trust him"—this SLO would be best for the community. Patton publicly explained his actions, but rather than respecting community preference, CPAB served only as an outlet for the post-hire venting.

The fallout from such personnel decisions can be serious. In similar fashion, Sergeant David Guevara, in charge of the Community Relations Office, was the object of numerous CPAB complaints regarding his intransigence, an issue that continued into Coleman's tenure and began to escalate. In a hand-recorded phone interview, Coleman expressed her frustrations in working with Guevara and his CROs to Aaron:

Aaron's fieldnotes

Julie tells me flat out that there is a "culture of not a whole lot of cooperation between CROs and the CPAB." It's unclear to her what their role is and what the role of CPAB should be. Guevara, she suggests, is perfect example of this; he's very my-way-or-the-highway. I note that Ricardo Diaz identified this concern as well when he spoke of Guevara. I ask whether Vera Fisher had ever mentioned this to Julie. Julie equivocates at first, but eventually comes out and says that Vera had alerted Julie about Guevara soon after she took over co-chair duties.

"Regardless" of the role of the CROs, she says, "it takes a certain mind-set to get along with your community. And if you have no people skills, how's that going to work?" The "comfort zone" for Guevara and his assistant, who is much like him, "is working with the Explorers. They're children. You can't have those people working community relations," if they're going to treat the CPAB like children as well. We have Jan Green, she admits, who is a warm fuzzy "people person" but Jan's on leave right now and as a civilian doesn't hold the same authority as Guevara, a sworn police sergeant.

Julie is curious to understand if Guevara is required to operate within some set of policy and procedures. If that's the case, "fine, do that, follow the rules. We don't have to hold hands and sing kumbaya, but there has to be a fair amount of respect." The obvious corollary is that if there's no manual that he's following, then Guevara is really falling down on the job. This, I learn, is the reason that she wanted to talk to me—to know if I had any insight into the nature of community policing in LA, specifically Sgt. Guevara's duties or any sort of blueprint for those duties that he was supposed to be following. I responded that this is exactly the sort of information that I am after. I mention as an afterthought that obtaining quantitative data from LAPD administration downtown has been a challenge for me. That's the way they are, she agrees, they don't want input or accountability.

As co-chairs, both Coleman and Fisher appealed directly to Captains Patton and Himura about Guevara without success. Notably, this issue was never agendized or broached at meetings. The meeting forum and control structure in place seemed ill-fitted to such confrontations—Guevara, for example, often attended—and so these concerns existed essentially in a back channel. Julie's efforts were considerable, but never existed officially within the format of the meeting itself. Guevara's eventual transfer back to patrol after at least four years as CRO Sergeant was the result of Guevara's own missteps within the LAPD's political culture rather than a reaction to resident concerns.

Like many institutions accused of breaching public trust, when LAPD admits fault, it tends to rely on a "bad apple" defense—an isolated bad actor is to blame. This defense limits the scope of damage: at worst, the institution is at fault for employing the bad apple (see Kaplan 2009). More subtly, the bad apple defense functions to support a political rhetoric of institutional accountability, incorporating both complaint and public outcry into the process of adjudication. By drawing these together, an institution can demonstrate that the system functions just as it ought: a bad apple was found and discarded before the rest of the barrel could be tainted. The identification of the problem and the subsequent fallout constitutes "accountability" and the institutional structure that facilitated the transgression can remain intact.

CRO Robert Smith absorbed many of Guevara's duties. In the wake of Guevara's transfer, we interviewed him about the role of CPAB in holding LAPD accountable for such problems. While Vera and Hector competed over who might partner with police, we questioned Smith regarding the nature of that partnership. Smith gave different answers to the same question asked in five different ways: How does community—of any sort—hold LAPD accountable and check police power? He provided the following answers: officer surveillance by other officers; Internal Affairs review of microphone and video recordings; the LA Police Commission, composed partly of civilians, some of whom had held "very very negative beliefs about the police" before "actually learning" about the department; and the complaint system, where civilian complaints are reviewed by an immediate superior.

When asked directly about the Guevara situation, Smith turned the tape off, explained the politics behind Guevara's transfer—Guevara had irritated the brass downtown in a minor nepotism scandal—and then allowed recording of the following:

> SMITH: Sometimes we get people in positions that shouldn't be there. That's definitely true. And like I said, I do believe that our department is one of the most progressive in the world, if not the most progressive. We really try to work on community engagement and I think that

> Captain Martín is taking it to the next level. . . . It's important because I need voluntary compliance—we need voluntary compliance. The LAPD and every police department needs voluntary compliance from the community. Because we're outnumbered typically a thousand to one. So if we don't have that voluntary compliance from the majority of the residents, we're not going to have any compliance. Because—when we've lost voluntary compliance, we've lost control.

Smith's allusions to LAPD's progressive vision shed light on the politics of partnership. In his discussion, he substituted "trust in police" when asked about "accountability." LAPD enthusiastically educates all comers about its operations so long as police control the discourse. After police killed a Guatemalan man in LA's Westlake neighborhood, for example, HO officials took meeting attendees down to the station's basement to try the police use-of-force training simulator. Because many residents did predictably poorly on a video simulator designed to lead subjects passively through scenarios to engineer a shooting moment, residents walked away indoctrinated with police training, expectations, and perspective on "officer involved shootings."[5] Smith's argument is the same—if the public were simply better educated about police virtue, they would trust LAPD's decision making without question. Smith's take easily renders as, the more trust in police can be generated, the less accountability is required.

Smith goes on to demonstrate how this framework can cope with controversy, from the present issue of Guevara to more "malicious mistakes":

> SMITH: [B]eing a Community Relations Officer, you're building good credit with the community. Look, we're all human beings and the Police Department is made up of human beings. Mistakes are going to happen. I would like to think that every mistake was an honest mistake, if you can call it that, meaning it wasn't on purpose, it wasn't malicious. But we are going to get malicious mistakes as well. Guys with bad tempers. Guys with whatever going on. If you've done your job as a police department, if you've integrated with your community, they're not going to hold the actions of one or a few against all of you. They're going to say, you know what? That officer, you know

> what, I had dealings with him before and I should have told Officer So-and-so about it. I should have told the Captain about it, I should have told the supervisor.

Smith began with the bad apple defense, but quickly transitioned to blaming the community itself for failing to appropriately utilize the chain of command. Despite the repeated complaints by Coleman, Fisher, and other CPAB members about Sergeant Guevara to Captain Himura, he laid the fault at the feet of the community, who he considered insufficiently dedicated to resolving the issue. While Coleman cast her complaint as a systematic violation of the idea of partnership, Smith saw each transgression by "one or a few" officers as isolated incidents. Smith was quick to criticize Guevara personally when the tape was off, but seemed incapable of identifying a systemic community mechanism for handling the problem. Most strikingly, in answering the accountability question in so many different ways, Smith was satisfied that he had not only answered the question, but answered it thoroughly. The idea that "community partnership" might entitle residents to speak back against their partners, or even have a hand in choosing them, never materialized despite repeated pressing.

At a similar time, Coleman's own report to the Police Commission came due. Between this and several other issues, she felt pressured to support police publicly while believing that they were acting illegitimately—the commission format, like CPAB, was organized to produce legitimacy, not controversy. After an event that she felt was baldly a "photo-op" using her as a prop, Coleman decided to resign her position as co-chair. Captain Martín, Himura's eventual successor in the Lakeside division, reappointed Vera Fisher as co-chair. HO, meanwhile, continued apace through CRO Juanito Ruiz, speaking every month to a new and largely anonymous group in an ever-shifting setting.

Intercommunity Conflict

> JOHNSON: Understand that in 1950, you couldn't be Black and own a home in Compton. You know what I'm saying? It's real difficult to talk about Blacks and Mexicans in Los Angeles without including White people.

Antoine Johnson, who spent many years as a community organizer, reminded us that however fraught the tensions between the Black and Latin@ communities in South LA, they are driven by conditions of impoverishment and racial segregation imposed by the larger White society. The very existence of community policing in LA is the product of South LA's 1992 protests—by both Blacks and Latin@s—against the brutal conditions of oppressive community confinement (Valle and Torres 2000). Unlike Julie Coleman and Vera Fisher's institutional efforts, the uprisings were successful in effecting personnel change in the form of Daryl Gates. Since that time, LAPD has erected a community policing apparatus that has provided rhetoric of community accountability, but, at least in Lakeside, has also succeeded in platforming divisive community politics.

The English/Spanish meeting dynamic, coupled with the constant reshuffling of the Spanish meeting, provides insight into the interlocking issues of race, language, and citizenship that underlie CPAB's claims to community representation. The different orientations, processes, and membership requirements of each meeting made it clear that absorbing HO directly into CPAB would be difficult if not impossible. HO attendees seemed mainly uninterested in the business of cogovernance, largely because of the precarious relationship with citizenship that many experience and the broken relationships with police from their countries of origin. Latin@ residents lacked standing and leadership within the official CPAB meeting as well and steady attendance went unrewarded. Captains could shift the status of the Spanish meeting without regard, because the attendees had no stake in the institution—elaborate trappings of cogovernance were not required and the institutional memory of each HO meeting faded quickly. Unlike English CPAB, there was little documented HO legacy to celebrate. This is not to suggest that Lakeside's Latin@ population had no inclination to public service, but only that it was not possible to express such an inclination within the police institution.

The precarity of the Spanish meeting was largely a byproduct of strategic moves to maximize Latin@ leadership talent in the name of outreach. Latin@ leaders responsibilized through this structure were all used outside the formal structure of CPAB to increase turnout at a meeting which lacked the status of the official CPAB, while the few

Latin@ CPAB attendees were ignored. As far as Lakeside was concerned, Mendoza's function was not to deliberate police engagement strategies, disseminate official information to residents, or even perpetuate the meeting itself as a body, but to advise police on how best to encourage Latin@ governmental cooperation. Mendoza's attempt to broker his power produced Captain Himura's decisive break with the meeting format altogether. Mendoza's power was always as tenuous as the legal status of his constituency.

The roles of Latin@ and Black residents as political subjects within their respective meetings were different as well. The legacy of Black CPAB members is an important part of the post-1992 era of public relations. Agentive and legally aware individuals, CPAB members could (officially at least) lay claim to a full set of citizenship rights. Individual members seldom declared that they were speaking for the larger community, but rather considered themselves to be part of a deliberative community body. They arrived with the expectation of active participation in the CPAB process and took seriously their responsibilized roles as eyes, ears, and mouths. Few took this more seriously than Vera Fisher, who expected her representational authority as co-chair to be respected by police as well as the community, or Julie Coleman, who expected police to respect community preference. Having visible support from Black residents remains crucial for maintaining police legitimacy in an era politically sensitive to the police shooting of Black people; this, together with the official markers of CPAB, elevated the community status of Black CPAB members. Yet when co-chairs attempted to use their elevated status on behalf of the community, they found a brick wall instead of partnership.

The best example of a successful independent political initiative is Vera Fisher's historical subcommittee. That Fisher's avenue for independent authority extended over preserving the history of the CPAB itself suggests two possibilities for resident power over police resources: (1) enhancing CPAB as a means to strengthen LAPD's legitimacy and (2) elevating one community group over another. Whether her push was a direct result of her anti-Latin@ views or not, the effect was to position CPAB as a body of Black citizens against a rising Latin@ majority. That she was encouraged in this effort while discouraged in so many others speaks to the politics of partnership as well—solidarity was once again discouraged and neither Hector Mendoza nor other prominent Latin@s were consulted for their input. Despite her limited successes, Vera took her deflections on substantive issues like homelessness in stride, although she was also eventually deposed and then subsequently reinstated in undemocratic fashion.

Freed of the co-chair contest with Hector, Julie Coleman's brief activist-oriented tenure centered around a quest for accountability from LAPD itself. Both Vera and Julie tried to leverage their authority to make demands of police and discovered in the roots of their power contingency on police approval. As CRO Robert Smith suggested, the only way to affect substantive issues like hiring, firing, and transfer of officers was to take on the role of supplicant and appeal to the chain of command, but police decisions were final. Hector and Vera fought a political battle over representation, but that representational space was generated within a project that lacked the ability to exert much influence over LAPD. In this sense, community leaders, relegated to symbolic roles and engaged in symbolic fights, were limited in their capacity to produce neighborhood or police change. If we measure the success of community policing in Lakeside by its ability to cultivate the community's capacity to organize through mutual trust, collaboration, and coalitional politics, ongoing community antagonisms rendered police efforts a failure. Whatever the possibilities of community policing might be, the prominent divisions within Lakeside's community also challenged the possibility of community solidarity, which could exert sustained pressure on LAPD to relinquish such power.

Conclusion

On February 12, 2013, Christopher Dorner killed a police officer and barricaded himself in a snow-covered log cabin in the San Bernardino Mountains. Dorner, a Black former LAPD and Navy officer, was fired in 2009 after an incident in which he claims his training officer kicked a mentally ill man in the face and chest. Dorner reported the incident, the officer denied the accusation, and Dorner was fired for making false statements, subsequently appealing the ruling several times to no avail (Leonard, Rubin, and Blankstein 2013; Rubin, Leonard, and Linthicum 2013). Dorner maintained not only that his complaint was accurate but also that LAPD was institutionally racist and reported numerous instances of civilian abuse by officers. Dorner, who had made several previous complaints about departmental racism, posted a lengthy statement on Facebook outlining his complaints and began a private war with area law enforcement. Police were terrified, setting up round-the-clock guards on fellow officers and shooting wildly at vehicles only vaguely resembling Dorner's truck. Large men of color in LA took to wearing T-shirts that proclaimed "I am not Chris Dorner" (Alsop 2013; Blankstein and Therolf 2013; Hanna and Yan 2013; Leonard, Rubin, and Blankstein 2013). Police eventually found the cabin where Dorner was hiding and fired tear gas canisters known as "burners" into the structure, which burned to the ground with him inside. Police later recovered his body and found that Dorner had taken his own life before the smoke and flames could (Clinton 2013).

The hunt for Dorner revealed several things. First, the case proved to be something of a racial Rorschach test: Whites, including most of the popular media, saw Dorner as insane and read his manifesto as the incoherent rantings of a lunatic. Many Blacks and Latin@s, however, while condemning the killing of innocents, saw the Facebook manifesto as a lucid and accurate description of racism and the LAPD (e.g., Frazier 2013). In a form of carefully worded solidarity, several other Black former LAPD officers came forward in the media with similar stories of racist treatment from the department (Cannick 2013a, 2013b; Romero 2013). In the words of a former LAPD Sergeant, "I am not surprised that it happened. I am surprised it took this long and I'm convinced that it will happen again if the department doesn't start to treat their employees better" (Cannick 2013b). At the next Police Commission meeting, many angry public commenters made similar statements. One young Black man referred to Dorner as LAPD's "only good cop" and that "we respect what he did." Another Latina woman reminded Commissioners that there were "so many people rooting for Dorner" and that the violence is "not just Dorner's responsibility, but all of our responsibility."

Equally important was the police reaction to the crisis. In searching for Dorner, law enforcement seemed more interested in protecting police than in protecting the public of any color or class: both from the substance of Dorner's allegations and from him directly. In the course of defending themselves, police actually shot at more civilians than Dorner did. Officers fired one hundred shots at a truck that was a different color, make, and model than Dorner's, injuring Margie Carranza and her elderly mother, Emma Hernandez, and destroying their truck (Winton 2013; Winton and Blankstein 2013). Police of nearby Torrance shot at David Perdue, an early morning surfer whose truck also bore little resemblance to Dorner's—both he and his truck suffered injuries. The protective function of law enforcement, the cornerstone of its public legitimacy, seemed much more self-protective than public-protective.

The Lakeside CPAB meeting normally scheduled for two days after Dorner's death was postponed for a week. Chief Charlie Beck instead held a last-minute town hall meeting to address public comment regarding Dorner. He denounced the LAPD officers' reckless behavior in the mistaken identity cases and promised a swift and thorough investigation into Dorner's firing. Captain Himura, confirming LAPD scuttlebutt that a Lakeside appointment was proving grounds for promotion, had indeed been promoted outside of Lakeside, giving way to Captain Victor Martín. A light-skinned Latino man with a muscular build and a shaven head, he joked quietly that he joined the force in 1988 after one of LAPD's minority recruitment efforts. His previous posting was in a division referenced as a model for collaborative programs, so SLOs were excited about what the Captain would bring. According to CRO Robert Smith, Martín would take outreach "to the next level." A quiet man with a restrained smile, Martín appeared deferential and apologetic to residents. A small camera crew of CROs shadowed and recorded him for monthly episodes on the Lakeside website. He and CRO Robert Smith decided to move this meeting to a local McDonald's as a way to get one step closer to the community while talking about the delicate issue of Dorner.

This McDonald's franchise, by no coincidence, was owned by a Black former LAPD officer. About fifty of us crowded around tables, booths, and stools, in the back corner of the lobby. Smith greeted us with coffee—employees, repurposed into table service, circulated with cups, stir sticks, cream, and sugar. Martín, Smith, and the SLOs clustered awkwardly around a counter in the middle, even though some attendees were behind them. Employees shouting food orders from behind the register and the intermittent beeping of the fry cooker interwove with the meeting discourse making concentration essential. Few customers stopped to check out the meeting, if that was a goal; in fact, one man entered the lobby and immediately exited the building upon seeing the collection of cops. We listened as the Captain addressed the Dorner case.

Aaron and Danny's fieldnotes

Martín: "It's been a busy, emotional week" for LAPD. Our hearts and prayers go out to those families who have been affected. "The investigation is still in flux," but Lakeside Division has played its part by providing security for officers and their families in sixteen different locations in LA, San Bernardino, and Orange counties. "It's been grueling and taxing on officers," but there has been no hesitation on the officers' part. There were over a thousand clues to sift through, not to mention separating real sightings from people who just looked like Dorner. The one-million-dollar reward generated lots of interest. Martín didn't like it to end the way that it did, but says that Dorner made it inevitable with his manifesto.

Chief Beck hosted an open forum at the local Church of Scientology last night. The community asked tough, probing, sometimes unfair questions of the Chief—which Martín says he is glad of—and Beck answered over fifty of them. The Chief is committed to opening a transparent investigation into Dorner's firing and making the results of that investigation publicly available.

Nicole Williams: Will there be a chance to ask more questions of Chief Beck? Will there be more appearances?

Martín: Right now, the Chief is a busy man, including appearance on talk radio and in community forums, but there will be many more, maybe not in South Bureau, but within driving distance. Check out "LAPD Online" for details—the Chief will be a very busy man for the next few weeks.

Ms. Carter: We don't know where the next forum will be? A forum was held at the central office a few days ago but no one was told. The community was not apprised of these meetings! I only found out yesterday! I don't know what happened.

Martín: Yesterday's was a last-minute thing, hopefully we'll do better in the future.

Ms. Carter: The chief has mentioned that it will take six to eight months for a complete investigation of Dorner's case.

Martín: Yes, it will take that long to ensure transparency on the part of the LAPD.

Nicole: What do you mean when you say "transparent"?

Martín: Many investigations are done which are open to public record. There is a lot of information that can be made available through the Freedom of Information Act, which can be requested by anyone. Transparency means that we'll do our best to put all that information out there, but we have to consider the rights of the officers as well—they have some legal rights to privacy, just as we can't violate the rights of some informants. Many people in this room have been involved in making LAPD more accountable. We're not there yet, but we're getting better. In my twenty-five years on the force, the department has come a long way. We've made good strides. "To the best of our limitations," the department will be thorough in investigating this case.

Bruce Palmer: A while back, LAPD was under the federal consent decree. Under that decree there were independent arbiters that were in charge of the investigation. Will there be civilian oversight for this?

Martín: That was only a few years ago that LAPD was released from that, and yes, there will be oversight. Gerald Chaleff is a civilian member of the police department. Google him, look at his record. He was a staunch activist, a public defender, a president of an ACLU chapter here in Southern California. He is in charge of constitutional policing—he keeps us accountable. He is the main reviewer as well as the Inspector General Alex Bustamonte. Some people think this still looks like it's being run internally, but this is in "capable hands." The department will be fair, transparent, and impartial.

Ms. Carter: For the sake of the community, will anyone from the community be on that panel?

Martín (consults with SLO Smith, others): They will publish the names of the panel and I will let you know, but it's not likely the review board will consist of any community members.

Vera, sitting next to Aaron, has been keeping up a running commentary to him the whole time on how and what on earth could they possibly be investigating? Aaron offers up the ending of the manhunt—i.e., the fire and the self-inflicted gunshot—as a possible answer, since it's not clear from Martín's words whether it is this, allegations of racism within LAPD, or specifically Dorner's firing. Partly to stem the flow so he can hear better, and partly because he wants to know the official answer, he urges her to ask.

Vera Fisher: What on earth are they investigating? What he did seems pretty clear!

Martín: Not the crimes themselves, but the internal issues over his firing are what will be investigated.

As he answers this, Gerry Torrance, in his walker-cum-seat-with-wheels, rolls over and starts to tell Vera the same thing.

Perhaps not satisfied with Martín's bland response, Mr. Palmer also speaks up—not *quite* angrily, but aggressively: "They're not investigating the facts of the crime, but the crime against him that he gave up his life to have investigated!"

As discussed in Chapter 3, this was a textbook moment of messaging, rather than a moment of dialogue. The Captain, despite his mild demeanor, was in tight control of the Dorner discourse, leading off by framing the issue as one of LAPD heroics, mourning police victims and highlighting their ordeal. In the introductory chapter, SLO Fernandez laid the blame for the Rodney King Uprisings squarely on the shoulders of one of the men who attacked Reginald Denny; in a curious congruence, Captain Martín highlighted Dorner as controlling the entire situation. Of the actions of these men, there is little doubt, but the police response in both cases revealed a basic narrative of police innocence and justification that has remained largely unadjusted since 1992. Like the OIS in Chapter 2, the officers framed their respective situations as simplistic matters of individual action and responsibility while presenting police as reacting helplessly to a situation that they had no hand in creating. In the narrative to the public, the unwinding of events in all cases was made necessary by the non-police parties—in all cases, and despite community policing themes of proactivity and responsibility, police had no choice but to handle things aggressively and reactively.

The Captain rushed to reinforce the department's legitimacy before residents even began to question him. He reassured CPAB members that Beck was committed to transparency, using the town hall as evidence. Entertaining tough questions was proof that the department was responsive and transparent. Mr. Palmer, a keen community advocate, sharply questioned Martín and remained unsatisfied with the lack of community voice in the investigation—throughout the course of our research, no community member ever pointed to the Police Commission as anything more than the same institutional appendage that maintained Daryl Gates in power for fourteen years. Martín reassured Palmer that the department would be "fair, transparent, and impartial" in their handling of this case. In the absence of community involvement, however, the message from police seemed to be "trust us."

Many in the community—mainly people of color—remained concerned about the role of race in Dorner's allegations, the manner in which he was treated, and the ongoing racism of LAPD that created the conditions for the events in February 2013. The interpretations and choice of descriptors of Dorner by the media tended to emphasize his insanity directly (e.g., "depraved") or indirectly by using incredulity and distancing words to evince a misunderstanding of plain English (Dorner was "apparently seeking to explain or justify murder" and it "seems to be Dorner's belief" that he was fired for making a false report). Indeed, those writing against such a narrative felt it necessary to begin by emphasizing that Dorner and his concerns were not "entirely crazy" (M. Martinez 2013; M. Simon 2013). LAPD's legitimacy—bolstered through community policing after Rodney King and the Rampart scandal—was the primary defense against these charges. Yet despite intense public interest, police limited the community from participating in the accountability process. Even Lakeside's CPAB, hardly a bastion of police hostility, evinced anger and skepticism of police accountability and found Dorner's credibility to be probative, but could not force their involvement in the investigation.

In the end, Special Assistant to the Chief for Constitutional Policing Chaleff conducted the investigation and wrote the reports that were distributed to the Police Commission later that year. The internal investigation found that the decision to fire Dorner was "sound and just" (Chaleff 2013, iv). A second report, a mixed-methods study of LAPD's internal disciplinary system, also conducted by the LAPD's Constitutional Policing Assistant (assisted by external reviewers), found significant complaints of internal bias in the process, but that these included both excessive discipline and excessive protection of women and minorities. The report's summary statistics (complaint data were not released) claim that disciplinary actions taken are racially proportionate across the board.[1] Perhaps more telling, between 2010 and 2013, 10 percent or less of the complaints filed by trained law enforcement officers against their own organization were sustained by that organization (Chaleff 2014).

Police and Community Governance in the Post–Civil Rights Era

Los Angeles is one of many urban areas where police espouse community governance (Los Angeles Police Department 1992; Parks 1999). The general rise in such partnerships, discussed in policing literature as the "community policing era," has begun to dominate the field in criminal justice initiatives (Brown 2010; Herbert and Brown 2006; Hughes and Edwards 2002; Myers and Goddard 2013). When Chief Beck, a product of the Gates era, became LAPD Chief in 2009, he promised to carry forward LAPD's community-oriented approaches, which, in addition to CPAB meetings, seem to include enforcing a broader range of quality-of-life offenses and adopting cutting-edge technology, including the latest in crime analysis software to identify hot spots, direct patrol resources, and predict crime and recidivism (Brayne 2017; Newton 2015). How can we best understand these efforts?

Community policing purports to be the opposite of militarization: running carnivals, promoting an Officer Friendly image, and playing baseball with local gangs. Yet these trends need not oppose one another. Williams (2011) identifies the increased sharing of strategies by police and the military. While we traditionally might think of this as military transfer of weapons and training to police departments, Williams shows how the military has strategically adopted community policing strategies as counterinsurgency, isolating Richie's (2012) feared populations from society in various ways while building bridges with moderates. This is the approach used in the wars in Iraq and Afghanistan; it also resembles the approach that we have described here. The implications of this challenge directly the dichotomy of community policing and police militarization outlined by police scholars and President Obama's Task Force on 21st Century Policing (2015)—it is not community policing *or* militarization, but rather community policing *and* militarization. Community policing is not a rollback of repression and endorsement of cooperative cogovernance, but the same ethos in a more palatable packaging.

As we briefly outlined in Chapter 1, the early twentieth century was an era of state building, which included criminal justice reform (Platt 1977). The US state took shape as a classed society organized to support its capitalist engine. At the same time, it also built its apparatus to subordinate and exclude Black and Brown communities, expanding the category of "White" to include all Europeans and measuring it against the immiseration of African Americans, Mexican Americans, and other subjected groups that provided the grist for society's mill—property and labor. As time has passed, the state has grown and changed, from a booming postwar economy to the present politics of austerity. Just as the conquest—"primitive accumulation," in the terminology of Marx—of the Mexican-US War provided the expansionist need for White terrorist militias to secure land, and the postwar industrialization boom required a regulated and professional police force to combat organized labor and maintain the color line, the contemporary moment sees an expansion of police power diffusing itself into community life. The increased willingness of the US Supreme Court to provide police with a blanket general warrant—beginning right as the Civil Rights Movement succeeded in abolishing race-specific legal barriers to justice—must be understood as a major enabler of such community infiltration.

Community policing does this in a number of ways. Its very nature is to normalize the presence of police in everyday settings, which officers define as noncoercive. Captain Martín's meetings in public spaces like McDonald's were conducted with increasing regularity even before his tenure. Himura held meetings and outreach events in restaurants, schools, and churches. Although these certainly bring the police to the community, they also make the community an inhospitable place for precisely those who avoid the station. Surveillance—for which police are trained, even when maintaining a friendly demeanor—becomes ubiquitous. Everywhere becomes a precinct.

Herbert (2005, 2006) argues that the community policing framework fails because it responsibilizes citizens in ways that they are ill-equipped to manage. He positions the relationship as one of devolved authority, an overstatement that we challenge, but his overall point is a good one—in Lakeside, civilians like Nicole Williams and Vera Fisher serve police functions. This, as Captain Patton explained in Chapter 3, involves learning not only the contours of police action, but also ways to displace personal victimization in the neighborhood. Moreover, residents are told that if they "see something, say something"; that is, they become the eyes and ears of the department, providing intelligence to officers. Residents learn when and how to channel crime complaints to police and facilitate the centralization and legitimation of computational crime statistics. From their positions as members and leaders of other community groups, police also task these civilians as "mouths," with messaging on police narratives about a variety of neighborhood situations and conditions.

As part of the partnership bargain, residents demand that their complaints be heard. These complaint encounters involve frequent negotiations, challenges, and deflections between police and their civilian volunteers. When space is made for civilians to complain about crimes and disorder that inhibit safety or neighborhood desirability, police can limit, restrict, and constrain those complaints. It is crucial that residents be induced to denounce others as outsiders (immigrants, gangs, taggers, etc.), but residents are not given the keys to enforcement either. Police discuss their potential actions in response to these crimes, but retain the ability to choose which activities upon which to act and report. Some police officers deny that they and the department can take responsibility for enforcing a given complaint. They might call attention to, for instance, a departmental policy, a city budgetary constraint, or a law that expressly prohibits them from taking action. Otherwise, they might redirect the complainant and offer to connect residents with other city services, or tell residents to seek out those others themselves.

This dynamic represents perhaps the biggest misconception about community policing initiatives. Devolved authority from police to the citizenry—cogovernance—is at the heart of the legitimacy of the community policing project, as outlined in numerous LAPD documents (e.g., Los Angeles Police Department 1992, 1999, 2009). These collaborations are presented as equitable and coequal, but there is great deal of distance between bringing crime complaints to police and codirecting police strategy, ethos, funding allocations, and personnel deployments and employments. The former feels supplicatory, while the latter sounds democratic. The Dorner exchange and many others throughout this book demonstrate that public engagement is used to gather information, push out messaging, and provide opportunities for venting, but not to provide the public leverage to direct police action. Neither CPAB nor HO—nor even the Police Commission—served as forums to hold police accountable, as police were free to deflect even minor complaints, much less major structural adjustments in priority. This one-sided dynamic gives us little hope that such "partnerships" can be equal. Police leadership over CPAB and HO meetings, however friendly and benevolent, is the result of police strategy, not the cause. This is not only a misconception, but a calculation used to placate the citizenry after the violence of 1992. We must cease mistaking additional forums to alert police of criminal activity with cogovernance or "democratic policing." As Herbert (2006) suggests, this may be difficult.

Complicated Collaborations

If this is the scaffolding of community policing in Lakeside—a cooptation of community leaders for informational, bridge building, and denunciation purposes without a commensurate sharing of power—then the ground-level interactions are a study in racial community politics under an umbrella of White dominance. Contextualization of the economic and racial structure of communities is a necessary but understudied aspect of community policing. Skogan's (2006) evaluation of community policing in Chicago, for instance, examines Blacks, Latin@s, and Whites in isolation as though they were, as the title implies, three separate cities. Insights about each group's different relationships with police are well taken: whereas Whites have a trusting and cooperative relationship with police, the intense repression in Black and Brown neighborhoods and the fear of deportation among Latin@ immigrants certainly prevent these groups from having a similar relationship. Skogan, however, does not examine the interrelationships between these racial groups or the power structure that creates community conditions. Similarly, Herbert (2006) limits his discussion of neighborhood conflict to that of an external factor that shapes the ways residents interact with one another and police, without addressing the larger racial dynamics of Seattle and its neighborhoods.

South LA has for decades been a geographic space reserved for housing the poor and working class, although this may change as LA's urban core gentrifies. Lakeside's rapid demographic changes have resulted from the massive reshaping of LA's labor market niches, producing a divided neighborhood where solidarity is compromised in a number of ways. As job opportunities for citizens decline, degrade, and increasingly bar those with criminal records from employment, LA's Black population, long under violent siege from the criminal legal system, is quickly giving way to Latin@ immigrants who are grudgingly tolerated so long as they quietly fill low-wage and secondary labor market positions. This is the context in which Lakeside Division has decided to linguistically separate its (English) CPAB and (Spanish) HO meetings.

Because police are empowered to define community insiders, they select those most acquiescent to police control and ensure that collaboration means centering police strategies. This dynamic positions Black and Latin@ community police leaders to adopt a White racial frame, wherein both groups adopt negative racial attitudes toward one another that reflect White supremacist narratives, encouraging the emergence of mutual antagonism (Feagin and Cobas 2014). While ethnoracial conflict is certainly real (C. G. Martinez 2016) and the tensions between Hector Mendoza and Vera Fisher encapsulate in many ways the views of other residents we spoke with, LAPD seems uninterested in crafting solidarity between these groups or in power sharing in a way that would make resources available to either group, much less both. Under such contrived conditions of scarcity, conflict is hardly a wonder.

Complaint encounters highlight such tensions between perceived insiders and outsiders. Greenhouse, Yngvesson, and Engel (1994) argue that community identity is tied to remembered history and belonging, particularly when demographic changes result in new neighbors. Complaints trace these boundaries of community social and moral order by identifying those people and behaviors that threaten or violate it. Complaints give voice to community conflicts, highlighting how those with a robust community identity, such as Ms. Carter and Mr. Palmer, imagine themselves in contrast to outsiders, such as Sra. Santos. Insiders see themselves as consumers of police service and civilians whose rights the police are chartered to protect. In contrast, outsiders see themselves as uniquely vulnerable to law enforcement. That Whites in Beverly Hills have an entirely different relationship to law enforcement than either group in Lakeside is not foregrounded. This cleavage along ethnoracial lines does not prevent insiders from teaming up with officers to help police intracommunity divisions as well, groups so marginal that they were never eligible for CPAB's consensus space in the first place.

In this context, it is useful to compare and contrast the attitude of police toward the Black and Latin@ communities with close involvement of police in the business community. Policing a racialized community induces insider/outsider sorting, but LAPD has managed to achieve a gatekeeping role for newly investing businesses, allowing them in with a metaphorical (and sometimes literal) police escort and contractual leverage. Once businesses get through the door, police protect them, and in turn they become financially and discursively supportive of local law enforcement needs. Police are also then in direct control of the surveillance apparatus of these businesses, adding additional nodes to an already extensive network. Police carefully cultivate business relationships, taking a direct hand in crafting the economic landscape of Lakeside. In so doing, they continue to dabble in racial politics in more subtle ways, carving out space for Latin@ labor and housing while keeping Latin@s in check through vendor sweeps and checkpoints. Black mom-and-pop business are identified as less protected as officers maneuver subtly to push them out.

As things stand, insiders to Lakeside include a bastion of elderly Black middle-class home owners, the cooperative business community, and a small number of Latin@ activists willing to work with police to ameliorate the depredations against labor and the undocumented. As Lakeside's gentrifying edges creep inward, the question of who falls where in the insider/outsider dynamic will take on crucial importance, as will the question of who is empowered to make that distinction.

"For the Sake of the Community"

As Ms. Carter's appeal to Captain Martín above and the data presented throughout this book suggest, community crime collaborations are not the transformative projects that police claim them to be. Despite the rhetoric, civilians in the current structure cannot hope to have the sort of impact on police that they want; CPAB exists specifically to co-opt and shape community efforts, not to change the nature of the police institution. Additionally, they may not perform their practical function either—there is little evidence that such police-led initiatives have the crime reduction impacts that officials claim (e.g., Herbert 2001b). Crime is a multifaceted problem, related to a much broader set of conditions that community policing does not and cannot address. Yet the focus on crime and crime prevention proceeds to the exclusion of discussions of oversight.

Perhaps Chief Parker anticipated this. LAPD jumped out ahead of external oversight demands early on when Parker, one of the pioneers in crafting the police public relations playbook, began setting the department's strategy and institutions. Parker's first major post in IAD diverted cries for public oversight, leaving the existing police institution intact. All of this occurred while LAPD simultaneously built up and deployed police military capacity to devastating effect through such initiatives as SWAT, Operation Hammer, and the Metro division. Despite, or perhaps because of, the staggering number of police scandals to emerge from LA, LAPD has demonstrated for the world's police departments how to balance its public opinion while enhancing its regulatory, coercive, and military apparatus. Indeed, according to Fatal Encounters (2018), a journalistic effort to track police killings, LAPD leads all jurisdictions in the nation, including Chicago and New York, in deaths involving officers by a significant margin.

Readers at this point will not be surprised at our observation that police may not always have the community's best interests at heart (see, e.g., K. Williams 2007). In ways that the larger White society is perhaps just beginning to grasp, police violence against Blacks and Latin@s and the criminalization of Latin@ immigrants are defining features of governance in these communities. They shape the everyday life of such civilians in ways that most Whites, the wealthy, and self-segregated populations in upscale communities seldom have to think about. Launched just after we left the field, the Black Lives Matter movement has brought together voices at the forefront of the public debate on police use of force (Taylor 2016).

These shared struggles in particular are a place where Blacks and Latin@s can come together to effect change. Scholar and civil rights activist Angela Davis (2016) asserts that police reform activists should oppose all forms of police-led repression because the same mechanisms that affect one group affect them all. Police repression is carried out by police officers in LA, private prison guards throughout the United States, and Israeli military officers in Palestine. Immigrants' rights activists help to link contemporary Black and Brown struggles by broadening the focus to the merger of local and federal immigration enforcement efforts that target Latin@ refugees (Rios 2011; Zepeda-Millan 2017). Both implicate Richie's (2012) prison nation, knitting together enforcement, imprisonment, and surveillance capacities stretching horizontally throughout dark poor communities and up through local to federal levels of government and international private enterprise. These dynamics exist despite the fact that we are well into the "community policing era." Because resisting a police state is a shared struggle, multicultural coalitions can and must strengthen reform efforts. The data presented in this book offer a warning that we should beware the very real potential for interracial conflicts to complicate attempts at building multicultural coalitions. Given the degree to which the Trump administration has gone on a scattershot offensive, however, threatening reform efforts across the board, such conflicts may be sidelined anyway, as formerly disparate social movements come together under the banner of community resistance (Branson-Potts, Bernhard, and Do 2017).

Community discourse is powerful because it taps into something fundamental—no one is against more community. Yet we have spent a great deal of space criticizing the appropriation of the concept. We must step back from considering community as a mode for government and instead reconceptualize community as a mode of empowerment. Policing must be democratized in a way that it never has been for subjugated people of color and the poor in the United States. Police are public servants. The IRS carries out tax policy, but no one seriously suggests that they ought to be the arbiters of tax rate adjustment. Police, on the other hand, do largely as they please in the streets, so long as they limit their targets by race, socioeconomic status, and degree of political radicalism, and the courts have mostly abdicated their role in pushing back on behalf of civil and human rights (Alexander 2010; Balko 2013; Martinot and Sexton 2003). Rather, since the end of the civil rights era, the vast majority of cases pitting the general warrant of police to stop, search, seize, invade, detain, strip, assault, and kill civilians—in general to do what they like under the color of "public safety"—against the rights of civilians have been decided in favor of the police (Alexander 2010). In a literal sense, policing as an institution, rather than citizens, is the driving force behind the expansion of its own set of powers. As we have seen, this extends deeply into the community platforms intended to hold them accountable.

Long-term change strategies will require that civilians reclaim community discourse and mobilize grassroots efforts to pressure city governments to reform the police. Activists can reclaim community discourse in a way that draws upon the narratives of identity and belonging that are rooted in civil rights era struggles and speaks back against governmental co-optation. Popular protest might be the most fruitful way forward for those civilians seeking greater opportunities for police oversight (Epp, Maynard-Moody, and Haider-Markel 2014). Bass (2000, 174), examining community-based activism in Seattle, Washington, and Oakland, California, concluded that popular movements were vital in driving police reform efforts: "Change in policing is often a result of external forces advocating for reform. Community organizations and collective action play an important role in the politics of policing and police reform. They are critical for pushing reluctant or cautious political leaders to address difficult or unpopular police policy decisions. In several of the cases discussed, it is unlikely that the city would have addressed the issue were it not for community action."

Community-based organizations dealing with police reform have been instrumental in promoting criminal justice reform initiatives all over the United States (Bass 2000), including in our own backyards. The Coalition for Police Accountability in Oakland was key in drafting Measure LL, to rebuild the Oakland Police Department's oversight process, which passed with 80 percent of the vote. The new police commission, which not only contains significant community representation but was selected by community members, has powers to hold police accountable in cases of misconduct or abuse, up to and including dismissal of the Chief (*Post* Staff 2017). Protest action, legal campaigns, and grassroots appeals by groups like Critical Resistance Oakland were instrumental in dismantling the civil gang injunctions that prevented Black and Brown youth from moving about Oakland freely. Meanwhile, the resistance efforts of several groups in Portland, Oregon, including Black Male Achievement, have resulted in the closing of Portland's gang list, the first move of its kind in the nation (Saul 2017). Recent grassroots movements and electoral victories have also removed Portland's police from participation in the federal Joint Terrorism Task Force. None of these moves have resulted in democratic control of the institution of policing, but, quoting French socialist Andre Gorz, prison abolition organization Critical Resistance calls for "non-reformist reforms"—reforms that do not predicate their demands on the needs of the state.

The time is ripe for change, and we should be hopeful that it can happen. With an administration so distant from the hearts and minds of the average US resident, our only hope to bring about change is to support community-based organizations and criminal justice reform initiatives. We have every reason to believe that such movement is currently happening across the country, but we cannot be complacent; rather we must redouble our efforts.

ACKNOWLEDGMENTS

Neither of us really understood at the outset of this project how much work it would be. Intellectually, of course, we knew, we had been prepared, but it was not until the fourth week in a row of twelve-hour days, eighteenth revision and reworking of a chapter, and seemingly hundredth time turning down friends for happy hour that the reality of coauthoring your first book really sinks in. In moments like those, we were both grateful for the understanding, assistance, and support of our family, friends, and colleagues.

First, we would like to extend our endless gratitude to the residents, business owners, activists, organizers, and public service workers in Lakeside who were so generous with their time over the course of five years. We hope to have captured the thrust of the multiple perspectives that you all shared with us. The officers and administrators at the Lakeside Station were also extremely helpful, and we thank them as well. While many will not share our views on the police, we sincerely believe that some officers will read this and see themselves and their perspectives reflected within, even if that is not a popular thing to admit publicly.

The list of thank-yous for those from the University of California system is lengthy, so bear with us. Chronologically, John Hipp and George Tita are first: they probably never guessed that this book would result from their initial quantitative research project in South LA, but hey—you said you wanted assistants who would make the project their own, and here it is! Thanks also to our mentors and advisors over the years, both official and unofficial, who we mention by name below, for putting up with our scholarly and personal idiosyncrasies.

This project took an interesting turn with the Visualizing Governing through Crime in California joint venture between Irvine and Berkeley, which helped us hone our photography skills and introduced us to a supportive group of colleagues. Many thanks to Mona Lynch and Jonathan Simon for organizing that, as well as the crew of participants who were generous in their feedback (many of whom are thanked elsewhere). The symposium came at a crucial moment in our development as scholars and lent this project a legitimacy it probably did not deserve at the time.

NYU Press has been extremely supportive and patient with us throughout this lengthy process, and we mean that sincerely. Ilene Kalish, and her assistants, Joseph Dahm and Martin Coleman, all deserve a special thanks for their thorough reviews of our work at every step of the process. We were amazed at how chill you were with us. Nervous even, because our colleagues shared with us their editorial horror stories. (Honestly, Ilene, somewhere along the way we thought someone was pulling our leg—there was no book contract. But missed deadline after missed deadline, you hung in there with us, just saying, "I know writers need their space.") Thanks particularly to the anonymous reviewers for their insightful comments on the entire manuscript as well.

The interconference Critical Police Studies Working Group has been a source of support, friendship, and feedback. A special thanks to Seba Sclofsky for investing his time in us and taking on a leadership role when called upon. We are very grateful for our senior colleagues as well—Malcolm Holmes, Alex Vitale, Jeanine Bell, and Charles Epp—who have participated in panels with these young upstarts and continue to believe in us.

The data for our interviews were transcribed by a dedicated group of UCI undergraduate research assistants. Their help was invaluable—they basically made this book possible. So, a huge thank-you to Yaya Aranda, Lauren Bacchus, David Dominguez, Anthony Espinoza, Claudia Gavrilescu, Jen Lim, Preston Ong, Gina Perez, Allen Salgado, Letí Sanchez, and Van Truong. Congrats to Yaya and David on your union (you're welcome!) and a double thanks to Lauren, Letí, and Gina—the so-called "office moms"—for creating order from chaos.

We must also thank our close friend and colleague Matty Valasik for his amazing map-making skills, for his loyalty, and for always coming through in a crunch. You're the best, man!

DANNY'S PERSONAL ACKNOWLEDGMENTS

Much of the credit for the path I eventually took to become a sociology professor and book author goes to the faculty of the Criminal

Justice Department at Cal State San Bernardino—my intellectual home. Brian Levin's hate crime classes always left me buzzing with thoughts and questions. Crunching data for Dale Sechrest's policing lab (rest in peace) and James Kaufman's creativity project (in Psychology) gave me a respect for the craft of research. But it was the hallway chats with professors Steve Tibbets, Deborah Parsons, Gisela Bichler, and Pamela Schram that finally convinced me to apply to UCI.

I cannot remember my time at UCI without thinking of the tireless support of my mentors and friends there. Susan Bibler-Coutin: there were so many times I wanted to quit but just a few words from you kept me going till graduation day. Whether I complained about being unable to manage work projects or the absence of a social life, you always listened and motivated me forward. Diego Vigil: you were another important calming voice in my ear, and you showed me that professors have fun too! Thanks for reminding that even though it may not always feel like it, Latin@s have a place in the academy. Cheryl Maxson: Interviewing young prisoners up and down the state helped make me the researcher I am. Thanks for letting me join the DJJ team. Geoff Ward: I miss our pickup soccer games immensely, but not more than your crash-courses in critical race theory on the sidelines. Hope to meet you on the pitch for some footy and a discussion again soon! Steve Herbert at the University of Washington: thanks for picking up the phone out of the blue and agreeing to advise some random grad student. It's cool people like you that make this profession great! And to my dear friend and colleague Natalie Pifer: I have always admired your persistence. Hearing your voice kept me going on all those trips up and down the Five freeway, and up on all those late writing nights. Thanks for being there.

Thank you to the faculty of the Sociology Department at USF for giving me the time and space to complete this work. My deepest thanks go to my friends and mentors, Josh Gamson, Kim Richman, and Ceci Santos, for being there when I needed a sympathetic ear. Faculty brown bag presentations on my research organized by Karina Hadoyan (in CELASA), research and travel support from Pamela Balls-Organista and Marcelo Camperi in the Dean's Office of the College of Arts and Sciences, and Steph Sears's and Ev Ho's amazing Faculty of Color Writing Retreats all helped immensely in developing this book. Without your guidance, support, and encouragement, this project would not be possible!

If I were to say I had a second academic home, it would have to be the Racial Democracy, Crime and Justice Network (RDCJN). Ruth Peterson, Laurie Krivo, and Rod Brunson: thank you for accepting me into "academic summer camp," and the extended RDCJN family. A special thanks to Jody Miller. I knew, meeting you that foggy night in Stockholm, that we would be friends forever. Thank you for always having my back and answering all my annoying questions about this academic life. And, of course, I also have to thank *both* the 2014 and 2017 Summer Research Institute cohorts (the best cohorts!), especially Nicole Gonzalez-Van Cleve, Meli Guzman, Mando Lara-Millan, Pat Lopez-Aguado, Reuben Miller, and Mike Walker, for making the RDCJN another of my homes away from home. And to the leaders of the Latino Criminology Working Group, Robert Duran, Anthony Peguero, and Maria Velez: thank you for your continuing guidance and support as well.

To everyone who read drafts of the manuscript in process: you made it! You're alive and well. I'm glad. But I'm sure the journey tested you. Thanks to my close friends Erin Evans, Abner Morales, and Tina Garcia-Lopez for not pulling your punches; this work is much stronger for it. And thank you to Marjorie Zatz, Victor Rios, and Jamie Fader for pouring over chapters of this book and offering your genuine thoughts and insights. Also, thank you to Tony Platt and Jonathan Simon, organizers of the Carceral Studies Working Group at UC Berkeley. Our work benefited tremendously from your workshops.

Finally, let me thank my loving family. To my mom and dad, *Marína y Alberto: este libro es para ustedes, por cada sacrificio que hicieron para darnos nuestro pan de cada dia.* To my sisters, Cheech and Laura: you were my first role models. Both of you are so damn smart and successful that I knew I had to aim high! *Gracias por tu apollo incansable. Los quiero muchísimo!*

AARON'S PERSONAL ACKNOWLEDGMENTS

This ongoing academic journey of mine has been nearly as literal as figurative, spanning six different states and five different universities, and the list of personal thank-yous is long. I am incredibly appreciative. Beginning with the University of Wyoming, thanks always to Malcolm for taking me under your wing and showing me the craft. We may do it differently, but your guidance was crucial. Margie Zamudio, rest in power. You showed me how to be both an activist and an academic and pointed me toward both Marx and LA. This book bears more than a little of your imprint, and I am eternally in your debt.

At the UCI, in addition to the collective thank-yous, some specific individuals stand out. John Hipp, we may fundamentally disagree about a lot of things, but you trusted me and treated me like a colleague (even though your common sense might have suggested that was a mistake), and for that you have my gratitude. My "wacky ideas" are richer therefore. Simon Cole, you expanded my understanding of what academia is capable of. You helped me learn to think differently, and that's no small thing. Sora Han, my thanks for being a source of theory and critique. Cheryl Maxson, even though we never worked directly together, you were there at the beginning, middle, and end, and I can't thank you enough for your support. Raul Fernandez, thanks for helping me read and teach Marx with new eyes. To the UAW crew collectively, thanks for giving me a productive outlet for my activism and teaching me how to organize—blame for the results belongs to me alone. Special thanks to Erin Evans and Alfredo Carlos along those lines, as well as just for being super cool and inspirational friends and organizers.

The Criminal Justice and Criminology Department at Washington State University in Pullman provided a refuge for me for three years. Even though I left the place, I wish I could have taken the people with me. Melanie-Angela Neuilly, thanks for being my friend and confidante. Faith Lutze, your dedication, tirelessness, and basic decency kept me going sometimes. Dale Willits, I can't emulate your approach to scholarship, but I appreciate it, as well as your support and friendship. Amelie Pednault, keep your head up. David J. Leonard, your outside mentorship was fairly brief, but absolutely necessary at the time. Along with a few others, you showed me how to keep my integrity in this business.

Although I never actually taught for the University of Idaho, I almost feel like I did. Thanks to the faculty of the Sociology and English departments for allowing me to feel connected and involved. Specifically, thanks to Teresa Benz, Kristin Haltinner, Jody Nicotra, Dilshani Sarathchandra, and Brian Wolf for a very long list of things.

I've finally landed at Portland State University's Sociology Department, and my colleagues here have been extremely supportive. This project has taken an absurd amount of time and energy, and I hope to be a better, more sociable colleague going forward. Particular thanks to Julius McGee and Amy Lubitow for your friendship and support. Special thanks to Tina Burdsall as well for your support and our various collaborations and to Melissa Thompson for your patience. Kris Lucht Adams and Bahar Jaberi, thanks for making life here not only possible but fun.

A number of masochistic friends and colleagues also read drafts of chapters in addition to the official reviews, efforts for which words are simply not enough. Thanks to Tina Burdsall, Katy Lang, and Monica Williams.

Academics often thank their students for teaching *them*, and as a student I never quite understood why. Now I do. Thanks to my many students over the years, particularly my graduate students. Joy Mutare and Gisela Rodriguez-Fernandez in particular, I look forward to being your colleague and continuing to learn from you.

On a less institutional level, my family has been very tolerant of my sojourns and supportive of my career, and I have so much love and gratitude for this—Mom for showing me how to work and Dad for showing me what to work on. I sometimes just see myself as different mixed up bits of you. Nicole, thanks for reading, talking, and taking things and running with them—thanks also for being my friend as well as my sister. You outstripped me years ago.

Some family you're born with, some you choose, some chooses you. Akhila Ananth, you've always kept me honest and grounded. Véronique Fortin, I think we're a lot alike, you and I, in the ways that matter. Jasmine Montgomery, you are one of the most brilliant people I've ever met and I thank you for sharing a little bit of that brilliance with me. Lori Sexton, I'm super excited looking ahead, but also thanks looking back as well for both friendship and collegiality. Rafiya Mason, you're the worst and I wish you nothing but the worst, obviously. Celia Reynolds, you're one of the very few people who has checked in with me every step of the way, and I love you for it. Marisa Omori, my thanks for many things.

Last—but should be first by all rights—thanks to Cheyenne Foster who has worked some magic and turned me back into a person. I'm excited about the future.

METHODOLOGICAL APPENDIX

On Police and Partner Ethnography

You're undercovers, huh?
—Lakeside resident

The metaphor of social research as a detective story is well worn. Our particular research site and positionalities however meant that people in Lakeside would literally confuse us with law enforcement officials, as the resident quoted in the epigraph did during a community carnival event held in front of the Lakeside Station. Following ethnographic traditions, we immersed ourselves into the working lives of civilians and state actors collaborating to maintain social order in South LA's Lakeside Division. Easing into conversations, friendships, and interactions requires that ethnographers be acutely aware of themselves and others, making strategic choices about when and how to engage. Ethnographers have accepted that objectivity in fieldwork is elusive, instead seeking to understand the particularities of subjectivity. Social worlds are unstable and ethnographic observations are made within constantly shifting conditions. Each researcher's background, training, and life experiences will inevitably influence what and how they "see" the object of their study (May and Pattillo-McCoy 2000)—in this case, community policing. How much access ethnographers can attain, with whom they can build relationships, and the sorts of questions they are able to ask shape the data they collect. This appendix explores how we collected our data, various challenges we confronted, and the solutions we devised. We hope that our work, as the first long-term, in-depth ethnographic exploration of community policing at a single site, will inspire future policing scholars to conduct close examinations of social interactions between police and civilians, in addition to conducting surveys and counting meeting attendees.

Figure A.1. Photograph of our shadows.

TWO DETECTIVES

We'd been going to the Lakeside Station regularly by the time we began observing meetings, with most of that time spent deep in the station's Gang and Homicide units. Many of the officers at the station became used to our presence in that way. We eventually became official members of the CPAB and wore name tags advertising this within the building. Later, through a separate research project, Aaron applied for an LAPD contract worker badge, which enabled us to forgo the guard station and buzz ourselves into "personnel only" doors. No one asked any questions.

Early one morning, we met SLOs Phil Hackett and Adrian Nilo in the basement roll call room before a ride-along. Hackett thought it would be a good idea for us to witness their morning routine, so we started by observing the daily predeployment meeting:

Aaron's fieldnotes

A tall P2 [officer entrusted with enhanced responsibility] who looks like a young Rutger Hauer directs us sternly to the roll call room at about five minutes before 6 AM. The room is mostly empty, but it quickly fills up. We sit in the very back, the lone civilians in a room that eventually comprises some twenty-plus officers, SLOs, and Sergeants. Most of them appear as White males, but there are a few Latinos and women. SLOs Nilo and Hackett are there on time. Hackett sits in front of us and to the right, but straddles the bench the whole time so that he's looking right at us. He also spends a bit of time picking his nails with a large knife. Is this his normal MO, or is he asserting his dominance in a place where he is powerful? Tough to know—he's a quirky dude.

The Watch Commander, a portly middle-aged white male with an air I can only describe as "cop nerd," calls role and gives out assignments to each car. Then he gets a bit more casual. "Does anyone have a burning desire to help Narco run a warrant?" He asks the SLOs if they have any instructions or announcements (they don't).

A Sergeant in the back begins a long set of instructions and advice regarding searches—if you're ultimately responsible for the results of the search, he says, then go in and search yourself, even if another team has cleared the house. He speaks for a while, talking about everyone's duty to debrief, i.e., share experiences and information. He does so himself, telling us about suspects that he's found hiding under beds, in boxes in the closet, and even in a doghouse in the back of the yard. "Imagine," he says, "if he stays there all night and then rapes and kills someone!"

The Watch Commander wraps it up by announcing that there are two detectives here today, and would they like to say anything? Startled, Danny and I quickly realize that he means us, and we quickly disabuse him of the notion that we are law enforcement of any kind. He looks puzzled—which he shouldn't, since he should have been warned we were coming—and ends it, sending everyone into line to get their equipment.

Both our appearance and the spaces we observed marked us as cops. Lakeside is still recognized as a largely Black community, albeit with a quickly growing Latin@ presence. Most cops on the force are Latin@ or White, in their late twenties or early thirties (LAPD 2017).

Interactions like these signaled that we had become liminal actors. Anthropologist Victor Turner, in his classic work *The Ritual Process* (1966), characterized liminality as a quality of being in between two spaces or phases of development, by the end of which a person's social status becomes transformed. It also takes the form of simply standing between several worlds—those of officers, other government officials, and different communities of residents. Our liminality became clearest with respect to engagement with officers. When officers believed we were also cops, they saw us as insiders and tacitly accepted us. We entered the bowels of the building where no civilians could go unaccompanied—our very presence confirmed our legitimacy. When they learned we were not officers but instead researchers, we became outsiders as their perceptions transformed in an instant.

Civilians sometimes mistook us for cops as well, although, interestingly, perhaps less often than police. One afternoon, we got to Lakeside early and decided to pull up to a local park before heading to the station. There was a community soccer game going on. Both of us are avid soccer fans, so we wanted to watch. As we made our way from the parking lot and up the cement walkway toward a grassy patch, a young Black man crossed our path. Without changing stride, he said audibly to us, "Good afternoon, officers," smirking as if in on a joke. We looked at each other, surprised, and argued about who looked more like a cop, given that neither of us were wearing badges, insignia, or any sort of uniform.

While we managed to build rapport with many community members, particularly CPAB members, some were reluctant to engage with us at first and a few never did. It was uncommon for participants to refuse to be interviewed, but some did outright, and even after repeated requests. Tanika Mahoney, a domestic violence organization coordinator and lowrider, and Sra. Santos, whom we discuss in Chapter 5, were prime examples of community residents who steadfastly refused interviews; although both spoke to us informally, it seems likely that lingering suspicions that we might ultimately report to police persisted.

Our efforts to mitigate such concerns mainly took the form of persistence and verbal attempts to convince civilians of our lack of responsibility to police. Sometimes this paid off. In the instance below, which occurred early in our fieldwork, it seems likely that the combination of our physical separation from police, our persistent denials, and perhaps clear suspicion from police themselves (a rarity) helped win one woman over at a Lakeside carnival in front of the stationhouse:

Danny and Aaron's fieldnotes

We succumb to hunger and walk over to the taco stand, where reggaeton is booming from the speakers just behind the stand, and order two *tacos al pastor* [pork tacos] and a juice (five dollars). We notice that police have begun to patrol the carnival in earnest. Two officers seem particularly interested in us, most likely because they saw us taking notes. They seem attentive to our activity and frequently gaze at us with suspicion. Danny at this point has counted at least twelve police officers making their rounds. The two officers periodically glance at us; at one point, one of the officers even motions over to where we were sitting. The idea that we are *so interesting* to the officers makes us laugh quietly to ourselves. Three bike officers are now circulating throughout the carnival off in the distance.

Danny makes his way back to the seating area after throwing away his trash and sees a group of police officers now seated a few tables away from Aaron, including what appears to be two off-duty or undercover officers. Again, they make it known to us that we are being watched.

A Black woman, who appears somewhat intoxicated, sits at the table next to ours and begins speaking very loudly on her cell phone. Once off her phone, she faces away from the tables of officers and toward us, beginning to speak loudly in our general direction about her dislike of police. At first, Danny isn't sure whether or not she is talking to us.

"You know what I'm sayin', undercovers? You're undercovers, huh?" she says, looking for affirmation from us.

"Us!?" Danny says laughingly.

"Yeah, you are."

She continues to speak loudly and we continue to engage, attempting to persuade her that we are not, in fact, cops. We're also nervous that taking sides here could potentially imperil our project, not to mention our safety. The police officers near us ignore her though as she says several times, "I wish these muthafuckas would say some shit to me, cuz I'll get ignorant!" Apparently deciding to trust us, she begins to treat us as confidants and attempts to sell us on her dislike of police. She tells us that she especially does not like one of the officers sitting at the table across from us who has arrested her on several occasions. Further, she hates cops because they don't respect the rights of people in the ghetto. Sharpening her critique, she finishes by telling us that her brother was shot sixteen times by police, which solidified her attitude.

Both residents and officers with whom we had little contact viewed us with suspicion. In this space, we probably looked like undercovers; only our faces were unfamiliar to the actual undercovers. Over time we learned that long conversations and interactions with residents, or other such sustained engagements, were usually sufficient to convince them that we were not officers. Once they discovered that we were not police, however, officers' trust was more difficult to obtain and more easily lost.

THE INVESTIGATION UNFOLDS

Community policing was not our intended object of study when we originally began visiting South LA. We were doctoral students at UCI when criminology professors John Hipp and George Tita enlisted us to conduct fieldwork on a research project examining interracial violence funded by a Haynes Foundation grant. Following several well-publicized homicides and intergang conflicts resulting in the death of Blacks and Latin@s at the hands of one another, various commentators, including neighborhood activists, Chief Bratton of LAPD, Sheriff Baca of LA County, and notable reporters from the *LA Times*, began quarreling over whether these events represented racialized gang war, pure gang conflict, or "ethnic cleansing" (e.g., Baca 2008; Hernandez 2007; Quinones 2007, 2015). Attempting to answer some of these questions statistically, Hipp and Tita (with Boggess 2009), investigated the issue, confirming the standard criminological cant that interracial violence is statistically rare. One is significantly more likely to be assaulted or killed by a person of one's own race/ethnicity; the truth of the interracial violence claims perhaps lay outside of such a quantitative approach. Our task was originally to look qualitatively at the issue.

Fieldwork began in the summer of 2008, part of which involved collecting demographic information on interracial homicides throughout South LA. We met with LAPD Deputy Chief Donovan Butler, a figure beloved by many in South LA, as he was not only from the area but also one of the first Black administrators in LAPD's history. He connected us to a Detective in the Homicide Unit who became our contact at the Lakeside Station. Detective Ron Jeffries facilitated our entry into the station and provided us a cramped interrogation room to use as an office, which was conveniently situated across from the shelves that contained homicide investigation materials going back more than a decade.

These materials, collated into enormous binders known as "murder books," were intended to give us a baseline understanding of the nature and distribution of interracial gang homicides. They contained details on the victims, the circumstances of their deaths, and the offenders, gruesome photos of the crime scene, notes from witness interviews, warrants, and letters and cards from families. We learned to triage the important information and get through most of them in a matter of ten to fifteen minutes. Others contained such detailed and convoluted information as to fill more than one "book." We coded two hundred of these. Both of us were aware that such grim work was coloring our thinking toward South LA, and we sought as quickly as possible to exit the tedious and macabre task and speak to actual residents about their neighborhood, their neighbors, and issues of community governance. No one would want outsiders to understand their neighborhood only through the dead bodies of (mostly) young people, yet this seems all too common when urban communities of color meet academia.

We were therefore relieved to begin observations and interviews with residents and officers. Seeking to better understand responses to interracial violence, we left the interrogation room and began attending community events and observing gang-focused public safety forums throughout South LA as well as interviewing officers and others involved in the issue. Experienced LAPD officers did not buy into the "race war" narrative propagated by the media to explain gang violence. Instead, they attributed gang violence to territorial and drug conflicts.[1] Interestingly, community people tended to agree with LAPD. This is not to suggest that interracial violence is not a problem, but rather that the incidents we investigated through such methodologies tended to have more immediate causes than an organized campaign of ethnic cleansing. The definitive academic source on South LA's interracial violence, however, has become the ethnography by Martinez (2016), who argues that considerable "alternative governance" has arisen in overpoliced and underprotected Black and Latin@ neighborhoods to manage concerns of violence. We encourage those interested in the issue to consult this text.

Both cops and community residents felt that we were better off talking to neighbors arguing over loud parties or soccer games in the park, because that's where Black and Brown tensions most emerged. Much of it, according to community organizer Jaime Vargas, had to do with conflicts among older age groups.

VARGAS: I say the real problem with gangs, gang members, is not the kids. It's the adults. And that's the problem I've always seen with gang intervention. They always talk about the gang youth problem, but if you

> ever gone to Mesa Court Housing, [the gang members] are like fifty-five or sixty-five years old. That's intergenerational now, and so you have old-timers, old guys calling the shots and it's engrained in the system. A fourteen-year-old kid spray painting his neighborhood, that's not really the problem, you know? They're not politically aware. They're just a kid, you know?

Earlier in the week prior to our interview, Jaime had organized a community meeting for gang leaders and interventionists to understand some causes of local gang conflicts. This became one of several gang-focused public forums that we attended that were organized by a variety of community groups and local government agencies. CPAB members and officials sometimes participated in these meetings, cops and activists told us, although in our subsequent research, this issue seldom reappeared. Captain Patton was in charge of Lakeside when we began observations. We went to the Captain with a blessing from Deputy Chief Butler, told him who we were, and asked if we could sit in on his meetings. He agreed and introduced us to the entire CPAB as one of their monthly meeting began.

We remained on productive terms with Captain Patton until Captain Albert Himura took over. Himura was a generally friendly person and actively sought ways to leverage our research skills to better understand the community volunteers. Aaron, for instance, collaborated with Himura to devise an informal survey of Lakeside area residents to determine their level of engagement and satisfaction with the Lakeside LAPD station and personnel. Aaron later presented the results of the survey, distributed online, in the community, and at CPAB meetings, at a CPAB meeting. Danny became the CPAB's de facto photographer and began taking pictures during community events. Danny presented these during a CPAB meeting as well. We also spent several years attending CPAB meetings in a neighboring division (and we attended several in East LA as well through a separate project), but time constraints and, frankly, better rapport with the Lakeside residents and officers led us to focus our efforts there.

In addition to regularly visiting the Lakeside Station, we visited residents' homes and places of work and recreation to learn more about their daily experiences with community policing. Community volunteer events provided us ample opportunity to shadow residents and learn more about their volunteer work outside of the station. These events also became opportunities to ask how they got along with their neighbors, the sorts of problems they confronted, and whether they believed police were addressing, or could address, those problems. We discuss our relationship with community leaders, and their relationship with one another, directly in Chapter 6.

Slowly, we began to notice that while gangs were a perennial complaint, the degree to which residents adopted coded language to refer to racial "others" was equally persistent and seemed to shape their daily lives and conversational patterns. Beneath this, however, was a persistent tension between residents and officers when competing interests were at stake. Before long we dedicated our time solely to observing the community policing project. Observations of the CPAB and HO meetings, and interviews with community members and officers, as well as ride-alongs and community events, composed the core of our data collection strategy.

Our final phase of fieldwork involved observing other formal settings and interviewing actors whose work was intertwined with the CPAB/HO structure. In addition to attending zoning hearings (Chapter 5), we accompanied Dakari Hendricks, Lakeside's neighborhood prosecutor, to the arraignment of several vendors who had been arrested and ticketed following the vendor sweep that we discuss in Chapter 4. We attended the citywide CPAB forums, wherein CPAB members from each of LAPD's divisions would attend to socialize and hear presentations by various government officials and guests. Finally, we attended Police Commission meetings, where chairs and co-chairs from each CPAB made public reports on the division happenings, noting any significant limitations or challenges to expanding community policing.

GETTING BURNED

Perhaps ironically, being frequently mistaken for police officers did not go very far in helping gain police rapport. Police mistrust was a persistent challenge. Before setting out on the ride-along with SLOs Hackett and Nilo in the excerpt above, we followed the SLOs to the armory just outside the roll call room. They collected their shotguns, keys to the patrol car, and always-on recorders, or "burn boxes" as Nilo calls them. He explained that some officers are afraid of getting "burned"—disciplined or fired—for having a normal conversation over the radio that could be misconstrued if a review board reads a transcript later.[2] Nilo's reservations demonstrate the state of heightened suspicion under which cops work. It may come as no surprise that recruitment is a common problem in policing research.[3] Even though LAPD is technically supposed to grant ride-along requests from the public, at least with specific officers, the list of reasons why such a request can be postponed indefinitely is nearly infinite. And while it was relatively easy to build rapport with community volunteers or LAPD leadership, it was more difficult to be on friendly terms with SLOs and patrol officers.

Perhaps driven by the fear of being burned, note taking (the very heart of ethnographic fieldwork) sometimes roused officer suspicion. Most people did not react to our notebooks. We often carried them in our hands or tucked into the back of our pants and attempted to jot discretely. There were times, though, when we would alert one another that someone was staring at us as we wrote things down. SLO Hackett, in particular, made it known to both of us during the early years of fieldwork that he was uncomfortable with our writing. "Copious notes!" he would say, and while his tone was jovial, he could become quite passive-aggressive when upset. On one occasion, for instance, he jokingly threatened to lob spit balls at the two of us for writing our "copious notes." Strangest of all, we arrived to a police-sponsored event in the community at one point and exchanged odd pleasantries with Hackett. He asked Aaron directly how our project was going and then mocked him for pursuing a project that, unlike Hackett's own job, involved much "danger and daring." Despite regularly making his discomfort known, SLO Hackett became a close informant over time, taking us around on his beat, and inviting us to observe a Spanish-language police-community partnership meeting that he conducted.

There were other officers like Hackett with whom we had complex relationships. Initially, both of us got along well with SLO Liz Fairbanks, for instance. The three of us would often catch up and joke around before meetings. SLO Fairbanks couldn't get over the idea that we were, as she regularly described us, "liberals." We did not volunteer our political leanings. Our politics are much more complicated than this, but she made assumptions based on our answers to her questions about crimes in the neighborhood. She would playfully challenge our criminological acumen and chuckle at our worldview, seeing it as out of step with (her) reality. This was her general approach to everyone who was not an officer, however—so that we all could "feel [officers'] pain a little bit," she once informed the entire CPAB about a "transient" (homeless person) who "dropped his trousers" and "took a piss . . . fifteen feet away from two police officers." Eventually SLO Fairbanks began embracing us as we entered the community room, just as she would with community members. SLO Gus Fernandez, Fairbanks's partner, on the other hand, was far less interested. He tolerated us—at first. But after one heated conversation about politics, our professional relationships with both these officers took time to recover.

Danny's fieldnotes

We run into SLO Liz Fairbanks. Officer Fairbanks, apart from being very affable, likes to make fun of Aaron and I for being "Obama supporters" and "liberals" and excuses many of our opinions as idealistic and unachievable, and sometimes just plain wrong. She ribs Aaron for looking, as he puts it, "like a liberal," while looking to me and remarking that I look more like a cop.

Letting my guard down, I divulge that at one time I wanted to become a police officer.

SLO Fairbanks seems amused by this. She asks why I chose not to enter the profession.

I tell her I didn't want to be the one to make a decision—like an arrest—that could impact the rest of someone's life.

SLO Fairbanks shoots me a puzzled expression as if to say, why would anyone have a problem with that?

Most of the encounter involves similar exchanges about our liberalism and my change of heart. A few more officers join the discussion and jokingly disparage one of their fellow officers for being a "closet Obama supporter."

The conversation turns back to me, my decision, and why that means I "hate" police officers. [I never expressly said or meant to imply this, but somehow that's how the officers see it.]

Fairbanks saw us both as political opponents. She engaged with us playfully because our points of view were a novelty to her. Few others knew, but Liz and Gus reacted strongly to the fact that Danny turned away from a potential career in law enforcement. Perhaps they internalized this as rejection. Danny decided not to pursue a career in law enforcement for practical rather than political reasons. Though Liz was not involved directly in the argument and may not have argued with this logic, Fernandez certainly believed this meant Danny hated cops.

Following this encounter, SLO Fernandez became cold with us and could barely even muster a hello when we saw one another. He remained aloof for some time after this before he was transferred to a community outreach position out of police headquarters downtown. Only after he returned to Lakeside from this assignment did he again warm to us. He even began joking with us more than he had before. While we are uncertain as to what about the transfer prompted the change, we were grateful for the cessation of hostilities since Fernandez carried a lot of weight at the Lakeside Station.

SLO Fairbanks also became distant. At the next month's meeting, we saw her and both approached her for a hug as had become traditional, but she reverted to handshakes. It took her much less time to rebuild a relationship with Aaron. Her interpretation of Aaron seemed to be that he was simply naïve and in need of a copwise education, which she attempted to provide in a sometimes-aggressive manner. The political teasing also had an additional dimension of sexual tension, which perhaps helped smooth over the incident as well, but Fairbanks remained cool on Danny until we left the field.

As the above sampling of relationships suggests, we had uneven access to SLOs. At one point, Patton asked us to write out a list of officers with whom we were having trouble securing a ride-along, presumably to encourage them officially to participate in the project. We decided not to go this route because we felt it might further alienate those officers to be officially "shamed" for recalcitrance. Instead, we focused our energies on working with those officers with whom we did manage to forge close relationships. Over time, bonds with some SLOs changed and improved. This also affected our work, however, insofar as Lakeside's SLOs are divided evenly between Black, White, and Latin@. Our focus on renewing relationships with SLOs we knew already led us to focus on mostly White and Latin@ SLOs, although we were able to observe them all in other ways. Latin@ and White SLOs tend to move easily around one another, but both undermined the integrity and work ethic of the division's Black SLOs behind their backs and in front of us. As we became implicated in these networks, opportunities to build rapport with Black SLOs diminished, a dynamic that we did not notice until it was too late. Fortunately, interviews were supplementary to our participant observation and we were able to observe unhindered hours and hours of community-police interaction, but this remains a regret.

DOING RACE

Even before politics, the ways we each "did" race complicated our fieldwork.[4] The first year, Danny interviewed Detective Terry Farmer—a White woman in her late thirties, built like a basketball player. This first wave of interviews focused on understanding officers' experiences with interracial gang violence and strategies for investigation and enforcement. Midway through, Danny began asking about homicide investigations. When he proffered an example of a Latin@ neighborhood, suddenly the Detective asked Danny to stop the tape and abruptly left the room without explanation. Danny was unsure whether Farmer would return when she came back into the interrogation room where they were conducting the interview. Farmer plopped her own recorder down on the table between them, hit record, said he could do the same, and they continued the interview.

Perhaps, like SLO Nilo, Detective Farmer feared being burned and labeled as biased.[5] Perhaps Detective Farmer saw Danny—a Latino man—asking about policing Latin@ neighborhoods and quickly moved to protect herself against potential false allegations. On other occasions, Danny noted that White officers would furrow their brows or shift in their seats or choose their words carefully when answering questions about race. But none of them reacted as Farmer did. Learning from Danny's experience, we modified our approach to race in interviews. Suspecting that other cops or residents might somehow react or be less forthcoming due to a specific line of questioning, we altered the wording of our pilot interview schedule so the cues would be subtler. In similar, inverse fashion, Aaron, as a White man, was likely able to gain a degree of racial candidness from White officers that may have been more difficult otherwise, despite his perceived "liberalness."

Our racial identities and language abilities influenced the relationships with residents in more positive ways. Both of us got along well with most residents, but the degree of closeness we shared with each of them varied. Residents we met in meetings—themselves activists and networkers—largely welcomed us and were curious as to why we had chosen to focus on South Los Angeles. Both of us got to know Vera Fisher well, as we discuss in Chapter 6. She was especially warm to us, and we would all embrace as we entered the meeting room. We'd ask about each other's families and talk about our progress with the project. We'd ask about recent activity in the neighborhood. Over time, however, Aaron became closer to Vera, in large part because he was available when it came time to conduct an interview with her. The interview took place at her home and proved to be a bonding session in which Aaron was able to talk with her for over two hours, meet her family, and attend and volunteer at a community event with her afterward. Interviews conducted by the two of us together tended to produce very thorough accounts, which is likely due to (1) three-way dynamics, which allow an interviewer to sit back and think while the other questions, and (2) the combination of two brains probing for answers. On the other hand, interviews conducted one-on-one often produced closer relationships with the interviewees thereafter.

With Latin@ residents, the dynamics were slightly different. Aaron speaks some Spanish but feels insecure about his abilities. Many of the Spanish-speaking residents spoke to him encouragingly in Spanish, but it was difficult to address complicated topics. Still, his willingness to embarrass himself linguistically seemed effective in projecting sincerity, and residents seemed to appreciate it. It was much easier for Danny, as a native speaker, to communicate and connect with Hector Mendoza and other Spanish speakers. As such, Danny also conducted solo interviews with Hector in Spanish, which helped bring them closer together as well. Later Danny went along with Hector to visit the school where he is a PTA leader. Like Danny's family, Hector is a Salvadoran migrant, which earned Danny near instant acceptance. In such a way, we were able to gain access to the leadership of CPAB in ways that would have been much more difficult for a single researcher alone.

We found ways to "do" race that enabled us to engage with a broader range of subjects. Community members leveraged our language abilities. Both of us acted as translators in meetings for non-Spanish speakers (Chapter 6), and Danny assisted Latino residents in filling out city documents (Chapter 3). We also began to pay attention to such dynamics in conducting interviews or even casual conversations. When discussing vending, for instance, Aaron would ask CPAB's members' opinions when Danny was out of earshot.

Indeed, like many of South LA's Black residents, Aaron is a southerner who left a Black (Virginia) neighborhood for the West Coast, albeit for very different reasons and with a very different reception. Recognizable dialect, culture, and social setting, if not racial positionality, provided him with an established respectful dynamic with older Black neighbors on which to draw and some commonalities to lay groundwork.

But Aaron's racial positionality also complicated relationships in the field. Aaron took a particular disliking to the one regular White CPAB member with whom we interacted and interviewed: Foster Gill. He was universally cantankerous. Gill regularly broke in to conversations loudly, privileging his own interests as the record keeper and newsletter writer over others or interrupting to ask for information that had just been covered. Aaron described him as "arrogant" and "self-important," neither of which, by Danny's estimation, was untrue, but Aaron was much more attuned to Mr. Gill's role in this space. We often joked that Aaron disliked him because he was White. Sometimes they were both the only two White people in the room, and Aaron did not want to be lumped in with people's perceptions of Mr. Gill. This was particularly the case after Gill conveyed to us (not quietly) his general fear of Blacks in his neighborhood—likely because neither of us are Black. Both of us felt uncomfortable by that, but still we visited his home for an interview and stuck around for a tour of his collection of old newspapers and newsletters afterward, but neither of us built close ties with Mr. Gill beyond that.

To be clear, we are not suggesting that Aaron only spoke to Blacks or that Danny only spoke to Latin@s or that we avoided Whites. In observing our setting, we agreed when and how to approach community members in situations where our racial identities might complicate or facilitate data collection. In the main, we both were able to build positive relationships with community members at both meetings. When cookouts, birthday parties, or funerals came around, community members would invite us both and seemed to consider us a team, an impression that we generally encouraged.

THE PROMISE OF ETHNOGRAPHIC PARTNERSHIPS

Despite the shadows we cast on the social worlds in our study, collaborative ethnographic techniques proved beneficial in several respects. Perhaps most importantly, these techniques allowed us to analytically center police-civilian relationships in ways that urban criminologists, and individual researchers, have so far overlooked. Working together enabled us to engage with a broader range of people than either of us might have on our own. Writing notes side by side allowed us to triangulate our findings and confirm, disconfirm, and sharpen observations. Training our lenses on one another helped us understand how we each saw and shaped the field. Simultaneous data collection allowed us to examine how multiple power structures intersect in and impact Lakeside community meetings. While some readers might interpret our observations as more biased toward one group than others, we believe our study provides a snapshot of the sincere yet frustrating moments that compose the process of collaborative governance in South LA. We hope that this book inspires researchers to critically assess criminal justice settings like CPAB meetings while situating these institutions within the historical backdrop of community governance in the United States.

PARTICIPANT APPENDIX

Who's Who in the Text

Fabricio Alcala: CPAB member, Latino, sixties; former Lakeside civilian employee

Enrique Alves: CPAB guest, Latino, forties

Bernadette Ayers: CPAB secretary, Black, early fifties; small business owner; ran Lakeside LAPD volunteer initiative

Marcus Beasley: LAPD SLO, Black, forties

Dan Buchanan: LAPD administrator, White, sixties; commanded Lakeside before Captain Patton

Melvin Cantrell: LAPD SLO, White, forties

Ruby Carter: CPAB member/CRT member, Black, mid-eighties; retired

Pedro Chacon: Resident, Latino, forties; witness at Dan Venkatesh's hearing

Julie Coleman: CPAB co-chair, Black, fifties; assumed office 2012, resigned 2013; social worker

Minerva Cooley: CPAB member, Black, sixties; anti–domestic violence organization director

Chris Cordoba: LAPD SLO, Latino, forties

Tomás De La Garza: HO attendee/helper, Latino, late twenties; assisted Hector Mendoza; prone to seizures

Frazier Delford: CPAB member/Religious Roundup member/CRT member, Black, fifties; Lakeside's on-call religious consultant

Ricardo Diaz: HO attendee/organizer, Latino (Salvadoran, first generation), forties; directed Latino service organization

Erika Dominguez: CPAB member/HO attendee/CRT member, Latina, thirties

Carlos Escobar: LA City associate zoning administrator, Latino, fifties; oversaw Venkatesh's hearing

J. D. Evans: CPAB member, Black, late sixties; unofficial sergeant-at-arms; semiretired landlord

Liz Fairbanks: LAPD SLO, White, late thirties

Terry Farmer: LAPD Homicide Detective, White, late thirties
Gustavo "Gus" Fernandez: LAPD SLO, Latino (Mexican), fifties
Elder Figueroa: CPAB member, Latino, forties
Vera Fisher: CPAB co-chair, Black/White/Asian, sixties; in office 2008–12; resumed co-chairship 2013
Foster Gill: CPAB member, White, seventies; retired; block club organizer
Dwayne Glover: LAPD SLO, Black, thirties
Jan Green: LAPD Police Service Representative, Black, fifties; civilian personnel
David Guevara: LAPD CRO Sergeant, Latino, fifties
Phil Hackett: LAPD SLO, White, fifties
Sylvester Harris: FBI agent, Black, forties
Marlene Haywood: CPAB member, Black, eighties; retired
Dakari Hendricks: Neighborhood prosecutor, Black, thirties
Albert Himura: LAPD Lakeside Commander/Captain III, Asian, forties; Lakeside command 2010–13
Ron Jeffries: LAPD Homicide Detective III, White (Italian), forties
Antoine Johnson: Community labor nonprofit project director, Black, thirties
Roland Keller: Former LAPD administrator, White, sixties
Sun Kwon: CPAB member, Asian (Korean, first generation), sixties; grocery store owner
Carla Lewis: Resident, White, fifties; witness at Dan Venkatesh's hearing
Devron Lewis: LAPD SLO, Black, forties
Richard Lucas: LAPD Watch Commander/Captain I, Black, sixties
Carlos Macias: LAPD Watch Commander/Captain I, Latino (Cuban, second generation), forties
Tanika Mahoney: CPAB member, Black, forties; domestic violence organization coordinator; lowrider
Victor Martín: LAPD Lakeside Commander/Captain III, Latino, late forties; Lakeside command 2013
Teresa Mayfield: CPAB member, Black, seventies; retired university administrative assistant
Hector Mendoza: HO organizer/translator, Latino (Salvadoran, first generation), fifties; ran HO until 2011; high school PTA liaison
Mario Montes: LAPD Vice Unit, Latino, forties
Lilly Morgan: LAPD SLO, White, forties
Niccolo Nazario: HO attendee, Latino, late sixties

Paul Nguyen: CPAB/Business Car meeting guest, community/liquor store owner, Asian (Vietnamese, first generation), sixties

Adrian Nilo: LAPD SLO, Latino (Puerto Rican), fifties

Jeff O'Malley: LAPD administrator, White (Irish), fifties

Bruce Palmer: CPAB member, Black, sixties; business owner, retired LAUSD, ham radio/emergency preparedness enthusiast

Lydia Palmer: CPAB member/neighborhood council chair, Black, sixties; business owner

Rick Patton: LAPD Lakeside Commander/Captain III, White, fifties; Lakeside command 2007–10

Aldo Peralta: Temporary HO liaison to CPAB, Latino, thirties

Andres Peralta: USCIS Immigration Officer, Latino, fifties

Mario Pesci: LAPD Vice Detective, Latino, late forties

John Peters: CPAB member, Black, forties; sergeant-at-arms, never assumed office

Marvella Quito: HO organizer, Latina (Salvadoran, first generation), sixties; Mendoza's "left hand"

Rick Rinaldi: Community development organization director, Black, forties

Juanito Ruiz: LAPD CRO, Latino, late thirties; runs HO after 2012

Adriana Sanchez: Community labor nonprofit hiring coordinator, Latina (Mexican, 1.5 generation), thirties

Georgina Santos: HO attendee, Latina, sixties

Marge Sierra: LAPD SLO, Latina, sixties

Robert Smith: LAPD CRO, Asian (Indian, second generation), thirties; directs Business Car under Captains Himura and Martín

Abril Solis: HO organizer, Latina (Honduran, first generation), forties; Mendoza's "right hand"

Cynthia Stacy: CPAB member, Black, fifties; retired professor; lowrider

Maddy Stephenson: CPAB member, Black, forties; catering business owner

Gerry Torrance: CPAB member, Black, late sixties

April Umimoto: CPAB member, Asian (Japanese, second generation), mid-seventies; retired

Jaime Vargas: Community labor nonprofit program director, Latino (Mexican), forties

Dan Venkatesh: CPAB attendee, Asian (Indian, first generation), forties; 7-Eleven franchisee, owns other restaurants/convenience stores in Southern CA

Jim Washburn: HO attendee, White, sixties; supports Ricardo Diaz's leadership of HO

Nicole Williams: CPAB member, forties; involved in after-school program Mission: Responsibility

Carolina Zometa: CPAB member/HO attendee, Latina (Mexican, second generation), forties; high school security officer

NOTES

INTRODUCTION

1 LAPD pursued nineteen-year-old Abdul Arian for driving erratically, at one point into oncoming traffic. When he finally stopped on the side of the freeway and attempted to flee on foot, officers shot and killed him. Police claimed Arian called 911 himself. Police reported that he claimed to be unafraid of police or of using his gun. However, during their investigation of the scene, police recovered no weapons. After the shooting, his uncle told the *LA Times* that Abdul had wanted to become a police officer; he had participated in LAPD's junior officer program, the Police Explorers, but "disciplinary reasons" saw him discharged from the program (Curwen and Blankstein 2012).

2 In ways that closely mirror community policing, the US military uses community-based strategies to cultivate informants among civilians and maintain control of towns in Middle Eastern war zones. Research suggests that they are working from the same playbook (Kraska 2007; K. Williams 2011).

3 The US Supreme Court cases *Tennessee v. Garner* (1985) and *Graham v. Connor* (1989) underlined the deference of the court to the perceptions of the officer over the rights of the citizen—officers need only establish afterward that an individual could possibly have been a public safety harm in order to open fire, and they need not even be correct in their estimation. In 2018, the US Supreme Court, petitioning *Kisela v. Hughes*, affirmed this immunity for officers, provoking Justice Sonia Sotomayor's dissent in which she argues that the ruling "tells officers that they can shoot first and think later" (Sotomayor 2018).

4 Administrators widely recognize Lakeside as the sort of division where rookie officers cut their teeth. Because of its reputation as a high-crime community, working this beat is a stepping stone for career advancement. How this plays out in street-level interactions is a subject yet to be formally explored.

5 This system, known as CalGangs, has recently been criticized by the California State Auditor for overinclusivity. Among other concerns, the CalGangs list contained forty-two babies and toddlers (Mata 2016). See the auditor's report (Howle 2016).

6 Before conducting observations, we introduced ourselves to new meeting participants in both English and Spanish, as appropriate. We followed this same process and obtained verbal consent to participate in the study throughout the course of our observations.

7 We expand the discussion of our fieldwork dilemmas and the necessary shift in focus from the original goals of this collaboration in the Methodological Appendix.
8 These documents were gathered and provided by police to help Dr. Maxson and her LAPD evaluation team understand the 1990s vision for community policing (Hennigan et al. 2002; Maxson, Hennigan, and Sloane 2003).
9 In all we conducted sixty-eight formal interviews. Participants comprised forty-one men and twenty-seven women; twenty-three Latin@s, twenty Whites, nineteen Blacks, and six Asians. They ranged in age from their late teens to mid-seventies, but the majority were in their mid-forties or fifties. In a different sense, this sample comprises twenty police officers and administrators, eighteen residents, community organizers, and meeting participants, four school officials, fifteen community organizers (also often residents), three criminal justice practitioners, an outside business owner, and a journalist. These figures do not include the in-depth conversations with many more individuals that did not rise to the level of formal interviews.
10 The only exceptions to the pseudonym rule are politicians and public figures. Chief Charlie Beck, for example, is referred to by name throughout, while SLO Fernandez name-checked the real Damian Williams. Alert readers may notice pseudonymic similarities to street names located in Irvine, California.

CHAPTER 1. ROOTS, REBELLION, AND REFORM

1 We consciously use the terms "uprising," "rebellion," and "disturbance," which many of our civilian participants preferred. There were occasions where civilians corrected our usage of the term "riot," particularly with respect to the 1965 and 1992 incidents. For instance, CPAB member Bruce Palmer noted, "The Rodney King disturbances . . . yeah, they never say, 'riot.' They never say in public, 'Oh, there was a riot!'" Community organizer Juan Vargas, correcting us, said, "We don't call it a riot down here. We call it an uprising." The rationale was that "riot" is a stigmatizing term used against people of color that obfuscates the social conditions (including state violence) in which such violent reactions were bred.
2 Only a very small percentage of young Angelenos adopted the zoot-suit style, but police and the news media began to see all young Chican@s as gang members, instigating public hysteria (Escobar 1999).
3 We use the terms "Mexican," "Mexican American," and "Chican@" interchangeably for the remainder of this chapter, which reflects a transformation in Mexican racial identity beginning in the 1940s.
4 The Los Angeles Rangers, an armed Anglo militia, formed in 1853, in the wake of the Mexican-US War, as a component of the Anglo effort to seize land from Mexicans, who had been promised they could keep their land in the 1848 Treaty of Guadalupe Hidalgo. Their first mission was to capture and lynch a Mexican man accused of murdering a county marshal. County sheriffs and federal marshals were responsible for maintaining order in the region, but would regularly enlist

the aid of the Rangers (Los Angeles Police Department n.d.-a). When the LA City Council discovered that several Rangers were involved in the lynching of scores of Chinese migrants on Calle de los Negros near the Mexican section of town, they established the Los Angeles Police Department (LAPD) to institutionalize local law enforcement, increase accountability, and diminish the need for militia action (Escobar 1999).

5 In 1913, for instance, Mexican members of the Industrial Workers of the World organized a protest against working conditions in Sonoratown's central plaza. Alarmed by the five hundred protesters, five officers attempted to break up the event but were stymied despite killing one of the protesters. That evening police raided the nearby restaurants, bars, and movie theaters, beating and arresting nearly eighty people—anyone who looked as though they might have been at the rally (Escobar 1999).

6 Unlike those of later commissions, the McGucken Committee recommendations were wide-ranging. Not only did the report discuss police reforms, but local courts, the probation department, parks and recreation, public housing authorities, schools, juvenile correctional authorities, and even military police were all listed among those institutions that should adopt reforms related to the outbreak of the Government Riot. It appears that McGucken recognized the systematic and institutional nature of racism in LA.

7 The car itself was also impounded, and Price never saw it again, even though she lived to be ninety-seven. It was removed permanently after the storage fees exceeded the value of the car (Woo 2013).

8 Clubs were the proto-gangs of this period. They formed in high schools and fought against boys from other neighborhoods (Vigil 2002). Before long clubs took on lives of their own, becoming the "cool worlds" for street-oriented youth (M. Davis 2006).

9 These conditions led to increasing Black male employment within the high-wage electronics and aerospace industries, rising from 16 to 28 percent through the 1960s and 1970s, while Black female employment rose from 17 to 50 percent (Sides 2003).

10 Parker resisted integration efforts by then-Wilshire Division Lieutenant Tom Bradley (LA's future Mayor) in 1958. White rank-and-file officers protested by calling in sick. According to Bradley: "When I came on the department, there were literally two assignments for black officers . . . you either worked Newton Street Division, which has a predominantly black community, or you worked traffic downtown. . . . You could not work with a white officer, and that continued until 1964" (Merl and Boyarsky 1998).

11 For example, "Bloody Christmas," when drunken police officers arrested and beat innocent Mexican men in their jail cells, drew considerable criticism. Councilman Ed Roybal, LA's first Chicano City Council representative, accused the department of "systematic brutality," citing over fifty racially abusive incidents. The FBI indicted eight officers, convicting three. Parker dismissed six officers and

disciplined another thirty-six, promising that the Internal Affairs Division would investigate further, but little came of the inquiry (Sides 2003).

12 Instead, the report painted residents as chronically "idle" and engaging in violence to gain "relief from the malaise" (McCone and Christopher 1965, 3). Far from recognizing the segregation and tokenization within the LAPD itself, the report notes that a proposal from Black community leaders to deploy only Black officers to Watts to curb the violence was impossible because "police had no means of determining where the Negro officers on the force were stationed" (14), a point directly refuted by Tom Bradley, then a Sergeant. It later admits without irony that "only 4% of sworn personnel are Negroes and fewer are Mexican-American" (36).

13 The commission admits outright to ignoring the bulk of the evidence in whitewashing Parker's record: "Despite the depth of the feeling against Chief Parker expressed to us by so many witnesses, he is recognized, even by his most vocal critics, as a capable chief who directs an efficient police force that serves well this entire community" (McCone and Christopher 1965, 28). Cohen (1970, as quoted in Abu-Lughod 2007) lists abuse and discrimination by Whites and police as the second most common grievance among those surveyed living in the affected communities. Such grievances correlated directly with participation in the uprising. As Abu-Lughod reports, "[s]ome 43 percent of the males and 35 percent of the females thought that the riots had helped the Negro cause" (Abu-Lughod 2007, 217).

14 One of the worst beatings was that of Reginald Denny. He was driving a diesel truck through the intersection of Florence and Normandie when four Black men (including Damian Williams) pulled him out and kicked and beat him before hitting his head with a brick. They danced around as Denny lay bloody and disoriented in the street and then stole his wallet and shoes (Cannon 1999). Initially, no police units responded to the site of Denny's beating (Domanick 2016).

15 These calculations, while instructive, tend to omit violence caused by the state or the White establishment. While this may be because records of racist violence against non-Whites have historically been poorly kept, this introduces an unacceptable degree of bias into rankings of civic destruction. For example, the destruction of "Black Wall Street," the Greenwood neighborhood of Tulsa, Oklahoma, in 1921 by White racists should arguably rank higher than either 1965 or 1992 in LA. The Black Wall Street massacre left hundreds dead and thousands homeless, and destroyed most of the neighborhood through fire (Oklahoma Commission to Study the Tulsa Race Riot of 1921 2001).

16 In 1982 there were 205 gang killings in LA County. Within five years there were 387 gang-related murders and another 452 in 1988; by the early 1990s, there were over 800 per year (Domanick 2016).

17 The McCone Commission's major tangible gain toward improving structural conditions was the freeing up of federal antipoverty dollars that should have long since been distributed. For two years, twenty million dollars in federal poverty relief funds sat unused due to bickering between city officials and community lead-

ers. At the time, 15 percent of Watts-area residents were un- or underemployed (Abu-Lughod 2007). The uprising resulted in the rapid creation of programs such as the Economic and Youth Opportunity Agency, a job placement program for local youth. Head Start schools served poor youth and families without access to adequate education services (Sides 2003). The rebellion finally brought Johnson's War on Poverty to South LA.

18 Harlins's murder fed into the growing racial hostility that helped produce the mass violence of 1992, of which Korean businesses became some of the very first targets (Abu-Lughod 2007).

19 At five thirty the morning of December 6, seventy-five SWAT officers dressed in black boots, jumpsuits, helmets, and flak jackets and carrying M16 rifles surrounded Panther headquarters. Surprise was key to the plan: SWAT would break through the entryways and arrest the occupants. The Panthers were ready, however, having blocked entryways with sandbags and fortified windows with steel grates. The event turned into a protracted gun battle as police and Panthers exchanged gunfire in a five-hour standoff broadcast on national TV. Gates deployed an additional 125 SWAT troops and planned to escalate his tactics, but the thirteen Panthers inside surrendered. Miraculously no one died in the gunfight, and only three Panthers and three officers were injured. The court ruled that the Panthers fired in self-defense and were eventually acquitted of all charges (Balko 2013; Bloom and Martin 2013).

20 Corresponding neatly with US census block groups and tracts, this created an early confluence of crime data and demographic information, even before Compstat made such analyses routine.

21 Ardrey's writings are part of a larger body of thought known as sociobiology, and his work specifically has been critiqued as biologically determinist and eugenicist, legitimizing White supremacy and colonialism as part of the natural order. Sociobiologists have attempted to distance themselves from this history, with mixed results (for a discussion, see Alland 2004; Lewontin, Rose, and Kamin 1984).

22 After thorough review, scholars have determined that "[s]tudents who receive DARE are indistinguishable from students who do not participate in the program" (Rosenbaum 2007, 817). Some studies have indicated an increase in drug use among DARE participants (e.g., Rosenbaum and Hanson 1998). Nevertheless, according to its website, DARE continues to receive more than two hundred million a year in public funding to ensure its presence in 75 percent of US school districts.

23 All it took to be labeled a gang member was a police stop in which officers ticked the box for gang member or associate on a field interrogation card. This information was centralized into the statewide database and justified nearly any sort of treatment. According to Charlie Beck, then Watts Gang Unit Sergeant, police routinely stopped and frisked pedestrians and pulled over vehicles of suspected gang members to rifle through their cars (Domanick 2016). Police deliberately encouraged intergang violence by writing over gang graffiti with rival monikers

and dropping off roughed-up gang members in rival territory (M. Davis 2006; Hunt and Ramón 2010).

24 HAMMER's first year resulted in fourteen hundred arrests, but the DA filed charges in only 103 cases (Domanick 2016). Controversial tactics, such as the battering ram, had little impact on sales of crack cocaine or gang violence (Hunt and Ramón 2010). By 1990, these operations had resulted in the arrest of more than fifty thousand civilians, but 90 percent were released without charges (M. Davis 2006).

25 Between 1989 and 1992, nine hundred people—80 percent of those cornered—were bitten. A study revealed that LAPD dogs, in contrast to those in other cities, were specifically trained to "find and bite" rather than "circle and bark" and that few rules whatsoever governed their deployment in South LA. Once LAPD was ordered to retrain their dogs, the bite rate fell below 5 percent (Domanick 2016).

26 As a point of comparison, New York, Chicago, San Francisco, and Dallas had one death each within the same period.

27 Gates tried to conceal the data, but a study conducted by the Police Commission found that between 1987 and 1990, 3,781 civilians were injured by baton strikes—more than 900 incidents per year.

28 Gates remained popular with rank-and-file officers long after he left office. We note in our fieldwork a strong current of continued support for Gates and an outpouring of grief at his death in 2010.

29 To its credit, the report did not stop at identifying the officers involved as bad apples, noting that "[t]he failure to control these officers is a management issue that is at the heart of the problem" (Independent Commission on the Los Angeles Police Department 1991, iv). As opposed to the McCone Commission, which had gone out of its way to hold LAPD blameless, this commission located the genesis and violent expression of police brutality within the structure of LAPD management.

30 In direct response to the concerns of the Christopher Commission in 1991, Gates grudgingly allowed a community policing pilot program to begin in one division. After the City Council voted to add five more divisions to the pilot, Gates announced that he would personally direct the program from downtown, a move that was controversial and seen by some as obstructionist (Berger and Tobar 1992). Williams, by contrast, came in with the mandate and grew the program throughout the city.

CHAPTER 2. THE MAKING OF LAKESIDE

1 We should note that this was largely Ms. Mayfield's own interpretation. Although the notion of CPAB members as SLO liaisons has at times jibed with official policy—under Captain Patton, for example, or in official statements (Pols 1995)—the precise roles of CPAB members in such relationships and networks were constantly in flux. On the other hand, the general idea of a community "point of contact" has been with LAPD since the 1970s, as Chapters 1 and 3 discuss.

2 As the Black Belt took shape, inter-neighborhood violence between gangs increased (Alonso 2004; Sides 2003). At first much of this violence was about com-

petition, to see which club had the best fighters. By the late 1950s and early 1960s, hand-to-hand combat had transitioned to fights with knives, tire irons, and other such weapons, although murder was still rare. Central Avenue became a classed division in the increasingly Black area. Tensions between poor, working-class Blacks east of Central Avenue and wealthier, middle-class Blacks to the west arose (Hunt and Ramón 2010). Eastside Blacks were seen as "ghetto," whereas Westside Blacks were seen as "Uncle Toms" because they grew up in relatively prosperous neighborhoods. Their resulting feuds would erupt into later street gang wars as prosperity deteriorated (Sides 2003).

3 As with many public policy statements, how Special Order 40 actually plays out on the ground can vary considerably from the stated text. In broad strokes, the order means that collaboration between federal immigration and LAPD is strictly regulated, but through the course of our fieldwork we were made aware of several instances when the rules were skirted or flouted entirely, either officially or by individuals acting independently. For a more extensive discussion of LAPD's treatment of undocumented migrants since the 1970s, see Domanick (2016).

4 As this book goes to press, the city of Los Angeles has officially legalized street vending. Such a move would support the idea of the rising political power of the new Latin@ majority in South LA and municipal attempts to regulate Latin@ labor power (*Los Angeles Times* and Friel 2018; Reyes 2018).

CHAPTER 3. ORGANIZING THE DIVISION

1 Wacquant (2009, 261) describes Compstat as "an electronic data-gathering and data-sharing system making it possible to track and scan the evolution and distribution of criminal incidents in real time. This pooling of geographically coded police intelligence is then coupled with monthly meetings of police commanders to 'brainstorm' over tactical moves and expeditiously reallocate staff and resources to 'hot spots.' . . . [Compstat is] not only [a] supreme tool of scientific policing, but [a] 'paradigm' for public management generally."

2 Eighty percent of all LA voters claimed that they "strongly" or "somewhat" approved of LAPD's performance, which was nearly a 20 percent increase in public approval since 2005. As we might expect, Whites were most likely to approve of police performance (81 percent), whereas Latin@s (76 percent) and Blacks (68 percent) were less likely (Rubin 2009). We note also, with some irony, the comparison of such good news to the late 1980s, just a few years before the King uprisings.

3 Some noted that LAPD officers had changed their "organizational culture" and were more willing to listen to public criticism and publicly admit their mistakes. Interviewees praised LAPD's community-minded efforts, such as partnering with organizers to prevent retaliatory shootings at funerals, reading books to schoolchildren, promoting cops of color to higher ranks, and renouncing their participation in the FBI's "mapping of Muslim communities" project (Stone, Foglesong, and Cole 2009).

4 For example, see Costa Vargas's *Catching Hell in the City of Angels* (2006), which details the plan by the Coalition Against Police Abuse (CAPA) to independently elect a community review board with the power to subpoena and fire officers. During our fieldwork twenty years later, this plan was still reliably referenced at LA Police Commission meetings during the two-minute "community comment" block.

5 Part 1 crimes refer to FBI Index crimes, considered the most serious—aggravated assault, arson, burglary, larceny, homicide, motor vehicle theft, forcible rape, and robbery.

6 This, of course, does not mean it is *necessarily* majority Spanish-speaking.

7 They are simply ID cards, unlike the ones carried by officers that open electronically locked doors to the rest of the station. As an LAPD "contractor" through a different project, Aaron received such an access card, and CPAB members routinely borrowed it (and him) on several occasions to open inconveniently locked doors.

8 LAPD is broken into area units but also several divisions that are not geographically bound and function throughout the city. Metro is one of these. As the LAPD web page states, LA's community policing efforts are bolstered by a healthy dose of Metro "suppression" (Los Angeles Police Department n.d.-b).

9 Such task forces require more than law enforcement—seizing vendor carts and "cleaning up" (dumping) homeless encampments, for instance, require the participation of the LA Health Department (for greater detail, see Stuart 2016).

CHAPTER 4. COMPLAINT ENCOUNTERS

1 Portions of this chapter were adapted from Roussell and Gascón's (2014) article "Defining 'Policeability': Cooperation, Control, and Resistance in South Los Angeles Community-Police Meetings."

2 Although there were certainly conflicts between police and city attorneys, within the confines of CPAB, their interests mainly aligned with respect to policeability.

CHAPTER 5. NO PLACE FOR THE MOM-AND-POPS

1 We made multiple attempts to ascertain the current state of the Lakeside Boosters. The email address provided on the official Boosters website bounced back our message immediately, while phone calls to the Lakeside front desk and calls and voicemails to the Community Relations Office went unanswered. Our fieldnotes suggest several layers of donations from foundations and corporations to LAPD generally, youth programs particularly, and Lakeside specifically, including the Ray Charles Foundation. According to Himura, Lakeside had verbal commitments from Chase Bank, BP, BMW, and Toyota totaling about sixty thousand dollars. The current website lists several local businesses as sponsors as well.

CHAPTER 6. THE POLITICS OF PARTNERSHIP

1 As may have become apparent, positions like "representative" and "liaison" are tossed off glibly by police. Seldom do these designations come with any real

authority or survive long enough to achieve institutional integration—or even a successor should the individual move on or fade out of organizing.

2 There was a great deal of discussion regarding the Historical Subcommittee as we exited the field. Our periodic contacts after the fact, however, did not demonstrate a great deal of movement as Captains came and went.

3 Residents are not alone in feeling this way. Both immigrant's rights groups and the Spanish-language media perceive these checkpoints as aggressive acts against LA's undocumented Latin@ community.

4 This was particularly the case when explaining how to report crimes. In one instance it took Hector and Captain Patton numerous exchanges to clarify when residents should call 911 versus 311, and the issue was never truly clarified. Also, the Captain urged residents, when calling from a cell phone, to call the Lakeside dispatch office directly to avoid redirection to Highway Patrol or Sheriff dispatch. Since these instructions would also shift based on which officer was asked, Hector was not the only one confused.

5 This is the method used as well for experimental shooting studies, where the context that produces a shooting is stripped away—e.g., the profiling that may have produced the stop, police overdeployment in the area, officer affect, officer aggression toward the victim—and only the shooting details vary. This creates the impression that only the shooting decision itself is problematic, rather than an engaged critique of the practices that produced the moments in the first place. For an expanded critique of such methodologies generally, see Bonilla-Silva and Zuberi (2008) or, specifically, Roussell et al. (2017).

CONCLUSION

1 This is not the place for a point-for-point critique of the report's methodology, but suffice it to say that many of the authorial choices were made in the direction of institutional absolution. First, it is simply difficult to take the charges of "reverse racism" seriously when Black officers sued the police union in 1995 over charges of overwhelming "white supremacy." "Hispanic," although an ethnicity, is treated here as a "race," which may work to undercount Whiteness. "Caucasians" do seem ultimately to be underrepresented in terminations, but no statistical significances are assessed and the demographics of those complainants were not released. Like any punishment proceeding, the pipeline of complaints results in attrition toward the ultimate punishment, where the initial pool is the product of an unknown environment. Just as the population of arrestees is unrepresentative of the population, complaints against officers also represent selection bias, and each choke point should be separately assessed. The experiences of Dorner, unusually vigilant (or inventive, depending on the perspective) in reporting the racism of his colleagues, may be a useful lesson in the construction of that pool. Finally, the extent of the involvement of the outside experts is unclear—when the legitimacy of an organization is at stake, it is difficult to fully trust its self-produced numbers.

METHODOLOGICAL APPENDIX

1 There were notable exceptions to this, including the violence between the Black P Stones (a Black gang) and Florencia 13 (a Latino gang) as well as the killing of a young Black girl named Cheryl Green by a Latino gang member.

2 This arose during a discussion of the Rodney King beating. Officers made several questionable statements on the night of the beating. Apart from likening their previous domestic violence call to a scene from the then-popular movie *Gorillas in the Mist*, they were overheard debating whether they should "kick" King, which the officers argued in court meant to "release" him (Independent Commission on the Los Angeles Police Department 1991).

3 Rowe (2007) had to constantly work to build and maintain the trust and confidence of police officers so they would take part in the research. This was a fine balance to strike because the officers' trust was easily lost and difficult to regain. At some point Rowe resorted to asking any available officer for an interview or ride-along to collect at least some data.

4 "Doing" or performing race in social interaction involves the ways people walk, talk, act, and dress, in addition to their skin color, which altogether produce a shared understanding of race (Flores-González, Aranda, and Vaquera 2014). People doing a racial performance have their own racial identity, and at the same time those with whom they are interacting attribute them a racial identity based on their own interpretations (Lewis 2003).

5 Racial performances in the field can hinder data collection. Black research participants, for instance, might feel alienated by a White researcher's line of questioning (see Best 2003), or Asian immigrants might feel that an Asian American researcher is a community outsider (see Kobayashi 1994). In both cases the researchers' access to the intended subjects of study was limited.

REFERENCES

Abu-Lughod, Janet L. 2007. *Race, Space, and Riots in Chicago, New York, and Los Angeles*. New York: Oxford University Press.

Alexander, Michelle. 2010. *The New Jim Crow: Mass Incarceration in the Age of Colorblindness*. New York: New Press.

Alland, Alexander. 2004. *Race in Mind: Race, IQ, and Other Racisms*. Hampshire, UK: Palgrave Macmillan.

Alonso, Alejandro A. 2004. "Racialized Identities and the Formation of Black Gangs in Los Angeles." *Urban Geography* 25 (7): 658–74.

Alsop, Harry. 2013. "Police 'Tried to Burn Out Christopher Dorner.'" *Telegraph*, February 13. www.telegraph.co.uk.

Ardrey, Robert. 1966. *The Territorial Imperative: A Personal Inquiry into the Animal Origins of Property and Nations*. New York: Atheneum.

Ariëns, Ilva, and Ruud Strijp, eds. 1989. "Anthropological Couples." *Focaal, Tijdschrift Voor Antropologie* 10.

Baca, Lee. 2008. "In LA, Race Kills." *Los Angeles Times*, June 12. http://articles.latimes.com.

Balderrama, Francisco E., and Raymond Rodriguez. 2006. *Decade of Betrayal: Mexican Repatriation in the 1930s*. Albuquerque: University of New Mexico Press.

Balko, Radley. 2013. *Rise of the Warrior Cop: The Militarization of America's Police Forces*. New York: Public Affairs.

———. 2014. "How Municipalities in St. Louis County, Mo., Profit from Poverty." *Washington Post*, September 3. www.washingtonpost.com.

Bass, Sandra. 2000. "Negotiating Change: Community Organizations and the Politics of Policing." *Urban Affairs Review* 36 (2): 148–77.

Baumer, Eric P., and Kevin T. Wolff. 2014. "Evaluating Contemporary Crime Drop(s) in America, New York City, and Many Other Places." *Justice Quarterly* 31 (1): 5–38.

Bayley, David H. 1986. "Community Policing in Australia: An Appraisal." Adelaide: National Policing Research Unit.

Beck, Charlie. 2016. "Relationship-Based Policing." *Police Chief* 83 (July). www.policechiefmagazine.org.

Beckett, Katherine, and Steve Herbert. 2009. *Banished: The New Social Control in Urban America*. New York: Oxford University Press.

Bell, Jeannine. 2013. *Hate Thy Neighbor: Move-in Violence and the Persistence of Racial Segregation in American Housing*. New York: New York University Press.

Berger, Leslie, and Hector Tobar. 1992. "Gates Takes Reins of Community Policing." *Los Angeles Times*, January 11. http://articles.latimes.com.

Best, Amy L. 2003. "Doing Race in the Context of Feminist Interviewing: Constructing Whiteness through Talk." *Qualitative Inquiry* 9 (6): 895–914.

Blankstein, Andrew, and Garrett Therolf. 2013. "Dorner Manhunt: $1-Million Reward Offered in Bid to End 'Terror.'" *Los Angeles Times*, February 10. http://latimesblogs.latimes.com.

Bloch, Peter B., and David Specht. 1973. "Neighborhood Team Policing: Prescriptive Package." Washington, DC: National Institute of Law Enforcement and Criminal Justice.

Bloom, Joshua, and Waldo E. Martin Jr. 2013. *Black against Empire: The History and Politics of the Black Panther Party*. Berkeley: University of California Press.

Bobo, Lawrence, Melvin L. Oliver, James H. Johnson Jr., and Abel Valenzuela Jr., eds. 2000. *Prismatic Metropolis: Inequality in Los Angeles*. New York: Russell Sage Foundation.

Bonilla-Silva, Eduardo. 2004. "From Bi-racial to Tri-racial: Towards a New System of Racial Stratification in the USA." *Ethnic and Racial Studies* 27 (6): 931–50.

Bonilla-Silva, Eduardo, and Tukufu Zuberi. 2008. "Toward a Definition of White Logic and White Methods." In *White Logic, White Methods: Racism and Methodology*, edited by Tukufu Zuberi and Eduardo Bonilla-Silva, 3–30. Lanham, MD: Rowman & Littlefield.

Bourgois, Philippe, and Jeff Schonberg. 2009. *Righteous Dopefiend: Homelessness, Addiction, and Poverty in Urban America*. Berkeley: University of California Press.

Boustan, Leah Platt. 2010. "Was Postwar Suburbanization 'White Flight'? Evidence from the Black Migration." *Quarterly Journal of Economics* 125: 417–43.

Branson-Potts, Hailey, Meg Bernhard, and Anh Do. 2017. "L.A. Pride Parade Morphs into #ResistMarch, as Tens of Thousands Hit the Streets." *Los Angeles Times*, June 11. www.latimes.com.

Bratton, William, and Peter Knobler. 1998. *The Turnaround: How America's Top Cop Reversed the Crime Epidemic*. New York: Random House.

Brayne, Sarah. 2017. "Big Data Surveillance: The Case of Policing." *American Sociological Review* 82 (5): 977–1008.

Brown, Elizabeth. 2010. "Race, Urban Governance, and Crime Control: Creating Model Cities." *Law & Society Review* 44: 769–804.

Cannick, Jasmyne A. 2013a. "An Open Letter to the Los Angeles Police Department and the People They Police." *Electronic Urban Report*, February 15. www.eurweb.com.

———. 2013b. "Retired LAPD Sgt. Cheryl Dorsey: The Stress on Officers Isn't the Public, It's the Department." *Electronic Urban Report*, February 15. www.eurweb.com.

Cannon, Lou. 1999. *Official Negligence: How Rodney King and the Riots Changed Los Angeles and the LAPD*. New York: Basic Books.

Carr, Patrick J. 2005. *Clean Streets: Controlling Crime, Maintaining Order, and Building Community Activism*. New York: New York University Press.

Chaleff, Gerald L. 2013. "Review of the Investigation Surrounding the Termination of Christopher Dorner." Los Angeles: Los Angeles Police Department, Special Assistant for Constitutional Policing.

———. 2014. "Perspectives on the Disciplinary System of the LAPD: Insights and Recommendations from the Men and Women of the Los Angeles Police Department." Los Angeles: Los Angeles Police Department, Special Assistant for Constitutional Policing.

Chávez-García, Miroslava. 2012. *States of Delinquency: Race and Science in the Making of California's Juvenile Justice System*. Berkeley: University of California Press.

Clinton, Paul. 2013. "SWAT Deputies Used Hot Gas on Dorner." *Police Magazine*, February 13. www.policemag.com.

Cohen, Nathan, ed. 1970. *The Los Angeles Riots: A Socio-psychological Study*. New York: Praeger.

Conley, John M., and William M. O'Barr. 1990. *Rules versus Relationships: The Ethnography of Legal Discourse*. Chicago: University of Chicago Press.

Cordner, Gary W. 1995. "Community Policing: Elements and Effects." *Police Forum* 5 (3): 1–8.

Costa Vargas, João Helion. 2006. *Catching Hell in the City of Angels: Life and Meanings of Blackness in South Central Los Angeles*. Minneapolis: University of Minnesota Press.

Coutin, Susan Bibler. 2003. *Legalizing Moves: Salvadoran Immigrants' Struggle for U.S. Residency*. Ann Arbor: University of Michigan Press.

Curwen, Thomas, and Andrew Blankstein. 2012. "Freeway Pursuit Ends in Youth's Death as LAPD Fires 90 Shots." *Los Angeles Times*, April 13. http://articles.latimes.com.

Davis, Angela Y. 2016. *Freedom Is a Constant Struggle: Ferguson, Palestine, and the Foundations of a Movement*. Chicago: Haymarket Books.

Davis, Mike. 1993a. "Uprising and Repression in L.A." In *Reading Rodney King/Reading Urban Uprising*, edited by Robert Gooding-Williams, 142–56. London: Routledge.

———. 1993b. "Who Killed LA? A Political Autopsy." *New Left Review I* 197.

———. 2006. *City of Quartz: Excavating the Future in Los Angeles*. 2nd ed. New York: Verso.

Delgado, Richard. 2009. "The Law of the Noose: A History of Latino Lynching." *Harvard Civil Rights–Civil Liberties Law Review* 44: 297–312.

Domanick, Joe. 2016. *Blue: The LAPD and the Battle to Redeem American Policing*. New York: Simon & Schuster.

Emerson, Robert M., Rachel I. Fretz, and Linda L. Shaw. 1995. *Writing Ethnographic Fieldnotes*. Chicago: University of Chicago Press.

Epp, Charles R., Steven Maynard-Moody, and Donald Haider-Markel. 2014. *Pulled Over: How Police Stops Define Race and Citizenship*. Chicago: University of Chicago Press.

Escobar, Edward J. 1999. *Race, Police, and the Making of a Political Identity*. Berkeley: University of California Press.

Ewick, Patricia, and Susan S. Silbey. 1998. *The Common Place of Law: Stories from Everyday Life*. Chicago: University of Chicago Press.

Fatal Encounters. 2018. "Fatal Encounters." http://numeracy.co.

Feagin, Joe R. 2009. *The White Racial Frame: Centuries of Racial Framing and Counter-Framing*. New York: Routledge.

Feagin, Joe R., and Jose A. Cobas. 2014. *Latinos Facing Racism: Discrimination, Resistance, and Endurance*. New York: Routledge.

Flores-González, Nilda, Elizabeth Aranda, and Elizabeth Vaquera. 2014. "'Doing Race': Latino Youth's Identities and the Politics of Racial Exclusion." *American Behavioral Scientist* 58 (14): 1834–51.

Foucault, Michel. 2010. *The Government of Self and Others*. New York: Palgrave Macmillan.

Frazier, Mansfield. 2013. "Black Support for Dorner Shows Lingering Mistrust of Police." *Daily Beast*, February 14. www.thedailybeast.com.

Garland, David. 2001. *The Culture of Control: Crime and Social Order in Contemporary Society*. Chicago: University of Chicago Press.

Gascón, Luis Daniel, and Aaron Roussell. 2016. "An Exercise in Failure: Punishing 'At-Risk' Youth and Families in a South Los Angeles Boot Camp Program." *Race & Justice* 8 (3): 270–97.

Gates, Daryl F. 1979. "Special Order No. 40." Los Angeles: Office of the Chief of Police, Los Angeles Police Department. http://assets.lapdonline.org.

Goldstein, Herman. 1987. "Toward Community-Oriented Policing: Potential, Basic Requirements, and Threshold Questions." *Crime & Delinquency* 33: 6–30.

Greene, Jack R. 2000a. "Community Policing in America: Changing the Nature, Structure, and Function of the Police." *Criminal Justice* 3: 299–370.

———. 2000b. "The Road to Community Policing in Los Angeles: A Case Study." In *Community Policing: Contemporary Readings*, 2nd ed., edited by Geoffrey P. Alpert and Alex R. Piquero, 123–58. Prospect Heights, IL: Waveland.

Greene, Jack R., and William V. Pelfry. 1997. "Shifting the Balance of Power between Police and Community: Responsibility for Crime Control." In *Critical Issues in Policing: Contemporary Readings*, edited by Roger G. Dunham and Geoffrey P. Alpert III, 393–423. Prospect Heights, IL: Waveland.

Greenhouse, Carol J., Barbara Yngvesson, and David M. Engel. 1994. *Law and Community in Three American Towns*. Ithaca, NY: Cornell University Press.

Grinc, Randolph M. 1994. "'Angels in Marble': Problems in Stimulating Community Involvement in Community Policing." *Crime & Delinquency* 40 (3): 437–68.

Gupta, Akhil, and James Ferguson, eds. 1997. *Culture, Power, Place: Explorations in Critical Anthropology*. Durham, NC: Duke University Press.

Hadden, Sally E. 2003. *Slave Patrols: Law and Violence in Virginia and the Carolinas*. 2nd ed. Cambridge, MA: Harvard University Press.

Hagedorn, John M. 1988. *People and Folks: Gangs, Crime, and the Underclass in a Rustbelt City*. Chicago: Lake View Press.

Hanna, Jason, and Holly Yan. 2013. "Timeline in Manhunt for Ex-L.A. Cop Turned Fugitive." *CNN*, February 13. www.cnn.com.

Hennigan, Karen M., Cheryl L. Maxson, David Sloane, and Molly Ranney. 2002. "Community Views on Crime, and Policing: Survey Mode Effects on Bias in Community Surveys." *Justice Quarterly* 19: 565–87.

Herbert, Steve. 1997. *Policing Space: Territoriality and the Los Angeles Police Department*. Minneapolis: University of Minnesota Press.

———. 2001a. "'Hard Charger' or 'Station Queen'? Policing and the Masculinist State." *Gender, Place and Culture* 8 (1): 55–71.

———. 2001b. "Policing the Contemporary City: Fixing Broken Windows or Shoring Up Neo-liberalism?" *Theoretical Criminology* 5: 445–66.

———. 2005. "The Trapdoor of Community." *Annals of the Association of American Geographers* 95: 850–65.

———. 2006. *Citizens, Cops, and Power: Recognizing the Limits of Community*. Chicago: University of Chicago Press.

Herbert, Steve, and Elizabeth Brown. 2006. "Conceptions of Space and Crime in the Punitive Neoliberal City." *Antipode* 38: 755–77.

Hernandez, Tanya K. 2007. "Roots of Latino/Black Anger: Longtime Prejudices, Not Economic Rivalry, Fuel Tensions." *Los Angeles Times*, January 7. www.latimes.com.

Hipp, John R., George E. Tita, and Lyndsay Boggess. 2009. "Intergroup and Intragroup Violence: Is Violent Crime an Expression of Group Conflict or Social Disorganization?" *Criminology* 47: 521–64.

Hipp, John R., George E. Tita, Luis Daniel Gascón, and Aaron Roussell. 2010. "Ethnically Transforming Neighborhoods and Violent Crime among and between African-Americans and Latinos: A Study of South Los Angeles." Los Angeles: John and Dora Haynes Foundation of Los Angeles.

Howle, Elaine M. 2016. "The CalGang Criminal Intelligence System: As the Result of Its Weak Oversight Structure, It Contains Questionable Information That May Violate Individuals' Privacy Rights." 2015-130. Sacramento: California State Auditor.

Hughes, Gordon, and Adam Edwards. 2002. *Crime Control and Community: The New Politics of Public Safety*. Portland, OR: Willan.

Human Rights Watch. 1998. "Shielded from Justice." New York: Human Rights Watch. www.hrw.org.

Hunt, Darnell, and Ana-Christina Ramón, eds. 2010. *Black Los Angeles: American Dreams and Racial Realities*. New York: New York University Press.

Independent Commission on the Los Angeles Police Department. 1991. "Report of the Independent Commission on the Los Angeles Police Department." Los Angeles: Independent Commission on the Los Angeles Police Department.

Jamison, Peter, and Emily Alpert Reyes. 2015. "State of City: Garcetti Focuses on Public Safety; Wants Uber, Lyft at Airport." *Los Angeles Times*, April 15. www.latimes.com.

Johnson, Calvin C., and Jeffrey A. Roth. 2003. "COPS Program and the Spread of Community Policing Practices, 1995–2000." Washington, DC: Urban Institute.

Johnson, Gaye Theresa. 2013. *Spaces of Conflict, Sounds of Solidarity: Music, Race, and Spatial Entitlement in Los Angeles*. Berkeley: University of California Press.

Johnson, Lydia D. 2015. "The Politics of the Bail System: What's the Price for Freedom?" *The Scholar: St. Mary's Law Review on Minority Issues* 17 (2): 171–217.

Kaplan, Paul J. 2009. "Looking through the Gaps: A Critical Approach to the LAPD's Rampart Scandal." *Social Justice* 36: 61–81.

Katznelson, Ira. 2006. *When Affirmative Action Was White: An Untold History of Racial Inequality in Twentieth-Century America*. New York: Norton.

Kelley, Robin D. G. 1996. *Race Rebels: Culture, Politics, and the Black Working Class*. New York: Free Press.

Kelling, George L., and Mark H. Moore. 1988. "The Evolving Strategy of Policing." *Perspectives on Policing*, no. 4: 1–15.

Kirk, David S., and Sara Wakefield. 2018. "Collateral Consequences of Punishment: A Critical Review and Path Forward." *Annual Review of Criminology* 1 (1): 9–24.

Kirk, Michael, director. 2001. "LAPD Blues." *Frontline*. WGBH Educational Foundation, Public Broadcasting Service.

Kobayashi, Audrey. 1994. "Coloring the Field: Gender, 'Race,' and the Politics of Fieldwork." *Professional Geographer* 46 (1): 73–80.

Kraska, Peter B. 2007. "Militarization and Policing—Its Relevance to 21st Century Police." *Policing* 1 (4): 501–13.

Kroeker, Mark A. 1994. "In South Los Angeles, a Call for Citizens against Crime." *Los Angeles Times*, March 28. http://articles.latimes.com.

Kun, Josh, and Laura Pulido. 2014. *Black and Brown in Los Angeles: Beyond Conflict and Coalition*. Berkeley: University of California Press.

Leonard, Jack, Joel Rubin, and Andrew Blankstein. 2013. "Dorner's LAPD Firing Case Hinged on Credibility." *Los Angeles Times*, February 10. http://articles.latimes.com.

Lewis, Amanda E. 2003. "Everyday Race-Making: Navigating Racial Boundaries in Schools." *American Behavioral Scientist* 47 (3): 283–305.

Lewontin, R. C., Steven Rose, and Leon J. Kamin. 1984. *Not in Our Genes: Biology, Ideology, and Human Nature*. New York: Pantheon.

Lipsky, Michael. 2010. *Street-Level Bureaucracy: Dilemmas of the Individual in Public Service*. 30th anniversary ed. New York: Russell Sage Foundation.

Loader, Ian. 2000. "Plural Policing and Democratic Governance." *Social & Legal Studies* 9 (3): 323–45.

Los Angeles Police Department. 1992. "Building Public Safety Confidence in Los Angeles." Los Angeles: City of Los Angeles.

———. 1997. "Ideal Basic Car." Los Angeles: Los Angeles Police Department.

———. 1999. "Definition of Community Policing: A Staff Report." Los Angeles: Los Angeles Police Department, Management Services Division.

———. 2009. "Celebrating the Community-Police Partnership." Los Angeles: Los Angeles Police Department, Community Policing Unit.

———. 2017. "Report PR91: Sworn & Civilian Personnel by CS Class, Sex, and Descent." http://assets.lapdonline.org.

———. n.d.-a. "The LAPD: 1850–1900." www.lapdonline.org.

———. n.d.-b. "Metropolitan Division: K-9, Mounted Unit, S.W.A.T." www.lapdonline .org.

Los Angeles Times and Courtney Friel. 2018. "After 5 Years, L.A. City Council Approves Plan to Legalize Street Vending." *KTLA News*, April 17. http://ktla.com.

Lynch, Mona, Marisa K. Omori, Aaron Roussell, and Matthew Valasik. 2013. "Policing the 'Progressive' City: The Racialized Geography of Drug Law Enforcement." *Theoretical Criminology* 17: 335–57.

Lyons, William T. 2002. *The Politics of Community Policing: Rearranging the Power to Punish*. Ann Arbor: University of Michigan Press.

Manning, Peter K. 1997. *Police Work: The Social Organization of Policing*. 2nd ed. Prospect Heights, IL: Waveland.

Manza, Jeff, and Christopher Uggen. 2006. *Locked Out: Felon Disenfranchisement and America Democracy*. Oxford: Oxford University Press.

Marcelli, Enrico A., Manuel Pastor, and Pascale M. Jossart. 1999. "Estimating the Effects of Informal Economic Activity: Evidence from Los Angeles County." *Journal of Economic Issues* 33: 579–607.

Martinez, Cid Gregory. 2016. *The Neighborhood Has Its Own Rules: Latinos and African Americans in South Los Angeles*. New York: New York University Press.

Martinez, Michael. 2013. "Ex-LAPD Cop Gains Sympathizers on Social Media." *CNN*, February 15. www.cnn.com.

Martinot, Steve, and Jared Sexton. 2003. "The Avant-Garde of White Supremacy." *Social Identities* 9: 169–81.

Mata, Hector. 2016. "Beware of Gangster Babies: Calif. Database Slammed." *CBS News*, August 15. www.cbsnews.com.

Maxson, Cheryl L., Karen M. Hennigan, and David Sloane. 2003. "Factors That Influence Public Opinion of the Police." Research for Practice. Washington, DC: National Institute of Justice.

May, Rueben A. Buford, and Mary Pattillo-McCoy. 2000. "Do You See What I See? Examining a Collaborative Ethnography." *Qualitative Inquiry* 6 (1): 65–87.

McCone, John A., and Warren M. Christopher. 1965. "Violence in the City: An End or a Beginning?" 23. Sacramento, CA: Governor's Commission on the Los Angeles Riots.

McGucken, Joseph T. 1943a. "List of Projects Undertaken in the Los Angeles Area in Accordance with the Recommendations of the Governor's Committee." Attorney General, Law Enforcement, 1943–53. Inventory of the Earl Warren Papers, 1924–53.

———. 1943b. "Report and Recommendations of Citizens Committee: Investigation of the 'Zoot-Suit' Riots in Los Angeles." Attorney General, Law Enforcement, 1943–53. Inventory of the Earl Warren Papers, 1924–53.

Merl, Jean, and Bill Boyarsky. 1998. "Mayor Who Reshaped L.A. Dies." *Los Angeles Times*, September 30. http://articles.latimes.com.

Metzl, Jonathan. 2011. *The Protest Psychosis: How Schizophrenia Became a Black Disease*. Boston: Beacon.

Mirandé, Alfredo. 1987. *Gringo Justice*. Notre Dame, IN: University of Notre Dame Press.

Morales, Armando. 1972. *Ando Sangrando (I Am Bleeding): A Study of Mexican American-Police Conflict*. La Puente, CA: Perspectiva.

Morgan, Rod. 1985. "Setting the P.A.C.E.: Police Consultation Arrangements in England and Wales." Bath, UK: Centre for Analysis of Social Policy.

Morris, Aldon D. 2015. *The Scholar Denied: W.E.B. DuBois and the Birth of Modern Sociology*. Oakland: University of California Press.

Muñiz, Ana, and Kim McGill. 2012. "Tracked and Trapped: Youth of Color, Gang Databases, and Gang Injunctions." Los Angeles: Youth Justice Coalition. www.ushrnetwork.org.

Murakawa, Naomi. 2014. *The First Civil Right: How Liberals Built Prison America*. New York: Oxford University Press.

Myers, Randolph R., and Tim Goddard. 2013. "Community-Driven Youth Justice and the Organizational Consequences of Coercive Governance." *British Journal of Criminology* 53: 215–33.

Newton, Jim. 2015. "Police and Trust: Charlie Beck Reflects." *UCLA Blue Print*, Spring. http://blueprint.ucla.edu.

Oklahoma Commission to Study the Tulsa Race Riot of 1921. 2001. "Tulsa Race Riot: A Report by the Oklahoma Commission to Study the Tulsa Race Riot of 1921." February 28. www.okhistory.org.

Ostrow, Ronald J. 1990. "Casual Drug Users Should Be Shot, Gates Says." *Los Angeles Times*, September 6. http://articles.latimes.com.

Pager, Devah. 2007. *Marked: Race, Crime, and Finding Work in an Era of Mass Incarceration*. Chicago: University of Chicago Press.

Parks, Bernard C. 1999. "Strategic Plan on Community Policing: A Staff Report Prepared by Management Services Division, October 27, 1999." Los Angeles: Los Angeles Police Department.

Pelfry, William V. 2000. "Precipitating Factors of Paradigmatic Shift in Policing: The Origin of the Community Policing Era." In *Community Policing: Contemporary Readings*, 2nd ed., edited by Geoffrey P. Alpert and Alex R. Piquero, 79–92. Prospect Heights, IL: Waveland.

Peralta, Stacy, director. 2008. *Crips and Bloods: Made in America*. Verso Entertainment.

Pino, Nathan W. 2001. "Community Policing and Social Capital." *Policing* 24: 200–215.

Platt, Anthony M. 1977. *The Child Savers: The Invention of Delinquency*. Chicago: University of Chicago Press.

Pols, Mary F. 1995. "L.A. Police Official Delivers Pep Talk to Thousand Oaks Crowd." *Los Angeles Times*, February 2. http://articles.latimes.com.

Post Staff. 2017. "New Citizens' Police Commission Could Become among Strongest in Nation." *Oakland Post*, August 17. www.oaklandpost.org.

President's Task Force on 21st Century Policing. 2015. "Final Report of the President's Task Force on 21st Century Policing." Washington, DC: Office of Community-Oriented Policing Services.

Pulido, Laura. 2006. *Black, Brown, Yellow, and Left: Radical Activism in Los Angeles*. Berkeley: University of California Press.

Quinones, Sam. 2007. "How a Community Imploded." *Los Angeles Times*, March 4. http://articles.latimes.com.

———. 2015. "A Change in the Landscape: L.A.'s Parks No Longer Belong to Street Gangs." *Los Angeles Times*, February 7. www.latimes.com.

Raco, Mike. 2003. "Remaking Place and Securitising Space: Urban Regeneration and the Strategies, Tactics and Practices of Policing in the UK." *Urban Studies* 40 (9): 1869–87.

Rampart Independent Review Panel. 2000. "Report of the Rampart Independent Review Panel." Los Angeles.

Reiman, Jeffrey. 1979. *The Rich Get Richer and the Poor Get Prison*. Boston: Allyn & Bacon.

Renauer, Brian C., David E. Duffee, and Jason D. Scott. 2003. "Measuring Police-Community Coproduction: Trade-Offs in Two Observational Approaches." *Policing* 26: 9–28.

Reyes, Emily Alpert. 2018. "L.A. Shops Would Get Voice, Not Veto, in Sidewalk Vending." *Los Angeles Times*, April 17. www.latimes.com.

Richie, Beth E. 2012. *Arrested Justice: Black Women, Violence, and America's Prison Nation*. New York: New York University Press.

Rios, Victor M. 2011. *Punished: Policing the Lives of Black and Latino Boys*. New York: New York University Press.

Romero, Dennis. 2013. "Joe Jones Manifesto: Black Ex-LAPD Cop Says of Dorner, 'I Understand.'" *L.A. Weekly*, February 11. www.laweekly.com.

Rose, Nikolas. 1996. "The Death of the Social? Re-figuring the Territory of Government." *Economy and Society* 25: 327–56.

Rosenbaum, Dennis P. 2007. "Just Say No to D.A.R.E." *Criminology & Public Policy* 6 (4): 815–24.

Rosenbaum, Dennis P., and Gordon S. Hanson. 1998. "Assessing the Effects of School-Based Drug Education: A Six-Year Multilevel Analysis of Project D.A.R.E." *Journal of Research in Crime and Delinquency* 35 (4): 381–412.

Rousey, Dennis. 1996. *Policing the Southern City: New Orleans 1805–1889*. Baton Rouge: Louisiana State University Press.

Roussell, Aaron. 2015a. "Holmes et al vs. City of Racine: Supplemental Expert Witness Report." 14-CV-208-JPS. U.S. District Court for the Eastern District of Wisconsin.

———. 2015b. "Policing the Anticommunity: Territory, Race, Exclusion, and Regulation." *Law & Society Review* 49 (4): 813–46.

Roussell, Aaron, and Luis Daniel Gascón. 2014. "Defining 'Policeability': Cooperation, Control, and Resistance in South Los Angeles Community-Police Meetings." *Social Problems* 61: 237–58.

Roussell, Aaron, Kathryn Henne, Karen S. Glover, and Dale Willits. 2017. "The Impossibility of the 'Reverse Racism Effect': Critical Implications for Criminology." *Criminology & Public Policy*. doi:10.1111/1745-9133.12289.

Rowe, Michael. 2007. “Tripping over Molehills: Ethics and the Ethnography of Police Work.” *International Journal of Social Research Methodology* 10 (1): 37–48.

Rubin, Joel. 2009. “LAPD Gains New Approval from the Public.” *Los Angeles Times*, June 22. http://articles.latimes.com.

Rubin, Joel, Jack Leonard, and Kate Linthicum. 2013. “Police Say Ex-Cop Was Bent on Exacting Revenge.” *Los Angeles Times*, February 7. http://articles.latimes.com.

Saul, Josh. 2017. “In a First for the Nation, Portland Police End Gang List to Improve Relations with Blacks and Latinos.” *Newsweek*, September 25. www.newsweek.com.

Scott, James C. 1998. *Seeing Like a State: How Certain Schemes to Improve the Human Condition Have Failed*. New Haven, CT: Yale University Press.

Scott, Jason D., David E. Duffee, and Brian C. Renauer. 2003. “Measuring Police-Community Coproduction: The Utility of Community Policing Case Studies.” *Police Quarterly* 6: 410–39.

Sexton, Jared. 2010. “People-of-Color-Blindness: Notes on the Afterlife of Slavery.” *Social Text* 28: 31–56.

Sides, Josh. 2003. *L.A. City Limits: African American Los Angeles from the Great Depression to the Present*. Berkeley: University of California Press.

Simon, Jonathan. 2007. *Governing through Crime: How the War on Crime Transformed American Democracy and Created a Culture of Fear*. New York: Oxford University Press.

Simon, Mallory. 2013. “Alleged Cop-Killer Details Threats to LAPD and Why He Was Driven to Violence.” *CNN*, February 9. www.cnn.com.

Skogan, Wesley G. 2006. *Police and Community in Chicago: A Tale of Three Cities*. New York: Oxford Press.

Skogan, Wesley G., and Susan M. Hartnett. 1997. *Community Policing, Chicago Style*. New York: Oxford University Press.

Skolnick, Jerome H., and David H. Bayley. 1988. “Theme and Variation in Community Policing.” *Crime and Justice* 10: 1–37.

Skolnick, Jerome H., and James Fyfe. 1993. *Above the Law: Police and the Use of Excessive Force*. New York: Free Press.

Smith, Neil. 1996. *The New Urban Frontier: Gentrification and the Revanchist City*. New York: Routledge.

Smith, Sharon. 2006. *Subterranean Fire: A History of Working-Class Radicalism in the United States*. Chicago: Haymarket Books.

Soja, Edward W. 2014. *My Los Angeles: From Urban Restructuring to Regional Urbanization*. Berkeley: University of California Press.

Sotomayor, Sonia. 2018. *Kisela v. Hughes*. Dissent. US Supreme Court.

Stone, Christopher, Todd Foglesong, and Christine M. Cole. 2009. “Policing Los Angeles under a Consent Decree: The Dynamics of Change at the LAPD.” Cambridge, MA: Harvard University, Program in Criminal Justice Policy and Management at the Kennedy School.

Stuart, Forrest. 2011. "Race, Space, and the Regulation of Surplus Labor: Policing African Americans in Los Angeles's Skid Row." *Souls: A Critical Journal of Black Politics, Culture, and Society* 13: 197–212.

———. 2014. "From 'Rabble Management' to 'Recovery Management': Policing Homelessness in Marginal Urban Space." *Urban Studies* 15: 1909–25.

———. 2016. *Down and Out and Under Arrest: Policing and Everyday Life in Skid Row.* Chicago: University of Chicago Press.

Sunshine, Jason, and Tom R. Tyler. 2003. "The Role of Procedural Justice and Legitimacy in Shaping Public Support for Policing." *Law & Society Review* 37 (3): 513–48.

Suttles, Gerald D. 1968. *The Social Order of the Slums: Ethnicity and Territory in the Inner City.* Chicago: University of Chicago Press.

Taylor, Keeanga-Yamahtta. 2016. *From #BlackLivesMatter to Black Liberation.* Chicago: Haymarket Books.

Telles, Edward, Mark Sawyer, and Gaspar Rivera-Salgado, eds. 2011. *Just Neighbors? Research on African American and Latino Relations in the United States.* New York: Russell Sage Foundation.

Turner, Victor. 1966. *The Ritual Process: Structure and Anti-structure.* New York: Routledge.

Tyler, Tom R. 1990. *Why People Obey the Law.* New Haven, CT: Yale University Press.

US Department of Justice. 1994. "Violent Crime Control and Law Enforcement Act of 1994: Fact Sheet." NCJ FS000067. Washington, DC: National Criminal Justice Reference Service. www.ncjrs.gov.

———. 2015. "Investigation of the Ferguson Police Department." Washington, DC: US Department of Justice, Civil Rights Division.

US Government Accountability Office. 2005. "COPS Grants Were a Modest Contributor to Declines in Crime in the 1990s." GAO-04-104. Washington, DC: Author.

Valle, Victor M., and Rodolfo D. Torres. 1992. "Enough of the Great Melodrama of Race Relations in Los Angeles." *Los Angeles Times,* December 6. http://articles.latimes.com.

———. 2000. *Latino Metropolis.* Minneapolis: University of Minnesota Press.

Vigil, James Diego. 2002. *A Rainbow of Gangs: Street Cultures in the Mega-City.* Austin: University of Texas Press.

Villaraigosa, Antonio Ramón. 2009. "Mayor's Budget Summary: Fiscal Year 2008–09." Los Angeles: Office of the City Mayor. http://lacity.org.

———. 2010. "Mayor's Budget Summary: Fiscal Year 2009–10." Los Angeles: Office of the City Mayor. http://lacity.org.

———. 2011. "Mayor's Budget Summary: Fiscal Year 2010–11." Los Angeles: Office of the City Mayor. http://lacity.org.

———. 2012. "Mayor's Budget Summary: Fiscal Year 2011–12." Los Angeles: Office of the City Mayor. http://lacity.org.

———. 2013. "Mayor's Budget Summary: Fiscal Year 2012–13." Los Angeles: Office of the City Mayor. http://lacity.org.

Vitale, Alex S. 2017. *The End of Policing*. London: Verso.

Wacquant, Loïc. 2002. "From Slavery to Mass Incarceration." *New Left Review* 13. https://newleftreview.org.

———. 2009. *Punishing the Poor: The Neoliberal Government of Social Insecurity*. Durham, NC: Duke University Press.

Wagner, Bryan. 2009. *Disturbing the Peace: Black Culture and the Police Power after Slavery*. Cambridge, MA: Harvard University Press.

Walker, Samuel, and Carol A. Archbold. 2014. *The New World of Police Accountability*. Los Angeles: Sage.

Walker, Samuel, and Vic W. Bumphus. 1992. "The Effectiveness of Civilian Review: Observations on Recent Trends and New Issues Regarding the Civilian Review of the Police." *American Journal of Police* 11 (4): 1–16.

Walker, Samuel, and Charles M. Katz. 2002. *The Police in America: An Introduction*. 4th ed. New York: McGraw-Hill.

Ward, Geoff K. 2012. *The Black Child-Savers: Racial Democracy and Juvenile Justice*. Chicago: University of Chicago Press.

Western, Bruce. 2006. *Punishment and Inequality in America*. New York: Russell Sage Foundation.

Williams, Kristian. 2007. *Our Enemies in Blue: Police and Power in America*. Cambridge, MA: South End Press.

———. 2011. "The Other Side of the COIN: Counterinsurgency and Community Policing." *Interface* 3: 81–117.

Williams, Willie L. 1993. "Administrative Order No. 10: Partnerships for Community Policing." Los Angeles: Los Angeles Police Department.

———. 1995a. "Commitment to Action: The Los Angeles Police Department's Strategic Plan 1995–2000: A Quick Look at the Planning Process." Los Angeles: Los Angeles Police Department.

———. 1995b. "Management Paper No. 2: Community Policing." Los Angeles: Los Angeles Police Department.

Wilson, William Julius, and Richard P. Taub. 2006. *There Goes the Neighborhood: Racial, Ethnic, and Class Tensions in Four Chicago Neighborhoods and Their Meaning for America*. New York: Knopf.

Winton, Richard. 2013. "Women Who Survived Flurry of LAPD Bullets Have Yet to Get Truck." *Los Angeles Times*, March 11. http://articles.latimes.com.

Winton, Richard, and Andrew Blankstein. 2013. "Women Whose Truck Was Fired on Will Receive $40,000 Settlement." *Los Angeles Times*, March 14. http://articles.latimes.com.

Woo, Elaine. 2013. "Rena Price Dies at 97; Her and Son's Arrests Sparked Watts Riots." *Los Angeles Times*, June 22. www.latimes.com.

Zamudio, Margaret M., and Michael I. Lichter. 2008. "Bad Attitudes and Good Soldiers: Soft Skills as a Code for Tractability in the Hiring of Immigrant Latina/os over Native Blacks in the Hotel Industry." *Social Problems* 55: 573–89.

Zepeda-Millan, Chris. 2017. *Latino Mass Mobilization: Immigration, Racialization, and Activism*. Cambridge: Cambridge University Press.

Zilberg, Elana. 2002. "A Troubled Corner: The Ruined and Rebuilt Environment of a Central American Barrio in Post-Rodney-King-Riot Los Angeles." *City & Society* 14 (2): 185–210.

———. 2011. *Space of Detention: The Making of a Transnational Gang Crisis between Los Angeles and San Salvador*. Durham, NC: Duke University Press.

Zimring, Franklin E. 2007. *The Great American Crime Decline*. Studies in Crime and Public Policy. New York: Oxford University Press.

INDEX

ABOUT THE AUTHORS

Luis Daniel Gascón is Assistant Professor of Sociology at the University of San Francisco.

Aaron Roussell is Assistant Professor of Sociology at Portland State University.

www.ingramcontent.com/pod-product-compliance
Lightning Source LLC
Chambersburg PA
CBHW020247030426
42336CB00010B/650

* 9 7 8 1 4 7 9 8 4 2 2 5 4 *